The Making of
Bourgeois Europe

The Making of
Bourgeois Europe

Absolutism, Revolution, and the Rise of
Capitalism in England, France and Germany

COLIN MOOERS

VERSO

London · New York

First published by Verso 1991

Verso
UK: 6 Meard Street, London W1F 0EG
USA: 20 Jay Street, Suite 1010, Brooklyn, NY 11201

Verso is the imprint of New Left Books

British Library Cataloguing in Publication Data

Mooers, Colin
   The making of bourgeois Europe: absolutism, revolution
   and the rise of capitalism in England, France and Germany.
   1. Western Europe. Transcripts of discussions
   I. Title
   940.28

   ISBN 978-0-86091-507-2

US Library of Congress Cataloging-in-Publication Data

Mooers, Colin.
   The making of bourgeois Europe: absolutism, revolution, and the
   rise of capitalism in England, France, and Germany/Colin Mooers.
      p.   cm.
   Includes bibliographical references and index.
   ISBN 0-86091-291-4. — ISBN 0-86091-507-7 (pbk.)
      1. Europe—History—18th century.   2. Europe—History—19th
   century.   3. Despotism—Europe—History.   4. Revolutions—Europe
   —History.   5. Capitalism—Europe—History.   I. Title.
   940.2′8—dc20

Typeset by BP Integraphics Ltd, Bath, Avon

Contents

Acknowledgements

Any work of this sort is bound to owe much to the efforts of others. This book, which began as a doctoral dissertation, has drawn on the inspiration and guidance of several individuals.

Thanks must first go to Ellen Wood, who is owed the greatest debt of gratitude. Through her guidance I was made aware of the many unresolved issues surrounding the rise of capitalism and the states-system in western Europe. Her patient encouragement and careful criticism of early drafts enabled me to strengthen my arguments considerably. Nick Rogers and Bill Irvine rescued me from several rash generalizations concerning English and French political developments. Geoff Eley was good enough to read through the entire manuscript. His comments on the chapter dealing with Germany were especially helpful.

Neal Wood provided extensive comments and detailed suggestions on earlier drafts of this book, while Robert Brenner helped me to avoid several errors of interpretation on the origins of capitalism in Europe. Although we have agreed to disagree on many points, George Comninel's comments on my treatment of the French Revolution were extremely helpful. Colin Barker and David McNally provided me with invaluable insights and moral support at various stages in the writing and rewriting of this book. I am especially grateful for the encouragement and good-humoured tolerance of my wife, Augusta Dwyer, who assisted me in completing this book while producing one of her own.

My final debt of gratitude far exceeds the bounds of intellectual life. This book is dedicated to my mother whose quiet perseverance, personal sacrifice, and unerring support has made all things possible.

Introduction

This book began as an act of theoretical clarification centring on two related areas of Marxist thought. The first deals with the long-standing debate over the origins and evolution of capitalism in Europe. The second has to do with the concept of bourgeois revolution and to what extent it remains a useful tool for understanding the great revolutionary upheavals of the seventeenth, eighteenth and nineteenth centuries.

What is striking about recent Marxist scholarship is how few writers have attempted to bring together in a systematic way the insights of these two areas of debate. The reasons for this are undoubtedly complex. Many former Marxists have now abandoned the field for the apparently greener pastures of post-Marxism. But even among Marxists the past decade has witnessed a marked retreat from the idea that historical materialism is capable of providing a comprehensive theory of history and society. Ill at ease with accusations of 'reductionism' and 'determinism', many Marxists have sought to distance themselves from the holistic claims of Marx's historical method with its insistence on the essential unity of material and social life, of politics and economics. For many, this has meant taking refuge in methodologies alternative to Marxism, such as post-structuralism's insistence on discrete and irreducible orders of reality, or the currently fashionable methodological individualism of analytic Marxism. It has almost invariably led to the abandonment of notions once considered basic to Marxism.

The concept of bourgeois revolution is a case in point. The assault on the Marxist concept of bourgeois revolution is by no means a recent occurrence. In England, anti-Marxist historians began to attack the

Marxist interpretation of the English Revolution as a bourgeois revolution in the early 1950s.[1] The 'revisionist' attack on the Marxist interpretation of the French Revolution dates from roughly the same period. Alfred Cobban, while declaring the importance of social forces in the French Revolution, explicitly rejected the Marxist claim that the revolution was a bourgeois revolution. It was, he concluded, 'not wholly a revolution for, but largely one against, the penetration of an embryo capitalism into French society.'[2]

But while the early assaults on the concept of bourgeois revolution had been more or less confined to the realm of historical scholarship, more recent revisionists have been much less timid about the underlying political implications of their work. François Furet, one of the most sophisticated of the French revisionist historians, explicitly associates the 'skidding out of control' [dérapage] of the revolution under the Jacobins with the horrors of Stalinist dictatorships in the twentieth century, 'Today the Gulag leads to a rethinking of the Terror, in virtue of an identity of project.'[3] The clear intent of Furet's attack on the Marxist interpretation of the revolution has been to discredit the whole idea of revolution in any form. He has declared that 'the revolution is over' in the West, because the most important ideas of the liberal phase of the revolution have triumphed.[4] This is an increasingly popular theme among right-wing intellectuals. Developments in eastern Europe have led some to proclaim the triumph of liberal values across the entire planet signalling 'the end of history as such ... the endpoint of mankind's ideological evolution and the universalization of Western liberal democracy as the final form of human government.'[5]

Attacks on Marxism and trumpeting the virtues of bourgeois democracy are nothing new. What is new is the extent to which Marxists have been prepared to accept the revisionists' rejection of the Marxist interpretation of bourgeois revolutions. The usefulness of many of the detailed historical studies undertaken by revisionist historians is beyond dispute. However, their interpretation of historical events is certainly questionable. It is, therefore, a bit premature to conclude, as one recent Marxist writer has done, that the 'long-standing claims to historical validity of the Marxist interpretation of the French Revolution have been exploded.'[6]

One of the central purposes of this book is to rehabilitate the Marxist concept of bourgeois revolution while at the same time avoiding the pitfall of attempting to deduce its inevitability from abstract notions of the transition from feudalism to capitalism. Nevertheless, it is important to insist upon the connection between the character of capitalist transition in various parts of Europe and the type of bourgeois revolution that was experienced. By far the most useful contributions to the 'transition debate' in recent years have insisted on a close relationship between forms of political power and the evolution of pre-capitalist class relations.[7] It should not, therefore, be surprising to find that the configuration of pre-capitalist class relations also affected the way in which pre-capitalist states were transformed into bourgeois states.

An additional consideration, however, also needs to be taken into account which is often obscured by the way in which the rise of capitalism is conceptualized. Although capitalism developed first in England, its impact was quickly felt beyond national boundaries. The emergence of English capitalism involved the internationalization of new forces and relations of production which profoundly influenced the character and the tempo of the transition to capitalism in other parts of Europe. The uneven character of capitalist development also played a considerable role in determining the form of bourgeois revolution which occurred in continental Europe in the late eighteenth and nineteenth centuries. It may be more accurate, therefore, to speak of more than one pattern of bourgeois revolution.

If there is no single pattern of bourgeois revolution, how then do we define bourgeois revolutions? Geoff Eley has offered the following definition. It is necessary, he argues, to distinguish

> between two levels of determination and significance – between the revolution as a specific crisis of the state, involving widespread popular mobilization and a reconstitution of political relationships, and on the other hand the deeper process of structural change, involving the increasing predominance of the capitalist mode of production, the potential obsolescence of many existing practices and institutions, and the uneven transformation of social relations.[8]

This definition of a bourgeois revolution is sufficiently broad to encompass a number of different historical situations. Moreover, it says nothing about the character of the social forces which carry through the 'reconstitution of political relationships' favourable to capitalism. It shifts attention away from the causes and conscious aims of those who made the revolution to its effects in fostering conditions suitable for capitalist accumulation. Thus it is entirely possible, as Eley and Blackbourn have shown in the case of Bismarckian Germany, for non-capitalist forces to undertake bourgeois revolutions.

The same argument I shall argue, can with some modifications, be applied to France. It should, therefore, be possible to meet the principal revisionist objections to the Marxist interpretation of the French Revolution without at the same time abandoning the notion of bourgeois revolution as an integral part of historical materialism.

These arguments are elaborated by first evaluating the major Marxist contributions to the debate on the transition to capitalism; secondly, by showing how these contributions help to illuminate the pattern of capitalist development in England, France and Germany, and by demonstrating how the 'uneven and combined' nature of capitalist development conditioned the form of bourgeois revolution experienced by each country. In the final chapter, I challenge the normative theory of bourgeois revolution put forward by Perry Anderson and others, which in my view mistakenly counterposes the 'backwardness' of the English Revolution to the supposedly more advanced bourgeois revolutions of the Continent.

This book covers a vast terrain. I have not shrunk from painting with a broad historical brush in many instances. Nor have I attempted to disguise my reliance on expert historians of the various countries I discuss. What I have attempted to do is gather together my own thoughts and those of others in a systematic fashion in the hope of shedding light on a number of theoretical issues of some importance to Marxists.

Notes

1. See Lawrence Stone, *The Causes of the English Revolution 1529–1642* (New York: Harper and Row Publishers, 1972) ch. 2.

2. Alfred Cobban, *The Social Interpretation of the French Revolution* (Cambridge: Cambridge University Press, 1968) p. 172.

3. François Furet, quoted in Alex Callinicos, 'Bourgeois Revolutions and Historical Materialism', *International Socialism* no. 43 (June 1989) p. 120.

4. Interview in the *International Herald Tribune*, 6 January 1989.

5. Francis Fukuyama, 'The End of History?', *The Globe and Mail*, 1 December 1989.

6. George Comninel, *Rethinking the French Revolution: Marxism and the Revisionist Challenge* (London: Verso, 1987) p. 3.

7. I have in mind the work of Robert Brenner and the various contributions generated by his writings. See T.H. Ashton and C.H.E. Philpin, eds, *The Brenner Debate* (Cambridge: Cambridge University Press, 1987).

8. David Blackbourn and Geoff Eley, *The Peculiarities of German History* (Oxford: Oxford University Press, 1984) pp. 82–3.

Marxist Theories of State Formation and the Transition from Feudalism to Capitalism

I. The Market-relations Model

A number of contemporary writers have insisted that the key to the rise of capitalism is connected to the emergence of trade, the spread of monetary relations and market exchange. This view is common to Marxist theorists such as Paul Sweezy, André Gunder Frank and Immanuel Wallerstein. But it is also a view which has deep roots in the non-Marxist tradition as well. It forms the guiding thread in the works of Fernand Braudel's study of the collapse of the Mediterranean trading economies and the rise of Atlantic trade in the sixteenth century. It is an approach extending back through the writings of the Belgian economic historian Henri Pirenne, through Karl Polanyi and Max Weber, to the work of Adam Smith, especially as set out in Book I of *The Wealth of Nations*.[1]

At the core of this conception is the belief that the rise of a money economy and the gradual incorporation of the individualized peasant economy which characterized European feudalism into the broad network of monetary and market relations was sufficient to 'dissolve' the feudal structure of society, opening the way for the full flowering of capitalism. Paul Sweezy, for example, argued that because of the inherent inertia of feudal society, which he characterized as a 'system of production for use', there existed no internal dynamic which would stimulate long-term growth and expansion, let alone supply the stimulus for the transition to capitalism. Accordingly, it was necessary to look for the dynamic element which led to the dissolution of feudalism in causes *external* to the system. According to Sweezy, 'long-distance trade could be a creative force bringing into existence a *system* of production for exchange alongside the old feudal system of production for use.'[2] On this view the rise of towns as 'centres and breeders of exchange economy'[3] was of crucial importance. Towns were seen as 'islands of capitalism' in an otherwise feudal world; it was on the growing commercial life of the towns that the feudal lords became increasingly dependent for their supply of luxuries and it was to the towns (and away from the land) that the serf population was drawn in order to escape the bonds of servitude.

There are a number of serious problems with this perspective. First of all, the view that towns were somehow external to the structure of feudal society is highly suspect. Towns, as one commentator has noted, were highly integrated into the structure of the feudal economy, functioning as a 'collective seigneur'; the urban economy was 'as internal to feudalism as the rise and decline of the seigneurial economy – indeed defined by this co-existence'.[4] The artisans and small craft producers who populated the towns and who may initially have come from the ranks of the serf or peasant population on the land were just as subject to feudal exploitation, even if by different means than those on the land. The lords who controlled the municipal centres extracted a surplus from the artisans through various exactions such as house and stall rents, mill and oven monopolies, tolls and taxes.[5]

Moreover, the bulk of urban-based production appears to have been devoted to the satisfaction of the feudal ruling classes' desire for luxury goods but not because it was somehow incompatible with feudal production as such. Such production (and consumption) was highly unproductive, in that very little of the economic surplus extracted from the subordinate classes found its way back into either agriculture or industry. In short, there was little in the way of an in-built stimulus towards innovation in the urban artisanal economy which would have given rise, on its own, to the expansive dynamic of capitalism. This judgement seems to hold not only for western European feudalism but even more so for its eastern variant.[6] There thus appears to be a firm basis for the view that 'the structures of urban society in feudal Europe duplicated those of the countryside.'[7]

The suggestion that the monetization of relations between the feudal lords and the mass of the peasant population somehow signalled the dissolution of feudalism and the rise of capitalism appears to be equally problematic. First, if we take only fourteenth-century England into account, even after the passage from serfdom based on labour services to money rents, we still have to wait a considerable time before we witness the emergence of anything resembling capitalism. Moreover, the rise of money rents tended to take place initially in areas furthest from the town markets and trade routes.[8]

On a Europe-wide scale, the pattern of rent forms appears to have been even more varied. Indeed, there seems to have been no strictly linear pattern whereby rents in labour services were gradually replaced by money rents. Money rents coexisted with labour service rents as far back as the tenth century in parts of England, northern France, the Rhine Valley and on the demesnes of central Italy, even though labour rent tended to predominate.[9] In eastern Europe, labour services and money rents tended to be combined well into the eighteenth century.[10] In any case, lordly exactions did not only take these forms. As Hilton has observed: 'by the twelfth century, peasant surplus was transferred to the landed aristocracy less in the form of rent calculated on the size of the peasant holding, whether in labour, kind or money, than in seigneurial taxation (tallage) and in the profits of jurisdiction.'[11] These new forms of surplus extraction, which included such things as court fines, profits from monopolies of various sorts, and statutes forcing peasants to grind their corn at the lord's mill, significantly increased ruling-class incomes as well as that class's hold over virtually every aspect of economic life in feudal society.

The general point to be stressed is that there appears to be very little evidence for the view that the emergence of money rents was somehow incompatible with feudal economic relations. 'Money rent', as Takahashi observed, 'in its "pure" form, is only a variant of rent in kind, or labour services and in essence "absorbs" profit in the same "embryonic" way as does rent in nature.'[12]

(i) *Wallerstein's world-capitalist system*

Despite these criticisms, which first emerged in the context of a debate between Paul Sweezy and Maurice Dobb in the 1950s, the market-relations approach has gained renewed vigour in recent years, and perhaps its most systematic development, in the 'world-system' theory of Immanuel Wallerstein.[13] Wallerstein insists that to ask whether feudalism in France or England disintegrated as a result of 'external' factors or 'internal' factors is in fact to ask the wrong question. The proper unit of analysis, he contends, should not be national societies but rather social systems. A social system, according to Wallerstein, is characterized by

> the existence within it of a division of labour, such that the various sectors or areas within are dependent upon economic exchange with others for the smooth and continuous provisioning of the needs of the area ... the only kind of social system is a world-system, which we define quite simply as a unit with a single division of labour and multiple cultural systems.[14]

Wallerstein distinguishes between two types of 'world-systems', which he calls world empires and world economies. World empires are essentially redistributive in nature and are dominated by a single political sovereignty such as existed in the pre-modern civilizations of China, Egypt and ancient Rome. World economies, on the other hand, are characterized by the predominance of trade and market exchange with a multiplicity of sovereign states within them.

The 'modern world economy' ostensibly arose in sixteenth-century Europe. It was here, according to Wallerstein,

> that we saw the full development and economic predominance of market trade. This system was called capitalism. Capitalism and a world-economy (that is, a single division of labour but multiple polities and cultures) are obverse sides of the same coin.[15]

On this view, the spread of market relations in the early modern period gave rise to an increasingly complex Europe-wide division of labour as various regions began to specialize in the production of specific agricultural commodities which they then sold on the international market. Specialization also led to differentiation, as some areas tended to gain a monopoly over the production of certain goods and thereby a greater share in the overall distribution of world-economic wealth.

According to Wallerstein, the increase in trade and the rise of an international division of labour also assigned each region of the world economy to a specific zone: core, periphery or semi-periphery. Similarly, each zone was assigned a specific form of labour control which corresponded to the specific form of economic activity the particular region had come to specialize in. Thus we see a particular pattern emerge: in the periphery which included regions of eastern Europe and Hispanic America, 'coerced cash-crop labour' in the form of serfdom and slavery respectively developed, corresponding to the form of productive activity which predominated: grain for sale on the world market in the case of the former, and 'labour-intensive' crops such as cotton and sugar in the case of the latter.[16] In the semi-periphery, sharecropping emerged as the dominant form of labour control; in the core, wage labour came to dominate owing to the greater need for 'skilled labour'.[17]

Thus, for Wallerstein, *class structure* is determined primarily by the form of economic activity in which a specific region specializes and the mode of labour control which 'corresponds' to that form of production. The class structure in the periphery is simple and highly coercive: lord and serf (as in eastern Europe) or master and slave (as in Hispanic America). In the core areas, the class structure is more complex and less directly coercive: lord, labourer, peasant, artisan, merchant and yeoman. In the semi-periphery, it is a combination of the two former class structures.

Political forms or states arise out of the needs of the dominant classes in the three zones. According to Wallerstein,

The three structural positions in a world-economy – core, periphery and semi-periphery – had become stabilized by about 1640. . . . The key fact is that given slightly different starting-points, the interests of the various local groups converged in northwest Europe, leading to the development of strong state mechanisms, and diverged sharply in the peripheral areas, leading to very weak ones.[18]

Each state, despite its relative strength or weakness has four principal functions: first, to establish territorial control over a given geographical region and the people who inhabit it; second, to legislate the mode of labour control; third, to establish taxation mechanisms which favour the accumulation of capital in the hands of the dominant class; and finally, to establish an armed force capable of furthering 'the concentration of accumulated capital within their frontiers as against those of rival states'.[19]

The emergence of strong states in the core of the world economy grew out of the growing complexity of production and the desire by core ruling classes to appropriate a disproportionate share of world economic surplus by appropriating a portion of that which was produced in other regions. Thus, 'once we get a difference in the strength of state-machineries, we get the operation of "unequal exchange" which is enforced by strong states on weak ones, by core states on peripheral areas.'[20]

For Wallerstein, the emergence of European absolutism in the core economies of the sixteenth century was an unmistakeably capitalist phenomenon. It was the chief means by which national groupings of commercial capitalists could assert their interests in the international economy. For the emerging capitalist class 'the strong state in the form of the "absolute monarchies" was a prime customer, a guardian against local and international brigandage, a model of social legitimation, a preemptive protection against the creation of strong state barriers elsewhere.'[21] The sixteenth century was decisive in the history of capitalism in that it represented the time frame in which all of the constituent elements of the capitalist world economy finally coalesced into a single process to form the modern world-system:

On the one hand, the capitalist world-economy was built on a world-wide division of labour in which various zones of this economy (that which we have termed the core, the semi-periphery, and the periphery) were assigned specific economic roles, developed different class structures, used consequently different modes of labour control, and profited unequally from the workings of the system. On the other hand, political action occurred primarily within the framework of states which, as a consequence of their different roles in the world-economy were structured differently, the core states being the most centralized. . . . [These] developments were not accidental but, rather, within a certain range of possible variation, structurally determined.[22]

Considered on its own merits Wallerstein's schematization of the 'world-system' is not without inconsistencies. It has been pointed out, for example, that Wallerstein's equation of 'coreness' with the existence of 'strong state structures' simply does not correspond to the historical evidence. For example, if we take 1550 as our point of departure, we find that many of the core economies cited by Wallerstein (the Netherlands, England, parts of Spain and southern Germany) in fact had *weak* state structures (the Netherlands and Germany). On the other hand, by 1700, the political and economic situation had changed dramatically such that England, France and the Netherlands represented the 'core' economies. And yet, neither Britain nor the Netherlands saw the development of absolutist states on a par with that which developed in France. At the same time, strong state structures did develop in countries outside the core such as those which emerged in Prussia, Austro-Hungary and Sweden. Contrary to Wallerstein's model, therefore, 'there were more and stronger absolutisms outside the core than in it.'[23]

Thus, as Gourevitch has observed, Wallerstein's principal argument, which links an international division of labour between the core and periphery to the emergence of strong and weak state structures respectively, does not hold up under the evidence:

> the argument concerning the peripheries does not account for the contrast between Poland and Prussia; the argument about the core does not account for the difference between the Netherlands on the one side, and Britain and France on the other, nor the differences between Britain and France.[24]

At certain points in his exposition, Wallerstein's market determinism pushes him into open contradiction with his general claim that equates core economies with strong states and peripheral economies with weak ones. With regard to the relationship between 'coerced cash-crop labour' and the state form he argues:

> the landowner [seigneur] was producing for a capitalist world economy. The economic limits of exploitative pressure were determined by the demand–supply curve of a market. He was maintained in power by the strength rather than the weakness of the central authority.[25]

Direct coercion, it seems, was a necessity for the eastern lords arising out of their need to control the labour force to take full advantage of the international market in grain.

At a later point, Wallerstein returns to his general assertion that the peripheral regions were characterized by weak states:

> While the sixteenth century was a period of the rise of state power in western Europe, it was an era of decline for state power in eastern Europe, both cause

and consequence of the latter's economic position.

Most people today associate the state of Prussia with two phenomena: the strong state and a strong *Junker* class. The sixteenth century precisely saw the rise of a strong *Junker* class in the areas which would later constitute Prussia. But it was also a century in which the state grew weaker, not stronger.[26]

If, in the first case, Wallerstein means by 'the strength rather than weakness of the central political authority' an *absolutist* state structure, he is clearly mistaken. The 'second serfdom' in eastern Europe actually preceded the rise of absolutist states in the east by approximately two centuries. The process of enserfment was 'under way in virtually all areas by 1400'.[27] And yet, in Prussia and Russia, 'strong' absolutist states never finally emerged until the latter part of the seventeenth century. Moreover, Poland, with a similar form of labour control, never developed anything resembling a strong absolutist state.

However, there is a sense in which the claim that political organization in eastern Europe during this period was stronger – and not weaker as Wallerstein's general line of argument would suggest – is much closer to the truth. But Wallerstein's ability to explain why this was the case and what was the actual form it took, is hampered by his claim that it was the 'central authority' which was strengthened. In the case of Poland, for example, while it is true that a strong central authority or absolutist state structure never emerged, there was at the same time a strengthening of lordly powers and political organization at the local level. Precisely because political authority was 'fragmented' between different lords throughout the region, political powers were capable of being concentrated much more effectively at the level of the demesne and local economy than at the level of the national economy. In Poland this was expressed in the growing strength of the local and provincial diets. As Robert Brenner notes:

> In creating these governing institutions, the lords of eastern Europe constructed a form of state peculiarly appropriate to their rather simple needs. It was a form in which they could represent themselves in the most immediate and direct way, and through which they could make certain that their rights over their land and peasants were protected, while insuring that the costs of any state administrative apparatus could be kept to a minimum.[28]

Thus, it was not the central authority which was strengthened, but the jurisdiction of the local lords; political power was decentralized. Consequently, Wallerstein's second claim which forms the basis of his general argument that the sixteenth century was a period in which 'the state grew weaker and not stronger' in eastern Europe is misleading.

In actual fact, this was a period in which the political powers and class organization of the eastern lords was dramatically strengthened, albeit at the local rather than the national level. The reason for this, however, was rooted in a wholly different dynamic than Wallerstein's trade-centred core-periphery model would lead us to believe. In the first instance, it lay in the eastern lords' need to strengthen their direct powers of exploitation over the enserfed peasant population – a phenomenon related to the pull of the international grain trade but, as we shall see in a moment, in no way explicable as a purely market-determined outcome.[29]

The first difficulty with Wallerstein's linking of the second serfdom with the rise of the international grain trade has to do with its timing. As mentioned above, the process of enserfment was well under way by about 1400. As one commentator has observed, 'Eastern grain exports to the West began expanding significantly around 1500 and achieved their most sudden and sizeable growth only between 1550 and 1600 ... after the foundations of the coerced labour system were fully established.'[30] Thus, as with the timing of the emergence of strong states in the periphery, the timing and linkage between the rise of the 'coerced cash-crop labour system' and the emergence of the grain trade is equally suspect.

There was undoubtedly a connection between the grain market – and the increased revenues it offered to the eastern lords from participating in such commerce – and the strengthening of lordly powers vis-à-vis the peasant population. In Poland, by the end of the sixteenth century, 'the real part of production passing through the market is tripled in case of the upper nobility, doubled in the case of the lower nobility, and cut to a quarter of what it was in the case of the peasant'.[31] Even so, the overall effects of increased market opportunities were dramatically different in different parts of eastern Europe. As Brenner has shown:

> the control of grain production (and thus the grain trade) secured through their [eastern lords] successful enserfment of the peasantry was by no means assured by the mere fact of the emergence of the grain markets themselves. In the rich, grain-producing areas of northwest Germany, the peasants were largely successful in gaining command of grain output in precisely the period of developing enserfment in northeast Germany – and they appear to have done so after a prolonged period of anti-landlord resistance. In fact, the peasants' ability in this region to control the commerce in agricultural commodities (a share of the Baltic export trade, as well as the inland routes) appears to have been a factor in helping them to consolidate their power and property against the landlords.[32]

In truth, the pull of the international market on the economies of eastern Europe was extremely limited. As Kula notes, in the case of Poland, 'the external market had a considerable importance in relation to commercial production in Poland – a very limited importance, however, for overall production.'[33] Despite its orientation to exports, the Polish economy marketed on average only 7 to 10 per cent of overall production during the sixteenth century and most of the seventeenth century. Moreover, participation in the grain market did not lead, over the long term, to an increase, but rather to a decrease in commercial trade: 'at the end of the eighteenth century, the exportation of Polish grain was much below the level attained at the beginning of the eighteenth century.'[34] The 'development of underdevelopment' in eastern Europe was rooted in a set of circumstances which are, for the most part, ignored by Wallerstein and other exponents of the market-relations approach. The long-term decline of marketable surpluses of grain was not simply the effect of a shift in terms of trade towards the end of the eighteenth century. It was due, ironically, to the relative inefficiency of the 'coerced cash-crop labour system' itself.

Since the lords could not affect the price of the grain they put to market, or the price of luxury goods which they purchased there, their only recourse – if they wanted to increase their marketable surplus, and hence their consumption of luxuries – was to exact a larger share of the peasants' surplus product. Thus the increase in market opportunities for the lords had the effect of an ever-greater tightening of the bonds of servitude of the peasantry. Good years, when production was high as a result of increased harvests, only led to a greater squeezing of surplus from the peasantry. Moreover, the higher revenues which the lords realized from these increased exactions were rarely reinvested in production; rather, they led to a greater expenditure on luxuries.[35] In this sense, the pattern of lordly response to increased revenues differed little from that which had characterized the whole of European feudalism.

The long-term effect of this pattern of lord/peasant relations in eastern Europe was a decline in overall productivity, the direct result of the lords' attempt to respond to expanded market opportunities by squeezing the peasantry rather than by improving their output through greater investment in agriculture. Declining productivity on the land was ultimately reflected in rising prices in grain. This, however, was not a sign of an enhanced market situation wherein greater profits might be realized as a result of increased prices, but of its opposite: a terminal crisis of productivity reflected in the growing exhaustion of serf-based production and declining harvests. The impact of this decline on the Polish economy was devastating:

> The shifts in terms of trade, which were apparently favourable to Poland in reality undermined Polish economic development, although they brought great economic advantages to a single social stratum. Due to the concurrence of great world-wide changes, the Polish nobility ... found themselves in the

position of Rentiers, 'coupon clipping' and profiting from the economic retro-gression in the country.[36]

Thus, Wallerstein's insistence that coerced cash-crop labour in the periphery formed the basis of economic advance in the West – through the mechanism of 'unequal exchange' – is misconceived since, as we have seen, the amount of transferable surplus product in the form of grain declined by at least half between the sixteenth century and the eighteenth. At any rate, the exported surplus was never more than a fraction of overall production to begin with. The important point is that eastern Europe was hardly in a position to fuel – through the transfer of wealth from periphery to core – the economic development of western Europe, least of all during the latter part of the eighteenth century when the West was first embarking on the path towards industrialization and hence most in need of surplus capital.

In sum, Wallerstein's insistence on the *capitalist* character of the second serfdom seems impossible to sustain: the eastern lords did not (and could not) respond to expanded market opportunities in a 'capitalist' manner; they relied instead on a form of peasant exploitation which, in the short term, increased their revenues, but which, in the long term, undermined productivity and exhausted the economy. Nor were they driven out of business when they failed to alter their methods of production as a result of their growing inefficiency. Moreover, market 'incentives' (such as rising prices) did not lead them to invest any greater share in improved methods of production either: when prices rose their marketing of grain actually fell. Rising prices reflected a crisis of production and not, as under capita-lism, a sign of growing prosperity and profitability.[37]

As Brenner has suggested, it was precisely the renewal of *feudal* social relations – and not any transition to capitalism – which explains why the economies of eastern Europe declined.[38] The key to understanding the chronically underdeveloped character of the eastern economies lies not with the influence of market forces but rather in the transformation (or lack of it in eastern Europe) of the *relations of production.*

The difficulties encountered by Wallerstein's attempt to derive both the causes of underdevelopment in eastern Europe and development in western Europe as well as the formation and structuring of the states-system from the effects of commerce and trade, serves to highlight the general theoretical shortcomings of the market-relations approach as a whole. What the market-relations perspective does in effect is transform the concept of 'the world market', as Banaji has suggested, into a 'formal abstraction' akin to the abstraction 'production-in-general' criticized by Marx in the *Grundrisse.*[39] That is, they fail to distinguish between the differences in the operations of the market and the various forms which

it assumes under different historical conditions and forms of social organization. As Kula observed of Poland during the second serfdom, 'market
phenomena are governed by completely different laws ... and above all
these phenomena have an altogether different effect on the non-market
sector and thus on economic life as a whole.'[40] Sweezy's failure to distinguish between the effects of the market under different social conditions
and on different social classes, and Wallerstein and Frank's failure to
understand why the growth of commerce in the sixteenth century in and
of itself was incapable either of underwriting western capitalist development or of moving the eastern economies in a capitalist direction, is rooted
in a common failure to distinguish between the historically unique forms
which 'the market' has assumed in different historical periods.

The failure of merchant capital to alter the institutional relationships
of feudal society – particularly the relations of dependence and coercion
between lord and peasant – was not simply a peculiarity of the way in
which the market operated in eastern Europe. As Rodney Hilton points
out, from the eleventh through to the eighteenth century the pattern of
merchant trade and commerce had always been to adapt itself 'both politically and socially to the feudal ruling circles. For these rulers were the
principal market for their luxury commodities, the recipients of private
and government loans.'[41]

For similar reasons, Marx insisted that 'the mere presence of monetary
wealth, and even the achievement of a kind of supremacy on its part,
is in no way sufficient for the dissolution into capital to happen.'[42] Marx
did not entirely rule out a role for merchants' capital in the transition
to capitalism; in specific historical situations it could aid in the dissolution
of the old mode of production, but only in conditions where the social
relations of production were already being transformed as a result of
other causes. Thus it is probably correct to say that the spread of commerce
may be a necessary, but not a sufficient, condition for the transition to
capitalism.

The 'original formation of capital' according to Marx,

> does not happen as is sometimes imagined with capital heaping up necessaries
> of life and instruments of labour and raw materials. ... Rather its original
> formation is ... through the dissolution of the old mode of production.[43]

It is, in other words, as Marx says of Adam Smith, an absurdity to speak
of a 'previous accumulation of capital' as the simple process of gathering
together huge quantities of money through trade and commerce, and
then employing this capital to produce more capital on an expanding
scale.[44] If this were possible, we would have to explain, as Marx insists,
why ancient Rome or Byzantium never gave rise to capitalism but instead

to the 'supremacy of the country over the city'.[45] Similarly, we would
have to account for why the great concentration of merchant capital,
credit and advanced exchange mechanisms which emerged in the Flemish
and Italian commercial centres in the thirteenth and fourteenth centuries,
along with considerable numbers of wage-labourers, did not result in
the rise of a new mode of production but rather remained entrenched
within the old. In short, as in the case of European commercial expansion
at the beginning of the sixteenth century, the growth of the market and
trade alone is insufficient to explain the transition from one mode of
production to another.

According to Marx, in order to understand the *specific* role of money
and market exchanges under capitalist conditions we must first grasp
the importance of the prior changes which must occur in the social relations of production *before* either money or commodities can function
as capital: 'In themselves, money and commodities are no more capital
than the means of production and subsistence are. They need to be transformed into capital.' But, Marx continues,

> this transformation can itself only take place under particular circumstances,
> which meet together at this point: the confrontation of, and the contact
> between, two very different kinds of commodity owners; on the one hand,
> the owners of money, means of production, means of subsistence, who are
> eager to valorize the sum of values they have appropriated by buying the labour-
> power of others; on the other hand, free workers, the sellers of their own
> labour-power, and therefore the sellers of labour. Free workers, in the double
> sense that they neither form part of the means of production themselves, as
> in the case with slaves, serfs, etc., nor do they own means of production, as
> would be the case with self-employed peasant proprietors. The free workers
> are therefore free from, unencumbered by, any means of production of their
> own. With the polarization of the commodity-market into these two classes,
> the fundamental conditions of capitalist production are present. The capital-
> relation presupposes a complete separation between the workers and the owner-
> ship of the conditions for the realization of their labour. . . . So-called primitive
> accumulation, therefore, is nothing else than the historical process of divorcing
> the producer from the means of production. It appears as 'primitive', because
> it forms the pre-history of capital, and of the mode of production corresponding
> to capital.[46]

Marx's critique of Adam Smith's conception of the 'previous accumulation' of capital has many parallels with contemporary critiques of mar-
ket-centred accounts of the origins of capitalism as expressed in the work
of Braudel, Frank and Wallerstein. What Marx said of the classical political economists holds true for the 'neo-Smithian'[47] theorists today: that
is, they fail to penetrate beyond the operations of the market to examine

the unique character of the social relations which characterize capitalist production.

II. Production Relations and Modes of Production

The idea that changes in the sphere of production are *causally* more fundamental than, say, developments in the sphere of exchange in determining large-scale historical transformations (such as those involved in the transition from feudalism to capitalism), is in many respects a commonplace of Marxism. Problems only emerge when we examine more closely how various Marxists have viewed the 'primacy of production' and how these changes in the sphere of production are thought to occur.

(i) *Forces and relations of production*

For many years the orthodox interpretation of Marx's theory of history expressed the view that the decisive element which determines the dynamic of historical change is rooted in the *independent* development of the technological forces of production. Thus, the transition from one mode of production to another occurs when the development of the technical/ material forces of production come into conflict with the relations of production. The relations of production, in this view, are usually defined as relations technically entailed by the labour process together with relations of property in the means of production. The materialist conception of history, in this view, as Lucio Colletti observed, is thus reduced to 'a technological conception of history'.[48] Indeed, certain of Marx's formulations appear to lend themselves to this kind of interpretation, particularly those passages where Marx attempted to render a shorthand summary of his historical method. Thus, in a well-known passage of the *Contribution to the Critique of Political Economy*, Marx refers to the 'mode of production of material life' as the determining element of the 'social, political and spiritual processes of life':

> At a certain stage of their development, the material forces of production in society come into conflict with the existing relations of production. ... From forms of development of the forces of production these relations turn into their fetters. Then comes the period of social revolution. With the change in the economic foundation the entire immense superstructure is more or less rapidly transformed.[49]

An equally famous passage from *The Poverty of Philosophy*, where Marx argues that 'the handmill gives you society with the feudal lord, the steam mill society with the industrial capitalist',[50] is just as often quoted as confirmation for the view that historical materialism is essentially a form of technological determinism. Central to this view of historical materialism is the idea that the forces of production causally determine the relations of production. The relations of production merely register the subterranean development of the productive forces. In other words, the assumption is that it is possible to locate a material substratum which is somehow separable from and independent of any social mediation. The development of the 'material forces of production' thus becomes the independent variable of historical change.

But is this Marx's view? If it were, it would make nonsense of his entire critique of classical political economy, one of the main purposes of which was to dispute the claim that production could be defined in purely technical terms. The 'trinity formula', espoused by the 'vulgar' political economists, which ascribed revenues to the various 'factors of production' – land, labour, and capital – was criticized by Marx precisely because it saw bourgeois *relations of distribution* already present in the technical conditions of the labour process. As Rosdolsky notes, vulgar political economy 'unthinkingly compounds the historically determined forms of production with the material aspects of the real labour process.'[51]

For Marx, relations of production are not separable from and in contrast to the material conditions of production. Unlike classical political economy which simply superimposes capitalist relations on the technical process of production by treating them as 'naturally' imposed relations, Marx saw the production process as *indissolubly* social and material, production of both material products and social relations. This comes out clearly in his critique of John Stuart Mill's contention that the basis of income distribution was already present in the material/technical labour process. Criticizing Mill, Marx writes:

Before distribution can be the distribution of products, it is: (1) the distribution of the instruments of production, and (2), which is a further specification of the same relation, the distribution of the members of the society among the different kinds of production. (Subsumption of the individuals under specific relations of production.) The distribution of products is evidently only a result of this distribution, which is comprised within the process of production itself and determines the structure of production. To examine production while disregarding this internal distribution within it is obviously an empty abstraction.[52]

This passage is important for a number of reasons. First, it clearly asserts the primacy of production over distribution and consumption. Second, it rejects the proposition that the production process can be conceived in purely technical terms. Production is both a material/technical and a social process; production conceived in isolation from social relations is 'an empty abstraction'. And third, the relations of production are determined by an 'internal distribution' of the means of production which in turn subsumes 'individuals under specific relations of production'.[53]

For Marx the relationship between forces and relations of production is an *internally* determined one; social relations are not simply mapped on to a pre-existing (that is, non-social) 'material' foundation. It is difficult, therefore, to see how Marx's views can be thought to sanction a 'technological' theory of society and history. Even the most sophisticated versions of the technological interpretation ultimately fail to specify how the development of the productive forces can be determined in abstraction from the relations of production.[54] By treating the forces of production as an independent variable of history, it effectively *dehistoricizes* historical materialism.

What, then, was Marx's conception of the relationship between the forces and relations of production? At the core of Marx's view was the idea that forces and relations of production were to be conceived as a *contradictory unity*.[55] Marx criticized the 'one-sidedness' of Ricardo's method of analysis precisely because it denied the contradictory basis of the capitalist mode of production. The essential contradiction of capitalism lay, for Marx, at the very heart of commodity production; under specifically capitalist conditions commodities embody both a material use-value and a socially determined exchange value. It was on the basis of this insight into the contradictory foundations of capitalist production that Marx was able to explore the developed forms of this elementary contradiction manifest in the distinction between concrete and abstract value-creating labour; between constant and variable capital and its ultimate expression in crises described by Marx as 'but momentary and forcible solutions of the existing contradictions'.[56] For Marx, Ricardo's method was ultimately reductionist because it collapsed these contradictory forms into a single 'unmediated identity'[57] in order to show, in Marx's words, 'that the various economic categories or relationships do not contradict the theory of value, instead on the contrary, of developing them together with their apparent contradictions out of this basis or presenting the development of this basis itself.'[58]

The contradictory unity of the forces and relations of production was not conceived by Marx as an abstract super-historical key to social development.[59] Rather, the specific form which this relation assumed could only be understood by examining how it was expressed historically in determinate social conditions. For Marx, it was not an *external* but an *internal* contradiction rooted in and mediated by the class struggle. In other words, the relationship between the forces and relations of production and conflict between classes are not two separate contradictions.

To treat them as such holds the danger of lapsing into some form of technological determinism. Rather, as Derek Sayer argues:

> the relevant contradiction lies not between technology and social relations *simpliciter* but between one set of emergent production relations which both constitute a productive force in their own right and are capable of sustaining a superior technology, and *another* within the framework of which they have operated hitherto.[60]

It is misleading, therefore, to suggest that Marx conceived of the relationship between the forces and relations of production as one of simple 'correspondence'.[61] It is difficult to see how, on such a view, the transition from one mode of production could occur, let alone variations within a single mode, without invoking a highly voluntarist conception of the class struggle. That is, it encourages the belief that the class struggle periodically intervenes to disrupt the functional unity of the forces and relations of production. However, simply inverting the relationship between the forces and relations of production – as Perry Anderson urges – does not solve the problem either, for it implicitly suggests that the technical/material dimensions of production are somehow separable from social relations – which is exactly what crude versions of historical materialism would have us believe.[62]

(ii) *Relations of production and forms of exploitation*

If many theorists have been unhappy with the exaggerated emphasis placed on the forces of production in traditional interpretations of Marx, few have questioned the concept of the relations of production inherent in this view. Despite their misgivings over the technological determinist implications of the traditional view, many Marxists have retained an excessively narrow conception of the relations of production similar to that which underpins the technological interpretation. The relations of production, it will be recalled, are from this perspective defined in terms of the technical requirements of the labour process. Relations of production are conceived as equivalent to forms of exploitation in the immediate process of production. Modes of production, accordingly, are defined by the direct relationship between exploiter and exploited at the level of the enterprise. The supersession of one mode of production by another is thus reduced to the process whereby one economic form of exploitation is replaced by another more technically efficient form.

This narrow conception of the relations of production has found its way into some of the more recent critiques of the 'market-relations' approach. In a well-known debate over the character of capitalist development in Latin America, Ernesto Laclau charged Frank and Wallerstein with confusing the meaning of the term 'mode of production'. Capitalism, according to Laclau, is defined by the 'fundamental economic relationship ... constituted by the free labourer's sale of his labour-power, whose necessary precondition is the loss by the direct producer of ownership of the means of production.' Feudalism is defined as 'a general ensemble of extra-economic coercions weighing on the peasantry, absorbing a good part of its economic surplus'.[63] The error of proponents of the market-relations perspective such as Frank and Wallerstein is to confuse 'the capitalist mode of production and participation in a world capitalist economic system'.[64] 'The world capitalist system', Laclau concludes, 'includes at the level of its definition, various modes of production.'[65]

According to Laclau, the expansion of European capitalism actually reinforced feudal forms of production in Latin America. The market-relations approach cannot explain these developments because it assumes that incorporation into the nexus of a world-wide system of exchange and division of labour necessarily entails that these relations be defined as capitalist. Laclau's general point, that the market-relations perspective neglects the relations of production in its account of capitalist transformation, is certainly valid. However, his conclusions are misleading and can result in a rather sterile set of theoretical conclusions, particularly as regards the transition from feudalism to capitalism.

For example, Laclau's position holds that wherever the relations of production are different from those of the dominant 'mode of production' – wage-labour in the case of capitalism, 'coerced' labour in that of feudalism – it can be said that different 'modes of production' coexist. If this were true, we would be forced to accept that the existence of hired labour throughout the medieval period was evidence of the existence of capitalism, in however limited a form. Maurice Dobb, in fact, comes close to arguing precisely this in his account of west European feudalism. Dobb contends that the use of hired labour on the feudal estates of thirteenth-century England meant that capitalist relations of production had been established even though feudal social relations still predominated elsewhere.[66] Pursued to its logical conclusion, this would imply that the simple numerical preponderance of hired labour is what ultimately determines the existence of capitalism.[67]

Modes of production are, in Dobb's words 'virtually identical' with specific forms of exploitation.[68] This view, however, is at variance with that of Marx. As we saw above, Marx's conception of the relations of production is much broader. For Marx, every mode of production is characterized by a 'specific economic form' through which surplus labour is appropriated; under capitalism wage-labour is the dominant economic form by means of which wealth is produced and eventually appropriated by capital in the form of surplus-value. But that does not mean that wherever wage-labour has been present, capitalism can also be said to have existed. 'Wage-labour' only becomes, in Marx's words, 'capital-positing, capital-producing labour' under certain historical conditions.[69] It is the *class relation* between capital and free labour which is the precondition for the appearance of the specific economic form which obtains between capital and wage-labour in the capitalist enterprise. If we only examine the particular relation which is established through the purchase and sale of labour we cannot discern any class relations. That is why, in *Capital*, Marx rebukes those 'who regard this superficial relation, this essential formality, this deceptive appearance of capitalist relations *as its true essence* ... [and] thereby gloss over the essential nature of the relationship.'[70]

The 'essential nature of the relationship' between wage-labour and capital only becomes evident if we take into account the conditions of competition and developed social division of labour within which the *individual enterprise* is located and within which the transaction between labour and capital takes place. What gives wage-labour its specifically capitalist character, in other words, is its appearance within a broader complex of social relations which are distinctively capitalist. By the same token, forced labour is only feudal when it is inserted within feudal class relations. In neither case is it possible to discover the true character of the form of labour or 'mode of production' by examining only the immediate labour process. Every mode of production exhibits a 'specific economic form' of exploitation, as Marx might put it, appropriate to its 'content'. That does not mean, however, that modes of production are reducible to these forms alone. Thus, of capitalism, Marx writes:

> When we consider bourgeois society in the long view and as a whole, then the final result of the process of production always appears as society itself, i.e., the human being itself in its social relations. Everything that has a fixed form, such as the product etc., appears as merely a moment, a vanishing moment in this movement. *The* direct production process itself here appears only as a moment. The conditions and objectifications of the process are themselves equally moments of it and its only subjects are the individuals, but individuals in mutual relationships, which they equally reproduce and produce anew.[71]

The important point here is that, for Marx, there was no intention of defining modes of production as 'virtually identical' with forms of exploitation. Forms of exploitation are certainly an essential part of his definition, but are not reducible to these forms. Since production was founded on the contradictory unity of the forces and relations of production there was no sense in which this unity – as it expressed itself historically in a given mode of production – could be conceived, in Ricardian fashion, as a series of 'unmediated identities' as Dobb's position suggests.

The particular relationship assumed historically by the forces and relations of production is what constitutes the economic 'laws of motion' of a given mode of production. Under capitalism, as we saw earlier, the essential contradiction inherent in this relation expresses itself in distinct and developed forms throughout the entire circuit of capital; the capital relation is merely a summary expression for the whole range of social relations embodied in the entire circuit of capital which includes exchange, price-formation, realization, and so on. The direct exploitation of labour appears only as a 'moment' in the production process as capital is forced beyond the direct labour process in order to reproduce itself.[72] That is why Marx was careful to avoid any reduction of his definition of capitalism to this relation pure and simple: 'the relations of production in their totality constitute what are called the social relations, society, and specifically at a definite stage of historical development.'[73]

Marx's reference to a 'definite stage of historical development' here is worth noting, for it implies that a purely theoretical solution to the problem of defining modes of production is inadequate. Judging a given set of production relations from the standpoint of 'their totality' may lead us to exactly the contrary conclusion from that drawn when we examine them from the standpoint of the immediate relations between appropriators and producers. This problem manifests itself most clearly in Marx's analysis of American and West Indian slavery. Marx made occasional reference to the capitalist character of American and Caribbean plantation slavery. What made American slavery capitalist was its insertion into a set of international economic relations which were dominated by capitalism and whose expansion was due to the expansion of production based on wage labour, especially in England. Marx writes that

> as soon as peoples whose production still moves within the lower forms of slave-labour ... are drawn into a world market dominated by the capitalist mode of production, whereby the sale of their products for export develops into their principal interest, the civilized horrors of over-work are grafted onto the barbaric horrors of slavery ... in proportion as the export of cotton became of vital interest to those states, the over-working of the Negro, and sometimes the consumption of his life in seven years of labour, became a factor in a calculated and calculating system. It was no longer a question of obtaining from him a certain quantity of useful products, but rather the production of surplus-value itself.[74]

Thus, 'forced labour' in this instance was compatible with capitalism, if only for a time. The plantation system used labour and land extensively rather than intensively; its form of expansion depended upon increases in the supply of slaves and new lands.[75] The exploitation of slave labour was an example of what Marx termed the 'formal' subsumption of labour to capital based on the extraction of absolute surplus-value. Slave labour was exploited to the point of exhaustion by lengthening the working day in order to obtain increases in productivity, and hence in the amount of surplus-value extracted. In other words, the *absolute* amount of time labour was employed was simply increased. Only when labour has been separated from direct access to the means of production, in this case, when the slaves had become transformed into wage-labourers, does capital begin to extract relative surplus-value on the basis of decreases in the length of the working day combined with an overall increase in productivity. It is only at this point that the capitalist mode of production comes fully into its own, where both labour and capital are combined in the most technologically efficient manner. 'The general features of the *formal subsumption* remain,' Marx writes,

> viz. the direct *subordination of the labour process to capital*, irrespective of the state of its technological development. But on this foundation there now arises a technologically and otherwise *specific mode of production – capitalist production* – which transforms the nature *of the labour process and its conditions.* Only when that happens do we witness the *real subsumption of labour to capital.*[76]

The important point here is that we do not need to consider plantation slavery as somehow 'outside' the social relations of capitalism to make sense of it theoretically. But this is only possible if we abandon the restrictive definition of capitalism as a mode of production which insists upon wage-labour in the simple sense as its defining feature. These observations are equally pertinent to the form taken by the transition to capitalism in parts of Europe. As we argue in the following chapters, fixation on the immediate relations of production can lead to disastrously wrong conclusions regarding the true nature of these societies.

To return to our present discussion, what these observations suggest is that the relations of production cannot be defined as narrowly as Dobb and Laclau wish to define them. The basic class relation – be it between capital and wage-labour or between lord and peasant – is in no sense a strictly 'economic' relation: it is a class relation which assumes different developed historical forms. One of the implications of this alternative view is that it avoids the tendency of Laclau's formulation to multiply the number of 'modes of production' found in a given 'social formation': since modes of production are not reducible to specific labour forms, any particular mode may be compatible with a variety of forms of labour. Indeed, as Jairus Banaji argues, 'the distinction between "modes of production" and "social formations" that is generally drawn in most recent Marxist literature may actually obscure and mystify the mechanisms of modes of production'.[77] In addition, this alternative view precludes any simple severing of the relation between economic and political structures since the latter are seen as grounded in the basic relation of production.[78]

One final point should be noted before returning to the historical dimensions of the transition debate. By saying that the relations of production cannot be adequately grasped on the basis of the traditional base/superstructure model with its excessively narrow and technicist definition of the 'economic', we should not fall into the trap of insisting that 'everything else' – all political, legal and ideological forms – are of equal weight in constituting the relations of production. This type of unitarian approach, which dissolves virtually all social forms into the relations of production, implies that changes in any one of the constitutive elements – in the state, for example – can also produce a change in the mode of production. Clearly some legal and political relations are constitutive aspects of the relations of production and others are not. Certain forms of legal property relations are central to the capitalist productive sphere, establishing the conditions under which capital and labour meet. As Wood argues:

> There are ... at least two senses in which the juridical-political 'sphere' is implicated in the productive 'base'. First, a system of production always exists in the shape of specific social determinations, the particular modes of organization and domination and the forms of property in which relations of production are embodied – what might be called the 'basic' as distinct from 'superstructural' juridical-political attributes of the productive system. Second, from an *historical* point of view even political institutions like *village* and *state* enter directly into the constitution of productive relations and are in a sense prior to them (even where these institutions are not the direct instruments of surplus-appropriation) to the extent that relations of production are historically constituted by the configuration of political power that determines the outcome of class conflict.[79]

The important point is that only through a historically informed analysis is it possible to 'resolve' the question of what constitutes a mode of production. If we simply collapse the totality of social relations into an undifferentiated unity, we have no real way of distinguishing one mode of production from another. If, on the other hand, we concentrate our attention only on the immediate process of production we may ignore other factors – juridical, political, and, critically, the impact of changes in the forces and relations of production at the international level – which help to determine the character of the relations of production.

In Dobb's case, reliance on an excessively narrow definition of the relations of production leads him to ignore crucial aspects of the transition to capitalism. Because of this, Dobb is unable fully to integrate the role played by the development of commodity and exchange relations into his account of the decline of feudalism. In addition, and for similar reasons, Dobb does not adequately grasp the centrality of the role of political power in feudal social relations and, therefore, underplays the influence of state structures in shaping the divergent paths followed by England and the continental countries following the crisis of European feudalism. His framework cannot account for why the transition to capitalism occurred in England in the seventeenth century while others in continental Europe failed to make a similar breakthrough. In the end, his account falls back on a conception of capitalist transformation similar to that held by the market-relations approach: capitalism invades the old mode of production 'from without'.[80] In other words, Dobb ends up presupposing precisely that which needs to be explained, namely, how capitalism emerged out of the internal social contradictions of feudalism. Despite these shortcomings, Dobb's historical treatment of the rise of capitalism remains one of the most insightful and deservedly influential accounts produced by a Marxist historian. It is worthwhile, therefore, examining his historical analysis in somewhat more detail.

(iii) *The role of petty commodity production*

Because of his definition of feudalism as 'virtually identical' with serfdom, Dobb's account remains ambiguous on the issue of how far the expansion of commodity relations contributed to the 'dissolution' of feudal society. This ambiguity is expressed in Dobb's characterization of the period between the end of serfdom in the fourteenth century and the English Revolution of 1640; this period is termed a *transitional* mode of production of an apparently indeterminate class character, variously defined as the 'petty mode of production' or simply 'feudalism-in-decline'.[81] Dobb summed up his assessment of this period in the following way:

> the disintegration of the feudal mode of production had already reached an advanced stage before the capitalist mode developed, and this disintegration did not proceed in any close association with the growth of the new mode of production within the womb of the old. . . . [And thus] an interval was necessary between the start of the decline of serfdom and the rise of capitalism.[82]

Despite his equation of feudalism with serfdom – which by all accounts was dead by 1500 – Dobb continued to insist that feudalism was only finally destroyed in England by the revolution of 1640. At the core of these inconsistencies is a failure on Dobb's part to see the growth of commodity relations not as something *external* to feudalism, but as an integral aspect of feudal relations of production. As Rodney Hilton has recently argued, petty commodity production was present not only as an expression of the ancient division of labour between agriculturalists, industrial craftsmen and petty traders but also as an element in the relations between landlords and peasants.[83]

Commodity production for the market, then, was not, as Sweezy's account suggests, an external factor grafted on to feudal society and fundamentally incompatible with its basic structure. True, feudal production was defined by a circuit of production geared to the immediate consumption needs of the feudal ruling class – whether these 'needs' were defined by the desire for costly luxury goods or materials for war. Peasant production, on the other hand, was geared to the immediate subsistence of the peasant household since any surplus above subsistence was subject to appropriation by the lord. This, however, was not a foregone conclusion: the lord's ability to appropriate surpluses above subsistence was dependent on his capacity to enforce his claim, just as the peasantry's ability to retain this surplus was dependent on the latter's ability to resist such exactions. The peasantry had a material interest in keeping as large a share as possible, thereby raising the ceiling of their own consumption.

The struggle over peasant surplus between lord and peasant formed the essential basis of the feudal dynamic both in the short and long term. And in the later phases of feudalism this struggle was in large measure a struggle over which class was to have greater access to the market. With the expansion in the world market in grains in the sixteenth century in eastern Europe, as we saw above, access to peasant surplus shifted decisively in favour of the feudal ruling class with the imposition of the second serfdom. In other cases, as in parts of Germany, the peasantry was able to resist these demands and thus won greater access to expanded market opportunities. From the standpoint of the peasantry, greater access to the market provided a basis of autonomy and the evasion of feudal obligations. It was also a hedge against bad harvests and famine. The expansion of commodity relations amongst the peasantry was thus inextricably bound up with the struggle over feudal rent between lord and peasant. Commenting on the remarkable growth of production for the market in the fourteenth century, Rodney Hilton writes:

The necessary basis for this market production was of course, an increase in the surplus production of agriculture – surplus that is to the subsistence of the basic producers. Undoubtedly this was made possible in part by increased technical efficiency, but improved organization and increased pressure by lords to transfer more of the surplus ... from the producers to themselves was even more important. The two problems, in fact, must have been interdependent to some extent: demand for rent sometimes stimulated peasant production, and at other times depressed it. Although lords participated in market production in their demesnes, it would seem that the bulk of the agricultural commodities which were offered for sale in village markets, in country towns and in the cities were produced by peasants in search of money to pay for rents, taxes, judicial fines and industrial products.[84]

The extent to which the growing independence of peasant commodity production was linked to the broader struggle of the peasantry to free itself from the combined weight of lordly exactions and the growing pressure of state exactions becomes evident when we consider the character of the major peasant revolts which in some measure precipitated the feudal crisis at the end of the fourteenth and early part of the fifteenth centuries. Almost without exception, the largest and – from the standpoint of the lords – most devastating revolts in this period occurred in areas such as the Paris basin, the environs of Barcelona, the Rhine valley, and, perhaps most spectacularly, in the English rising of 1381, all of which were characterized by high levels of peasant production for the market.[85]

In the English case, the peasant revolt was centred in the southeast, with the London market at its centre. It is true, as Dobb observed, that on the ecclesiastical and secular estates, serfdom and labour services were still much in evidence. Indeed the crisis of feudal revenues which had become acute by the end of the fourteenth century only served to stimulate attempts by estate owners to extend servile relations further, with demands for greater labour services and restrictions on the mobility of the peasant population. In addition, however, there was also a high proportion of peasants of free status. The uneven character of the social forms which co-existed in this region reflected the contrasting impact which the early development of production for the market had among the peasantry. Already, in the fourteenth century, the market in peasant land was beginning to produce a level of social differentiation within the ranks of the peasantry in substantial areas of southeast England. It was those sections of the peasantry which enjoyed the greatest degree of mobility and autonomy owing to their greater access to the market that the strongest resistance to the 'seigneurial reaction' developed: 'it was due to the early development of production for the market by peasants themselves, which strengthened the sinews of peasant war against such lords as might try to depress their status.'[86]

Here we must be careful to distinguish between the market as an opportunity and the market as a *compulsion*. The significant point is that peasant mobility was a sign of the extent to which the compulsions of the market, rather than production for subsistence, now governed the reproduction of the peasant community. The critical market was the market in tenancies, which implies a necessity to enter the market for the conditions of subsistence. It marks a situation in which direct producers were deprived of direct, non-market access to the means of subsistence through a system of competitive rents. In this sense, market-oriented peasants were compelled to do well; market opportunities *per se* could not have produced the results they did among the English peasantry. But where petty production and a growing market of free labourers who were increasingly dependent on the market for their means of subsistence came together, the logic was towards the dissolution of older forms of productive relations. In terms of our earlier analysis, these developments expressed the internal development of new forces of production, 'embodied' by a rising class, which contradicted the framework of the social relations within which they operated. 'The economic structure of capitalist society has grown out of the economic structure of feudal society. The dissolution of the latter set free the elements of the former.'[87]

By the end of the fourteenth and for the greater part of the fifteenth century, 'Rents were sufficiently low and the ability of both landowners and the state to control the free movement of peasants and labourers so minimal in practice that ... the feudal restrictions on simple commodity production virtually disappeared.'[88] Agricultural wages rose by 50 per cent and the peasantry gained *de facto* property rights as holdings were converted into copyholds. Conditions continued to improve throughout the fifteenth century. Stable land tenures and long-term leases, together with rising prices for agricultural products, served not only to stimulate peasant productivity but also to accentuate social differentiation and divisions within the peasantry. Peasant accumulation on the basis of a growing surplus above costs of production (that is, subsistence and rent) contributed to the rise of a stratum of rich peasants.

This layer of richer peasants, or yeoman as they came to be called in England, invested substantial portions of their income in agricultural improvements so as to increase the productivity of labour. The result was an overall expansion of petty commodity production, raising the yeomanry to 'the most important group amongst those who were farming for profit at the beginning of the sixteenth century...'[89] By the late sixteenth century, some copyholders held as many as 200 acres.[90] 'No wonder then', as Marx observed, 'that England at the end of the sixteenth century had a class of capitalist farmers who were rich men in relation to the circumstances of the time.'[91]

The rise of the yeomanry occurred to a substantial degree at the expense of the smaller peasantry. The accumulation of holdings by richer peasants meant that the less well-off were often forced to work on these larger holdings as agricultural labourers. A by-product of the dispossession of the smaller peasants was a breakdown in traditional peasant solidarity within the village community: 'Rich peasant families, now graziers and demesne farmers holding largely leasehold tenure, no longer stood as mediators between the lords and the communities of customary tenants. They were no longer potential leaders of the resistance.'[92]

The expansion of commodity production for the market which forced peasants into the market for their reproduction, the rise of a class of small capitalist farmers out of the ranks of the peasantry itself, and the consequent breakdown of peasant solidarity, were all essential links in a chain of events which culminated in the consolidation of capitalist relations on the land in England. As Rodney Hilton summarizes:

> peasant resistance was of crucial importance in the development of rural communes, the extension of free tenure and status, the freeing of peasant and artisan economies for the development of commodity production, and eventually the emergence of the capitalist entrepreneur.[93]

This was not, as we have argued, an inevitable process of commercialization. Peasant differentiation did not arise spontaneously from commodity production for the market, as though peasants were simply waiting to become capitalists, given half a chance. The capitalist impulse rather sprang from the fact that peasants were subjected to the market, in new ways. The character of their tenancies meant that recourse to the market was no longer merely a choice which could be foregone; it was compulsion imposed on them by the necessity to accumulate in order to survive.

The weakening of the village community in the seventeenth century as a result of differentiation represented an important opening for the larger landlords and gentry who wished to stem the tide of falling incomes and rents as a result of peasant gains of the earlier period. Large landowners, many of whom had arisen from the ranks of the yeomanry, were able to capitalize on divisions within the peasantry by mounting a full-scale assault on peasant rights. This involved practices such as 'rack-renting' – the imposition of multiple rent increases – and finally wholesale enclosure of properties formerly held by peasant tenants. Between 1590 and 1640, the combination of enclosure and the doubling of rents had dramatically shifted the balance of class power in favour of the landlords. Many of the lesser yeomanry now found themselves subject to expropriation as large landlords began to engage in capitalist farming on consolidated holdings. By the middle of the seventeenth century, the classic triadic pattern of capitalist farming referred to by Marx had been established: large landlords leased their properties to tenant farmers who, in turn, employed wage-labour drawn from the ranks of the now dispossessed peasant masses. Only in England – to which we shall return – did the primitive accumulation of capital, that is, the expropriation of the peasant producers from the land, assume, in Marx's words, its 'classic form'.

The expropriation of the peasantry by the landed classes themselves through the 'idyllic methods of primitive accumulation ... conquered the field for capitalist agriculture, incorporated the soil into capital and created for the urban industries the necessary supplies of free and rightless proletarians.'[94] Because Dobb's account neglects the internal factors which contributed to the dissolution of feudalism in favour of a conception of transition which locates the dynamic of change outside feudal relations *per se*, the phases of transition – from serfdom through the 'transitional' petty commodity mode to capitalism – appear as mere juxtapositions; there is no real sense in which the internal class conflicts of one phase can be seen to give rise to the next. Moreover, since capitalism simply invades the old mode of production from without, we are left with no explanation as to why the crisis of feudalism gave rise to such different outcomes throughout Europe; why, for example, did eastern Europe retreat into the second serfdom as the economies of the West began to move in the opposite direction? And why was England able to make the transition to agrarian capitalism while the economies of France and Germany stalled and receded?

(iv) *The role of 'political factors'*

It is obvious that the development of commodity relations within the peasantry did not give rise to a uniform transition to capitalism throughout Europe even though, as we have seen, this development appears to have given impetus to a Europe-wide pattern of resistance and revolt against feudal obligations in the late medieval period. The reason this did not occur is connected to the second major area of neglect evidenced in Dobb's account – that is, his failure to see differences in class organization and political power as the decisive element in determining the pattern of outcomes which emerged from the crisis of feudalism. Dobb's failure to place political compulsion at the centre of his analysis of feudal social relations prevents him from providing a satisfactory explanation of how the rise of 'feudal centralism' in the form of absolutist states stalled the transition to capitalism in large parts of continental Europe.

Dobb's main line of argument for the fall of serfdom is based on the dramatic decline in population following the Black Death and the Europe-wide famine of the fourteenth century. This reduction in the peasant population seriously affected seigneurial incomes and placed those who survived in a much better bargaining position vis-à-vis the lords. Moreover, the opening-up of untenanted lands and the colonization of peasant allods further threatened landlord control of the peasant population. At first, it seems as though Dobb wants to place political and social factors at the forefront of his analysis by arguing that:

The strength of peasant resistance, the political and military power of local lords, rendering it easy or difficult as the case might be to overcome peasant resistance and forcibly to prevent desertion of the manors, and the extent to which royal power exerted its influence to strengthen seigneurial authority or on the contrary welcomed an opportunity of weakening the opposition of rival sections of the nobility – all of this was of great importance in deciding whether concession or renewed coercion was to be the seigneurial answer to desertion and depopulation, and whether, if coercion was attempted, it was to prove successful.[95]

However, no sooner are these considerations raised, than Dobb dismisses them as, at best, secondary influences: 'political factors of this kind can hardly be regarded as sufficient to account for the differences in the course of events in various parts of Europe. ... All the indications suggest that in the deciding outcome, economic factors must have exercised the outstanding influence.'[96] For Dobb, 'economic factors' meant the scarcity or abundance of labour; it was this and not 'political factors' which determined the fall of serfdom in some areas and its strengthening in others:

it seems evident that the fundamental consideration must have been the abundance or scarcity of labour, the cheapness or dearness of hired labour in determining whether or not the lord was willing to commute labour services for money payment.[97]

What is missing from this account is any sense in which such choices were constrained by the balance of class forces between lord and peasant. This becomes clear from Dobb's treatment of peasant differentiation. Here, Dobb resorts to a curious line of argument by attributing peasant differentiation to 'inequalities in type of soil and situation and in fortune'.[98] Dobb seems to want to conflate here accidents of geography, such as 'inequalities in type of soil' with manifestly social causes, 'situation and fortune'. More important though, is the fact that when he does address the social basis of such developments, he treats them as though they were mere adjuncts of the reimposition of *lordly* power. For Dobb the significance of the rise of a 'kulak stratum' was that it led simultaneously to an increase in rural poverty as poorer peasants were dispossessed by their richer neighbours, and thus to an increased pool of hired labour at the disposal of the lords. On this view, peasant emancipation was a decidedly one-sided affair arising from 'a tendency to commutation at the lord's initiative'.[99]

Commenting on these passages from Dobb, Robert Brenner has aptly observed that

It is difficult to know what to make of Dobb's counterposition ... of 'economic' to political, when what appears to be at issue are decisive class struggles determining the maintenance of feudal class relations or their transformation. For was not the essence of feudalism as Dobb defines it the encasement of economic-productive activities within a determining structure of extra-economic relations of surplus-extraction directly by force?[100]

In an important sense Brenner is right; formally at least, Dobb does define feudalism in terms of class relations. But it is precisely the restrictive meaning which he attaches to this definition which is decisive in terms of his historical analysis; Dobb's focus is on the immediate relation between lord and serf within the confines of the feudal enterprise. That is why his analysis of the lords' response to the feudal crisis is presented as though it were simply a matter of the economic calculations of *individual* lords determined by the 'cheapness or dearness of hired labour' within their jurisdictions; broader considerations related to the balance of class power *between* the feudal ruling class and the peasantry simply disappear from sight.

This focus on the choices open to individual lords – whether to commute or retain labour services – also carries with it the implication that lordly power was paramount: lords could simply choose whichever form of labour best corresponded to their individual needs.[101] This orientation seriously misrepresents what was at stake; commutation, in England at least, did not represent merely the reimposition of serfdom in a new form, but the beginnings of an entirely new set of social relations which contradicted the traditional bonds between feudal lord and serf. Moreover, far from being the product of *conscious* design by any of the economic actors involved, the emergence of capitalist relations should properly be seen, as Brenner has suggested, 'as an *unintended consequence* of the actions of individual pre-capitalist actors and especially the conflicts between pre-capitalist classes'.[102] Dobb's tendency to see the results of peasant differentiation as a subsidiary aspect of the reimposition of landlord power leaves him powerless to explain not only the character of the peasant economy but also how differences in lordly *political* power throughout Europe affected the development of commodity relations (and hence differentiation within the peasantry) and thus the different trajectories of economic development from the sixteenth century onwards.

III. State Formation and Economic Development

The recent work of Robert Brenner on the origins of capitalism has gone some distance in redressing the shortcomings of Dobb's historical account. Moreover, despite his acknowledged debt to both Laclau and Dobb, he has been able to accomplish this only by implicitly breaking with the framework of these theorists. Brenner's analysis of the origins of capitalism goes significantly beyond that of Dobb by incorporating 'political factors', such as state-formation, as an essential element of his conception of production relations and economic development. Central to his viewpoint is the belief that 'a "fusion" . . . between "the economic" and "the political" was a distinguishing and constitutive feature of the feudal class structure and system of production.'[103] Following from this conception of feudalism, Brenner has coined the term 'political accumulation' to describe one of the key features of the feudal dynamic:

> the long-term tendency, prevalent throughout the feudal epoch (from circa 1000–1100), to 'political accumulation' – that is, the build up of larger, more effective military organization and/or the construction of stronger surplus-extracting machinery – may be viewed as conditioned by the system's limited potential for long-term economic growth, and, to a certain extent, as an alternative to extending or improving cultivation. Given the difficulties of increasing production, the effective application of force tended to appear, even in the short run, as the best method of amassing wealth.[104]

Through a comparison of the class relations of various countries, Brenner is able to show how different class structures and traditions of class organization determined specific historical outcomes in the transition to capitalism. For example, Brenner's comparative analysis of agrarian class relations in England and France convincingly demonstrates how, in the latter case, the relative strength of the peasantry and relative weakness of the landed classes undermined the ability of the latter to force through a transformation of agrarian relations similar to that which had been undertaken in England. Indeed, as Brenner's account makes clear, nowhere else in continental Europe was the classic pattern of primitive accumulation on the model of the English enclosures repeated on the same scale.

The development of political accumulation, according to Brenner, was not simply or exclusively a product of the fact that economic growth under feudalism was extensive – depending on territorial expansion – rather than intensive, the product of technological improvements which increase the overall productivity of labour. Since the application of force was the means through which surplus was extracted from the peasantry, and the guarantee that wealth would not be appropriated through a similar show of force by rival lords, the tendency towards political accumulation became 'self-perpetuating and escalating – the amassing of more land and men to more effectively exert force in order to collect the resources for the further application of power.'[105]

The long-term trend towards political accumulation was thus the construction of *feudal states* as the natural outcome of the military centralization required on the part of the lords to perpetuate themselves as a ruling class. According to Brenner, it is out of the different forms which political accumulation assumed in various parts of Europe that it becomes possible to chart the evolution of social-class relations, the divergent patterns of class conflict and systems of property. Thus, in France, we find two important developments: first, as a result of peasant conquests in the eleventh and twelfth centuries we witness a gradual evolution away from decentralized or fragmented feudal authority towards much more centralized forms of lordly political organization. The accelerated drive towards absolutism at the end of the sixteenth century is only the most obvious expression of this trend. Second, we find much stronger traditions of peasant solidarity and organization than elsewhere in Europe which, in conjunction with the protection of peasant rights offered by the absolutist state (as it increasingly found itself competing with local lords over peasant surpluses), enabled the French peasantry to establish strong property rights to their land. Over the long term, entrenched peasant property rights 'set in motion the developmental pattern familiar from the medieval period: demographic growth leading to the pulverization of holdings, accompanied by declining productivity, leading ultimately to stagnation and decline.'[106] In England by contrast, we find from the eleventh and twelfth centuries a high degree of coherence and self-organization among the lords which ensured that 'political accumulation' was carried out in a largely decentralized manner. As a result, 'there is no tendency to substitute an emergent system of centralized surplus extraction ... no embryonic rise of an absolutist form of rule.'[107]

Over time, according to Brenner, this decentralized form of surplus-extraction proved to be the trump card of the English aristocracy. For even in the face of the peasant advances of the late fourteenth and fifteenth centuries, the English lords were able to maintain their basic feudal property rights. It was the retention of these property rights which, in the end, were decisive: such rights ultimately allowed the English lords to undermine the customary rights and copyholds of the peasantry in the sixteenth and early seventeenth centuries and begin to farm their holdings on capitalist principles.[108]

Brenner's view that the different property systems which existed in England and France determined the long-term economic prospects of each, rests upon a more fundamental set of assumptions about the way in which property forms or property relations constrain or impel economic development. Brenner argues that in every social economy

property relations, once established, will determine the economic course of action which is rational for the direct producers and the exploiters ... the property relations will, to a very great extent, determine the pattern of economic development of any society; for that pattern is, to a very great extent, merely the *aggregate* result of the carrying out of the rules for reproduction of the direct producers and exploiters.[109]

The 'rules for reproduction' of pre-capitalist property relations, according to Brenner, are in essence inimical to economic development since:

> in allowing both exploiters and producers direct access to their means of reproduction, pre-capitalist property forms ... freed both exploiters and producers from the necessity to produce for exchange, thus of the necessity to sell competitively on the market their output, and thus of the necessity to produce at the socially necessary rate. ... In consequence, both producers and exploiters were relieved of the necessity to cut costs so as to maintain themselves, and so the necessity constantly to improve production through specialization and/or accumulation and/or innovation. The property relations, in themselves, failed to *impose* that relentless pressure on the individual producers to improve which ... is an indispensable condition for economic development.[110]

Brenner's analysis, with its emphasis on the decisive importance of political factors – that is, the build-up of absolutist state structures through the process of political accumulation – in the evolution of European feudalism represents an important advance over earlier Marxist accounts of the transition to capitalism. But it has also proved controversial. Guy Bois has objected that Brenner's political Marxism 'amounts to a voluntarist conception of history in which the class struggle is divorced from all other objective contingencies and ... from such laws as may be peculiar to a specific mode of production.'[111] However, Brenner does provide an account of such 'objective contingencies'. His argument is simply that the property relations which existed under feudalism set definite limits on the development of the productive forces and this, in turn, is what determined the drive towards 'political accumulation' and the construction of absolutist states. How effectively feudal ruling classes organized themselves determined their ability to resist peasant encroachments on the land.

The English ruling class, according to Brenner, was the most highly self-organized ruling class in Europe. Over the short term, this meant that the English aristocracy were able to exploit the peasantry extremely efficiently; over the long term, it meant that in the eighteenth century they were able to dispossess the peasantry through enclosures with relative ease. Brenner seems to want to assert that the emergence of capitalism was essentially a lord-centred initiative rooted in the long-standing powers of the English aristocracy. Now, there is no question that the most spectacular advances of agrarian capitalism occurred after the English Revolution and that large capitalist farmers, many of whom came from the traditional aristocracy, played a central role in this development. But we also need to ask where this leaves the idea that capitalism first emerged out of the ranks of the petty producers. How could the English aristocracy have been simultaneously too weak to re-enserf the peasantry and yet strong enough to drive them off the land through enclosures? By associating the emergence of capitalism exclusively with lordly initiative, Brenner comes close to short-circuiting the entire process. The ability of the English lords to carry through an assault on the peasant rights in the seventeenth century can only be explained by the prior weakening of the peasant community as a result of economic differentiation. The breakthrough from below by the yeomanry on the basis of petty capitalist accumulation was a crucial intervening stage in the later development of large-scale capitalist farming. How else is it possible to explain the unique triadic pattern of English agrarian capitalism? The tenant farmers who worked the large capitalist farms of the eighteenth century on the basis of wage-labour, had to have come from somewhere.

There is the implicit danger that Brenner's analysis could be interpreted in a voluntarist fashion. For if, in effect, the English lords always won the crucial class battles from the medieval period onward due to their superior class organization, then it becomes a short step to the conclusion that capitalism emerged essentially as a rational calculation based on ruling-class choice. In other circumstances, presumably, ruling classes could choose not to introduce capitalist methods. What gets lost is any sense in which ruling-class choices are constrained and shaped by changes in the forces and relations of production at the base of society.

It would be unfair to read too much into Brenner's analysis since it deals with the highly specific conditions of capitalist development in England. However, other theorists have been less constrained by the temptation to invest ruling classes with the power to dictate both the outcome of revolutions and the pattern (or lack thereof) of capitalist development. As we try to show in the next chapter on France, the failure to take seriously changes in the forces and relations of production at the base of society can lead to precisely the voluntarist vision of history that Bois warns against.

Before developing these points further we need to consider briefly the contribution of Perry Anderson. Like Brenner, Anderson emphasizes the importance of political factors in the transition from feudalism to capitalism. Despite this similarity, however, Anderson's account of the rise of European absolutism departs in important ways from the general approach adopted by Brenner. In his study of the rise of absolutism in Europe, Anderson gives particular weight to the 'superstructural' peculiarities which distinguished western European feudal development. It is Anderson's belief that 'what rendered the unique passage to capitalism possible in Europe was *the concatenation of antiquity and feudalism.*'[112] In particular, the tradition of Roman Law and urban concepts of citizenship are accorded an equal weight in the rise of absolute states and the transition to capitalism. 'Roman Law', Anderson writes,

> in Renaissance Europe was ... a sign of the spread of capitalist relations in towns and country: *economically* it answered the vital interests of the commercial and manufacturing bourgeoisie, ... *politically* ... Roman Law corresponded to the constitutional exigencies of the re-organized feudal states of the epoch.[113]

It was the incorporation of Roman Law into the western European conception of feudal sovereignty which Anderson views as central to the eventual emergence of capitalist absolute property rights. The system of parcellized or decentralized sovereignty and scalar property in the West and their relative absence in the east are said to explain the development of capitalist private property in the West and the retardation of capitalist development in the east 'since forms of private property could not develop at the same tempo.'[114] The emergence of capitalism out of the crisis of feudalism is summarized in the remarkable formulation: 'The classical past awoke within the feudal present to assist the arrival of the capitalist future, both unimaginably more distant and strangely nearer to it.'[115]

For Anderson, the long history of transition from antiquity through feudalism to capitalism in the West can be seen largely in terms of the historic perfection of a specific property form – absolute private property. Perhaps the most obvious problem with this view is that the tradition of Roman Law, which did have a great influence on the Continent, had very little impact in England where capitalism first arose. The English tradition of common law emerged in the medieval period, as Anderson himself points out, as 'an unpaid aristocratic self-administration ... which was later to evolve into the Justices of the Peace of the early modern epoch.'[116] It was in large part due to the decentralized nature of aristocratic organization that no absolutist state was able to gain a footing in England. Moreover, the 'parcellization of sovereignty' which Anderson singles out as one of the most important precursors of capitalist private property was of limited importance in England due to the early centralization of legal authority by the Crown which was administered at the regional level by agents drawn from the local aristocracy. As Sayer and Corrigan have observed: 'Growth of a nationally unified system of law is indicative of the limitation of "parcellization of sovereignty", bespeaking the declining power of feudal lords individually vis-à-vis the Crown, if not as a class vis-à-vis the peasants.[117]

When we come to France which, according to Anderson, 'conformed more closely to the archetypal feudal system than any other region of the continent',[118] the situation is not much better. France represents for Anderson something of a pure type and, in terms of the criteria he has set, *the* locus of evolutionary advance towards capitalism.[119] In France we find both parcellization of sovereignty and the growth of a commercially minded and urban-based bourgeoisie. As well, we find an absolutist state whose affairs are overseen by scores of legal experts – the *maîtres de requêtes* – schooled in the traditions of Roman jurisprudence and property law.[120] All of these considerations underlie Anderson's tendency to view the French Revolution as an almost archetypal bourgeois revolution against which all others pale by comparison.

We shall have more to say later on about Anderson's schematization of bourgeois revolutions. For the present it is sufficient to observe that there is little evidence to support Anderson's contention that juridical traditions played a determining role in the transition to capitalism either in England or in its subsequent development in France and elsewhere. The very fact that Roman Law was compatible with the very different relations of production and the property forms which existed in Roman antiquity, western European absolutism and continental capitalism proves that juridical traditions are remarkably pliable. Because of his overwhelming preoccupation with the *continuities* between the legal, political and economic traditions stretching between antiquity and capitalism, Anderson's analysis comes close at points to both evolutionism and functionalism. Because of the cumulative and endogenous inheritance of classical traditions in France, the transition to capitalism becomes almost retrospectively inevitable.

This orientation neglects the crucial *discontinuities* involved in the transition to capitalism, especially in continental Europe, where the transition was in large part brought about under the impact of external competition with English capitalism. Necessarily, therefore, the 'weighting' of the various social forces, institutions, and property forms contributing to capitalist development was much different from that in England. In those countries which had built up strong absolutist state structures there existed significant obstacles to capitalist development. In France, the conquering of state power by the bourgeoisie did not mean that the machinery of the state could be automatically directed towards the rapid advance of capitalist production. For a time, capital was forced to pursue alternative strategies of accumulation with little direct assistance from the state. But, once external pressures became compelling, the further development of capitalism was to a great extent only possible through the direct intervention of the state. The contradictory character of this process, we shall attempt to show, cannot be adequately grasped by resorting to normative models of bourgeois revolution of the sort advocated by Anderson.

It is important to stress in all of this that there are real differences in the approach of Anderson and Brenner. Brenner's primary concern is to delineate the origins of capitalism on the basis of the differing patterns of class relations which emerged out of pre-industrial Europe. The strength of Brenner's concept of state-formation as expressed in the concept of 'political accumulation' is that it grounds the state and the process of state-formation in the social relations of production. Anderson's framework is far more 'eclectic' in its apparent readiness to grant 'superstructural' factors such as law causal autonomy in the transition to capitalism.[121] In this sense, Anderson's approach borrows as strongly from Max Weber as it does from Marx.

Moreover, Brenner's general framework remains superior to that of both the market-relations perspective and the production-relations approach found in the works of Dobb and Laclau. In an important sense Brenner's account of how the characteristic logic of capitalism was first established in England and the barriers to its development elsewhere forms a necessary starting point for our analysis. The task which remains is to show how the compulsions of capitalism were transmitted and absorbed by those countries in western Europe whose pre-capitalist economic and political structures determined that the conditions for the emergence of capitalism there would be markedly different from the conditions of its origins in England.

Notes

1. See Fernand Braudel, *The Mediterranean and the Mediterranean World in the Age of Philip II* (Harper and Row, 1973); Henri Pirenne, *Medieval Cities* (Princeton: Princeton University Press, 1925); *Economic and Social History of Medieval Europe* (London: Routledge and Kegan Paul, 1936); Max Weber, in G. Roth and C. Wittich, eds., *Economy and Society* (New York: Bedminster Books, 1968); Karl Polanyi, *The Great Transformation* (Boston: Beacon Press, 1957).

2. Paul Sweezy, 'A Critique', in Rodney Hilton, ed., *The Transition From Feudalism to Capitalism* (London: Verso, 1978), p. 42.

3. Ibid., p. 43.

4. John Merrington, 'Town and Country in the Transition to Capitalism', in *The Transition*, p. 178.

5. Rodney Hilton, 'Introduction', in *The Transition*, p. 21; Hilton, 'A Crisis of Feudalism', *Past and Present* 78 (1980), p. 8.

6. Witold Kula, *An Economic Theory of the Feudal System* (London: Verso, 1976), p. 78.

7. Rodney Hilton, 'Feudalism in Europe: Problems for Historical Materialists', *New Left Review* (September–October, 1984), p. 91.

8. See Kahachiro Takahashi, 'A Contribution to the Discussion', in *The Transition*, p. 84; Maurice Dobb, 'A Reply', in *The Transition*, p. 67.
There is some dispute as to whether or not labour services had ever existed in the remote regions of the north and west of England in the medieval period. For the argument that they did not see: Jairus Banaji, 'The Peasantry in the Feudal Mode of Production: Towards an Economic Model', *Journal of Peasant Studies* vol. 3, no.3 (April, 1976), p. 312.

9. Hilton, in *The Transition*, p. 16.

10. Kula, *Economic Theory*, p. 72.

11. Hilton, in *The Transition*, p. 17.

12. Takahashi, in *The Transition*, p. 84.

13. André Gunder Frank, *Capitalism and Underdevelopment in Latin America* (New York: Monthly Review Press, 1969); *World Accumulation 1492–1789* (New York: Monthly Review Press, 1978); Fernand Braudel, *The Wheels of Commerce: Civilization and Capitalism 15th to 18th Century*, translated by Sian Reynolds (New York: Harper and Row, 1982). For a useful summary of Braudel's concept of capitalism and transition see his *Afterthoughts on Capitalism and Material Life* (New York: Harper and Row, 1977), especially ch. 2.

14. Immanuel Wallerstein, 'The Rise and Future Demise of the Capitalist World System: Concepts for Comparative Analysis', *Comparative Studies in Society and History* 4 (September, 1974), p. 390.

15. Ibid., p. 391.

16. Immanuel Wallerstein, *The Modern World System: Capitalist Agriculture and the Origins of the European World Economy in the Sixteenth Century* vol. 1 (New York: Academic Press, 1974), p. 87.

17. Ibid., p. 101.

18. Wallerstein, 'Rise and Demise', p. 401.

19. Immanuel Wallerstein, *Historical Capitalism* (London: Verso, 1983), pp. 48–56.

20. Wallerstein, 'Rise and Demise', p. 401.

21. Wallerstein, *Modern World System* vol. 1, p. 355.

22. Ibid., p. 162.

23. Theda Skocpol, 'Wallerstein's World Capitalist System: A Theoretical and Historical Critique', *American Journal of Sociology* vol. 82, no. 5, (March, 1977), p. 1084.

24. Peter Gourevitch, 'The International System and Regime Formation', *Comparative Politics* vol. 10 (April, 1978), p. 426.

25. Wallerstein, *The Modern World System* vol. 2 (New York: Academic Press, 1976), p. 90.

26. Ibid., p. 310.

27. Skocpol, 'Wallerstein's World System', p. 1082.

28. Robert Brenner, 'Agrarian Class Structure and Economic Development in Pre-Industrial Europe: The Agrarian Roots of European Capitalism', *The Brenner Debate*, pp. 282–3.

29. Robert Brenner, 'The Origins of Capitalist Development: A Critique of Neo-Smithian Marxism', *New Left Review* 104, (July–August 1977), p. 65.

30. Skocpol, 'Wallerstein's World System', p. 1082.

31. Kula, *Economic Theory*, p. 125.

32. Robert Brenner, 'Agrarian Class Structure, p. 37.

33. Kula, *Economic Theory*, p. 125.

34. Ibid., p. 116.

35. Kula, *Economic Theory*, p. 95.

36. Ibid., p. 133.

37. Ibid., p. 107.

38. Brenner, 'Origins of Capitalist Development', p. 72.

39. Jairus Banaji, 'Gunder Frank in Retreat?', *Journal of Peasant Studies* vol. 7, no. 4 (June, 1980), pp. 514–18.

40. Kula, *Economic Theory*, p. 17.

41. Rodney Hilton, 'Capitalism, What's in a Name?', in *The Transition*, p. 152.

42. Karl Marx, *Grundrisse* (Harmondsworth: Penguin Books, 1973), p. 506.

43. Ibid.

44. Karl Marx, *Capital* vol. 1 (New York: Vintage Books, 1977), p. 874.

45. Marx, *Grundrisse*, p. 506.

46. Marx, *Capital* vol. 1, pp. 874–5.

47. See Brenner, 'Origins of Capitalist Development', for an exposition of this concept in relation to Wallerstein and Gunder Frank.

48. Lucio Colletti, 'Bernstein and the Marxism of the Second International', *From Rous-*

seau to Lenin: Studies in Ideology and Society, trans, John Merrington and Judith White (New York: Monthly Review Press, 1972), p. 65.

49. Karl Marx, 'Contribution to the Critique of Political Economy' in Lewis S. Feuer, ed., *Marx and Engels: Basic Writings on Politics and Society* (New York: Doubleday, 1959), p. 43.

50. Karl Marx, *The Poverty of Philosophy* (Moscow: Progress Publishers, 1975).

51. Roman Rosdolsky, *The Making of Marx's Capital* (London: Pluto Press, 1977), p. 29.

52. Marx, *Grundrisse,* p. 96.

53. For a more detailed analysis of these passages see Alex Callinicos, *Is There A Future for Marxism?* (London: Macmillan, 1982), pp. 148–50.

54. See G.A. Cohen, *Karl Marx's Theory of History: A Defence* (Oxford: Clarendon Press, 1978) pp. 134, 172.

55. Simon Clarke, 'Althusserian Marxism', in *One-Dimensional Marxism: Althusser and the Politics of Culture* (London: Allison and Busby, 1980). The argument which follows is greatly indebted to Clarke's critique of 'structuralist' Marxism. See also his important: 'Socialist Humanism and the Critique of Economism', *History Workshop Journal* 8 (Autumn, 1979).

56. Marx, Capital vol. 3, p. 249.

57. Clarke, 'Althusserian Marxism', p. 45.

58. Karl Marx, *Theories of Surplus Value* vol. 2 (Moscow: Progress Publishers, 1977), p. 150.

59. Karl Marx, 'Russia's Pattern of Development' in Lewis S. Feuer, ed., *Marx and Engels: Basic Writings on Politics and Philosophy* (New York: Doubleday, 1959), p. 441.

60. Derek Sayer, *Marx's Method: Ideology, Science and Critique in 'Capital'* (Brighton: Harvester Press, 1983), p. 86.

61. See especially Etienne Balibar, 'The Basic Concepts of Historical Materialism', Sections 3 and 4, in *Reading Capital* tr. Ben Brewster (London: Verso, 1979). For a detailed critique of Balibar's discussion of the principle of 'correspondence and non-correspondence', see Clarke 'Althusserian Marxism'.

62. Perry Anderson, *Passages from Antiquity to Feudalism* (London: Verso, 1978), p. 204; *Arguments within English Marxism* (London: Verso, 1980) pp. 55–6.

63. Ernesto Laclau, *Politics and Ideology in Marxist Theory* (London: Verso, 1979), p. 28.

64. Ibid., p. 41.

65. Ibid., p. 33.

66. Maurice Dobb, *Studies in the Development of Capitalism* (New York: International Publishers, 1963), p. 55.

67. Jairus Banaji, 'Modes of Production in a Materialist Conception of History', *Capital and Class* 3 (Autumn, 1977), p. 7.

68. Dobb, *Studies,* pp. 17, 35.

69. Marx, *Grundrisse,* p. 463.

70. Marx, *Capital* vol. 1, p. 1064.

71. Marx, *Grundrisse,* p. 712.

72. I am indebted here to Colin Barker, 'Notes on "Industrial Society" and "Capitalism"', Manchester, 1982 (Mimeographed).

73. Marx, *Selected Works* vol. 1, p. 90.

74. Marx, *Capital* vol. 1, p. 345.

75. That is why Marx recognized that in the American Civil War, the 'war waged by the southern Confederacy is ... not a war of defence but a war of conquest, aimed at extending and perpetuating slavery.' Karl Marx, 'The Civil War in the United States', in David Fernbach, ed., *Surveys from Exile* (Harmondsworth: Penguin Books, 1977), p. 245.

76. Ibid., p. 1035. For a fuller discussion of this issue in relation to Caribbean slavery see Abigail Bakan, 'Plantation Slavery and the Capitalist Mode of Production: An Analysis of the Development of the Jamaican Labour Force', *Studies in Political Economy* 22 (Spring 1987) pp. 73–99.

77. Banaji, 'Modes of Production', p. 30.

78. Dobb, *The Transition*, p. 100.

79. Ellen Meiksins Wood, 'The Separation of the Economic and the Political in Capitalism', *New Left Review* 127 (May–June 1981), p. 80.

80. Robert Brenner, 'Dobb on the Transition from Feudalism to Capitalism', *Cambridge Journal of Economics* 2 (1978) p. 122.

81. Dobb, *The Transition*, p. 100.

82. Ibid., p. 100.

83. Hilton, 'Feudalism in Europe', p. 87.

84. Rodney Hilton, *Bond Men Made Free: Medieval Peasant Movements and the English Rising of 1381* (London: Methuen, 1973), p. 15.

85. Hilton, *Bond Men*, pp. 166–74; Anderson, *Passages*, p. 205.

86. Hilton, *Bond Men*, p. 166.

87. Marx, *Capital* vol. 1, p. 875.

88. Hilton, *The Transition*, p. 15.

89. G. A. Clay, *Economic Expansion and Social Change 1500–1700* vol. 1 (Cambridge: Cambridge University Press, 1984), p. 57.

90. Mildred Campbell, *The English Yeoman* (London: Merlin Press, 1942), p. 102.

91. Marx, *Capital* vol. 1, pp. 906–7.

92. Hilton, 'A Crisis of Feudalism', p. 17.

93. Hilton, *The Transition*, p. 27.

94. Marx, *Capital* vol. 1, pp. 895–6.

95. Dobb, *Studies*, p. 52.

96. Ibid., p. 53.

97. Ibid., p. 54.

98. Ibid., p. 61.

99. Ibid., p. 56.

100. Brenner, 'Dobb on the Transition', p. 128.

101. Ibid., p. 129.

102. Robert Brenner, 'The Social Basis of Economic Development', in John Roemer, ed., *Analytic Marxism* (Cambridge: Cambridge University Press, 1986) p. 26.

103. Brenner, 'Agrarian Roots of European Capitalism', *Brenner Debate*, p. 227.

104. Ibid., p. 238.

105. Ibid., pp. 38, 82, 239.

106. Ibid., p. 290.

107. Ibid., p. 264.

108. Ibid., p. 293.

109. Brenner, 'Social Basis of Economic Development', p. 26.

110. Ibid., pp. 28–9.

111. Guy Bois, 'Against Neo-Malthusian Orthodoxy', *Brenner Debate*, p. 115.

112. Perry Anderson, *Lineages of the Absolutist State* (London: Verso, 1979), p. 420.

113. Ibid., p. 26.

114. Ibid., p. 224.

115. Ibid., p. 422.

116. Ibid., p. 116.

117. Philip Corrigan and Derek Sayer, *The Great Arch: English State Formation as Cultural Revolution* (Oxford: Basil Blackwell, 1985) p. 31.

118. Anderson, *Passages*, p. 156.

119. For more on Anderson's France-centred preoccupation see Mary Fulbrook and Theda Skocpol, 'Destined Pathways: The Historical Sociology of Perry Anderson', in Theda Skocpol, ed., *Vision and Method in Historical Sociology* (New York: Cambridge University Press, 1984).

120. Anderson, *Lineages*, p. 129.

121. The term 'Eclectic Marxism' is borrowed from the sympathetic treatment of Anderson's work found in Robert J. Holton, 'Marxist Theories of Social Change and The Transition From Feudalism to Capitalism', *Theory and Society* vol. 10, (1981), pp. 854–62.

2

France: From Absolutism to Bonapartism

Writing in the latter half of the nineteenth century, Marx described the French state of the Second Empire as a 'frightful parasitic body, which surrounds the body of French society like a caul and stops up all its pores.' He goes on to note that the existing state

> arose in the time of the absolute monarchy, with the decay of the feudal system, which it helped to accelerate. The seigneurial privileges of the landowners and towns were transformed into attributes of the state power, the feudal dignitaries became paid officials, and the variegated medieval pattern of conflicting plenary authorities became the regulated plan of a state authority characterized by centralization and division of labour reminiscent of a factory. ... All political upheavals perfected this machine instead of smashing it. The parties that strove in turn for mastery regarded possession of this immense state edifice as the main booty for the victor.[1]

Marx's description of the French state in these passages is suggestive and compelling. The image of the French state as a field of conflict riven by the internecine struggles of the various competing interests which sought control of the state apparatus was a recurring one which could have been used accurately to describe virtually any period during the roughly three centuries spanning the rise of absolutism and the consolidation of the Bonapartist regime of the Second Empire. The idea of the state as the private 'booty' of those who controlled or aspired to control it was not a novel one; it was a conception which had deep material roots in the past. By alluding to the continuities between the absolutist state of the seventeenth and eighteenth centuries and the regime of Louis

Bonaparte, Marx was drawing attention to these profound links which the nineteenth-century state shared with the social and political structures of an earlier period.

Unfortunately, Marx was unable to pursue the historical roots of the Bonapartist state further than these few schematic remarks. 'The Eighteenth Brumaire' was after all, as Marx was later to note, written as a series of journalistic pieces 'under the immediate pressure of events, and ... its historical material does not extend beyond the month of February (1852).'[2] Marx's intention was merely to show how immediate conditions in France following the defeats of 1848, had allowed 'a mediocre and grotesque individual to play a hero's role'.[3] In other words, Marx was not claiming that his treatment of Bonapartism was based on any profound theoretical insights or even on any balanced assessment of the historical roots of the regime.

Despite these modest claims for his work, some contemporary Marxist theorists have seen in Marx's political writings on Bonapartism the basis for a 'theoretical construction of the concept of the capitalist state.'[4] Marx's treatment of Bonapartism is claimed to sanction a general definition of the capitalist state based on a 'regional theory of the political' in which the most essential characteristic of the state is its relative autonomy from the economic sphere.[5] This line of argument has, in turn, received much praise from what may be termed 'neo-Weberian' theorists such as Theda Skocpol who have insisted that political development must be sharply demarcated from economic development. To attempt to explain political development in terms of the evolution of class structures and relations is to do an injustice to the integrity and autonomy of political institutions; it is, according to such theorists, to lapse into a form of reductionism.[6]

The aim of the following discussion is to take up some of these more general theoretical claims within the context of French developments. For the central question which requires explanation is whether it is possible to account for the evolution of the French state as an expression of the relations of production without lapsing into the kind of mechanical economic reductionism which recent theorists have cautioned against. This question, however, cannot be satisfactorily dealt with at the theoretical level alone. It requires first of all an assessment of the historical role played by the state in the evolution of the social or class relations of production of France. In other words, it requires an analysis of precisely those historical continuities which Marx alluded to in his treatment of Louis Bonaparte's *coup d'état*.

I. The Rise of the Absolutist State in France

While England was taking the first tentative steps towards the consolidation of agrarian capitalism in the seventeenth century, France was embarking on a quite different historical path which would profoundly delay the transition to capitalism until long after it had been securely established in England. In England, as in most of western Europe, the crisis of feudalism at the end of the fourteenth century had resulted in the peasantry winning significant rights over the land. For a period of time, peasants were able to prosper in conditions where prices were rising, by marketing a portion of their surplus product. The growth of petty commodity production had given rise to differentiation within the peasant community and the emergence of a richer stratum of middling peasants who had begun to engage in small-scale capitalist farming. The subsequent breakdown in village solidarity which resulted from peasant differentiation sapped peasant resistance. Village communities now became vulnerable to the encroachments of enterprising landlords, who sought to enclose their estates as well as common lands and begin the consolidation of large-scale capitalist farms.

In France, for a brief period, it looked as though a similar evolution might be possible. Peasant gains were significant at the beginning of the fifteenth century; in many areas of France, village communities had won corporative status and the right to enforce their claims to common lands. In addition, individual peasants had won heritability rights over their tenures. Under these relatively favourable conditions a middling peasantry, similar to that which had arisen in England, began to prosper through the consolidation and even enlargement of its holdings and the advantages gained from marketing surplus production.[7] In short, for the peasantry as a whole this was a period of significant prosperity and economic advance.

On the other hand, during this same period, as Marc Bloch notes, 'the situation was very different with the seigneurial class, the only one superior to the small-holders, itself in disarray, shaken in its fortunes and mentally ill-prepared for the effort of adapting to an unprecedented situation. ... The lords were slowly becoming impoverished.'[8] Many landlords were willing to sacrifice their traditional powers of economic exploitation in return for urgently needed cash payments. At the same time, however, the impoverishment of the seigneurial class had led to the influx of bourgeois parvenu landowners who bought up estates and began to enlarge their holdings at the expense of the peasant tenants. The result was a concerted attack on peasant rights. New owners often forced out peasant tenants in favour of *metayers* or sharecroppers. *Metayers* were required to hand over between a third and a half of their produce directly to the landlord. Those peasants who had benefited from improved conditions now found themselves unable to take advantage of the market as rents reverted increasingly to rents in kind. Gains to be made from rising prices now fell to town-based interests. Through a combination of exorbitant new exactions, indebtedness to urban creditors and the growing burden of both royal and ecclesiastical tithes, the bulk of the French peasantry were driven deeper into poverty.

For the middling peasantry the results were disastrous. In the south, as one commentator remarks, 'the middling "yeoman" farmer tended to be squeezed out by morcellement from below and aggregation from above.'[9] Peasant plots tended to be subdivided, leading to fragmentation rather than expansion and consolidation:

> After the subtraction of seed, labour costs, rent, royal taxes, ecclesiastical tithes, and seigneurial dues, [the peasantry] retained an insufficient surplus to support a family even in good years. … Only those who rented a farmstead of 120 hectares or more were in a position to realize a substantial profit. Such *coqs de village*, who regularly brought a notable surplus to market, also collected seigneurial dues, provided credit and bought up holdings burdened with debt; they represented, however, scarcely 1 per cent of the peasantry.[10]

Here should be noted a significant difference between the position of the peasantry in France and that of England. The position of the French peasants was such that the landlords could engage in rent-squeezing, a strategy which was not possible in England. In England, the development of large landowners and the disappearance of landholding peasants contrasted with the maintenance in France of a peasantry which was at the same time land-hungry and thus subject to pressure as tenants. Under these conditions there was little incentive for landlords to engage in improvements since there was always a ready pool of land-hungry tenants available. For the peasantry, on the other hand, there was nothing in their position which would have compelled them to develop into a class of small-scale capitalist farmers akin to the English yeomanry. Rather, a tradition of relatively strong property rights over the land combined with the existence of a huge mass of land-hungry peasants looking for land led to a situation in which the majority of the peasantry were consigned to an equality of poverty barely above subsistence.

As the century wore on, the effects of this widespread impoverishment of the peasantry was expressed clearly in the massive revolts of the 1590s. Years of seigneurial reaction and the devastation wrought by the wars of religion resulted in widespread rebellion in many areas of France, most spectacularly in the southwest. At its height, the Croquants rebellion mobilized between 15,000 and 40,000 peasants. The demands put forward by its leaders were largely anti-seigneurial in nature. The insurgents appealed to the king to protect them from the harsh conditions imposed by local landlords.[11]

Despite the relatively conservative character of these revolts, they did represent a genuine threat to seigneurial interests. And the settlement which followed signalled a decisive turning point in the drive towards absolutism. As Salmon has observed:

> Faced with the revolt of the common people, the established classes themselves ultimately preferred royal authority to social anarchy, and had to put aside their factional struggles and selfish interests to acknowledge Henry IV. This was the basis on which Bourbon absolutism was constructed, and with it came permanent changes in the structure of society.[12]

Thus, in France, the beginnings of absolutism can be traced directly to the threat – or perceived threat – which revolts from below represented to feudal ruling-class interests. Perry Anderson has described the general nature of absolutism in similar terms; it was, he argues,

> a redeployed and recharged apparatus of feudal domination, designed to clamp the peasant masses back into their traditional social position ... a displacement of politico-legal coercion upwards towards a centralized militarized summit – the Absolutist state.[13]

From the standpoint of the peasantry, the consolidation of the absolutist state had a twofold effect. On the one hand, the peasantry benefited from the protection offered by the Crown against overly harsh exploitation by the seigneur. The Crown intervened to protect peasant property since its own fiscal health depended upon its ability to tax the peasantry. As a result, conflicts between peasants and landlords were often adjudicated by royal officials; more often than not these agents ruled in favour of the peasant proprietor by confirming the heritability of tenure. Thus, in a real sense, 'peasant ownership and the absolute state ... evolved in mutual dependence.'[14]

In so far as the absolutist state was forced to compete with the local nobility for a portion of peasant surplus, the Crown was naturally predisposed to the protection of the peasantry against intemperate exploitation by landlords. But the protection afforded by this intra-class competition, in the long run, only exacerbated the further fragmentation of holdings and general impoverishment of the peasantry. The combination of seigneurial dues and state exactions was generally so high that the majority of peasants were barely able to support their families, let alone retain anything to put to market. Between 1610 and 1644, state exactions from the *taille* rose from seventeen million *livres* to nearly forty-four million *livres*.[15] Total taxation increased by approximately sixfold as the state began to rely increasingly on extra-ordinary taxes to finance its military adventures; by 1654, around 63 per cent of all taxes collected came from the levying of extra-ordinary taxes.[16] The amount seized by the Crown at this time represented roughly 13 per cent of gross agrarian income, twice as much as at the turn of the century.[17]

Thus at the same time as the Crown moved to protect peasant property (and thus its revenue base), it clamped the peasantry into an equality of poverty from which, for the mass of rural producers, there was little hope of escape. Moreover, it prevented any significant differentiation within the ranks of the peasantry and thus the appearance of anything resembling a class of market-orientated petty producers comparable to that which had emerged in sixteenth-century England. At the same time, by preserving peasant property, the state made it virtually impossible for enterprising landlords to introduce new agricultural techniques, enclose their estates and undertake capitalist farming in a fashion similar to their counterparts in England. From the standpoint of rural development, therefore, the advent of absolutism did very little to alter the traditional pattern of feudal relations. Rather, the 'old mode of production was simply "sucked dry"; it was in no sense altered.'[18]

One of the recurring problems of the absolute monarchy in France was the conflict between the particularistic interests of the local nobility and the ever-increasing trend towards 'feudal centralism'.[19] For, even as the dominance of the monarchy had grown in the sixteenth and early seventeenth centuries, there still existed powerful corporate bodies which functioned to protect the traditional rights of the old feudal nobility. Throughout the medieval period, local nobles had enjoyed a high degree of autonomy, enforcing their rights and prerogatives through their own sovereign courts and through provincial estates. As seigneurial rights were eroded, the nobility had little choice but to look to the greater coercive power of the absolutist state to protect their interests. However, as the Fronde rebellion was to demonstrate, there continued to exist a high degree of tension between the exercise of noble rights at the local level and the centralized administration, which was often perceived to be acting against noble interests.

At a deeper level this conflict only reflected one of the central contradictions of absolutism; that is, while the state acted in the general interests of the nobility by preserving its class power through its superior military might, it also competed with it for a 'cut' of peasant surplus. Thus, the conflict between the state and the nobility was rooted in the struggle over the distribution of peasant surplus between rent and taxes.

A partial solution to this problem was to allow the nobility to appropriate a portion of the surplus which fell to the state through taxation.

This was done in the main through sales of office. From the reign of Francis I, the fiscal business of the state was overseen by tax-farmers, who purchased their offices and held responsibility for the collection of state taxes such as the *taille*. This was later systematized with the rise of the *intendants* who often combined military and fiscal offices.[20] The sale of such fiscal offices benefited the Crown in two ways: it received revenue from the sale of the office itself and the monies collected in taxes by fiscal office-holders. But, more importantly, it insured a measure of personal loyalty from nobles who bought such offices.

However, as the sale of offices grew in importance, the distinction between the performance of public duties and the private interests of the office-holders also increased. This confusion only worsened once offices became hereditary. Office-holders thus came to see their positions as part of their rightful patrimony, resenting any arbitrary measures taken by the Crown which might threaten either the value or heritability of venal offices.

This was most graphically illustrated by the Fronde rebellion which was precipitated by Crown attempts to impose an increase in the *paulette* – a tax on office which insured heritability. Opposition to the Crown by the *parlement* of Paris centred on the devaluation of venal offices which had resulted from the Crown's increasing resort to *rentes* (in effect, loans) and sales of office to meet its fiscal needs. In many cases, the value of office had dropped dramatically, which meant that some offices could become virtually worthless by the time they were passed on to the sons of their owners. Developments of this sort struck at the very heart of the patrimonial interests of the office-holding elite.

But despite the violent opposition to the Crown by large sections of the nobility, the rebellion never took the form of an anti-absolutist struggle comparable to that which had taken place in England during roughly the same period. The demands of the oppositionists emphasized rather the 'absolute yet limited power of the king'.[21] Neither the *parlement* of Paris nor any of the provincial or municipal *parlements* actually challenged the sovereignty of the Crown. The reason for the essentially conservative character of the revolt lay in the fact that to a very large extent the positions held by the *parlementaires* were granted by the Crown itself. Even the far-flung provincial *parlements* were heavily populated with royal office-holders.

In neither the case of noble nor non-noble office-holders was there any sign of an emergent 'bourgeois' opposition prepared to challenge the dominance of the absolutist state or the social structure which it sought to preserve. While in England the state was fast becoming what Barrington Moore has aptly called a 'committee of landlords'[22] acting in the interests of a self-confident class of enterprising agrarian capitalists, the *parlementaires* of France contented themselves with demanding only the most sectional and modest reforms of the absolutist state. Since their interests were indissolubly bound up with those of the state through an elaborate network of office-holding and patronage, it was less the case that opposition to the Crown *would not* mount a full-scale assault on absolutism than that they *could not* lest they threaten the very material basis of their own existence.

There was, of course, another reason for avoiding any such assault on the state. The Fronde had been punctuated by large-scale peasant revolts, most notably the revolt of Norman du Pieds and the Ormée uprising. As with the Croquants rebellion of the 1590s these were essentially anti-seigneurial in character. And they displayed the same limitations of these earlier revolts; in political terms this was no disengagement from the principles of monarchical rule. No social force emerged from the ranks of the immediate producers which was capable of offering an alternative social and economic blueprint for the restructuring of society. The rise of the absolutist state and the configuration of class forces which resulted precluded the emergence of any 'revolutionary' force on a par with the market-orientated yeomanry of England. As David Parker has observed of the Ormée revolt:

> Lack of political unity was reinforced by the low level of economic development which precluded the rapid evolution of classes capable of sustaining a general struggle against the monarchy. ... There was just no equivalent in France to the 'middling' class of independent small producers and yeoman farmers who provided the backbone of the New Model Army and much of the driving force behind the English Revolution.[23]

The settlement reached between the Crown and nobility which brought an end to the Fronde did little to alter the long-term economic prospects of France. Although the Crown had significantly undermined the fiscal and political autonomy of the nobility, it had also agreed that it would not tamper with the *paulette* or the patrimonial rights of office-holders. In addition, the Crown also agreed to partial payment of *rentes* and interest on loans from office-holders. Louis XIV was only able to make good these promises by resorting to the old practices of war finance, extra-ordinary taxation, the creation of new offices for sale and the flotation of further *rentes*. In so doing, however, the Crown only exacerbated its already shaky financial situation and bound itself more closely than ever to the interests of the great financiers of Europe.[24] By 1654, revenues from extra-ordinary taxation had grown to 63 per cent of the total. The total debt owed in *rentes* and loans from financiers was estimated by Colbert to be 451 million *livres* in 1661.

Despite the limited efforts of Colbert and his ministers to overhaul the financial apparatus of the state by greatly increasing the fiscal powers of the *intendants* and *commissaires*, the return to warfare in the last decades of the seventeenth century threw the economy once more into chaos. Payment of war debts in 1679–81 amounted to 130 million *livres*. It is estimated that nearly 70 per cent of state revenues were spent directly on war expenditures in the last years of Louis XIV's rule. The inevitable result was a renewal of the escalating cycle of extra-ordinary taxation and sales of office. In 1691, Parisian guilds paid 634,000 *livres* to the Crown for newly-created offices; in wholesale and retail markets 2,000 offices had been established. Between 1695 and 1715, a series of taxes, including the *capitation*, the *dixième*, and the *vingtième*, were revived to raise further revenues, but to little avail. By the end of Louis XIV's reign in 1715, the state deficit was roughly 45 million *livres* and anticipated revenues for several years to come were already committed to servicing the debt.

In the countryside, the combined weight of seigneurial dues and taxation by the state had bled the peasantry dry. The upturn in agricultural prices after 1730 was thus lost for the majority of rural producers. Indeed, their situation was only made worse as landlords sought to increase rents and reorganize their holdings.[25] Between 1720–29 and 1780–89, the rise in rents amounted to 142 per cent, while the weighted index of agricultural prices rose only 60 per cent. On the eve of the revolution, land rents stood some 50 per cent higher than in the second quarter of the century.[26] The impact of nearly two centuries of rising seigneurial rents combined with increased state exactions, meant that by the late eighteenth century approximately three-quarters of the French peasantry subsisted on less than five hectares of land, the minimum required for the economic independence of a single family. In most provinces, upwards of 25 per cent of peasant holdings were less than one hectare. For the overwhelming majority of the peasantry, then, the advances made in the early sixteenth century were but a dim memory. As Pierre Goubert points out: 'Were we to erect a social pyramid of peasant property, it would have a very broad base and absurdly slender apex.'[27] The breakdown of the peasant village community which resulted from peasant differentiation and the rise of the yeomanry which attended the beginnings of capitalism in England, was absent from the French rural landscape. The price paid by the French peasantry for the protection of their property rights by the absolutist state had thus been a high one; class solidarity and the integrity of the village community had both been preserved at the cost of immense suffering and poverty by the mass of peasant producers.

Very little of the income generated in the agricultural sphere found its way back into productive investment in agriculture. Despite the limited attempts by some landowners to emulate the agrarian system of England through land clearances, enclosure and consolidation of holdings and the introduction of new agricultural techniques, there was nothing resembling an 'agricultural revolution' in France.[28] The huge profits which resulted from improved agricultural prices in the second half of the eighteenth century fell to the recipients of rents and dues. The bulk of this wealth was then invested in office and forms of conspicuous consumption befitting a noble lifestyle. This pattern – which saw agricultural income flow into offices and *rentes* – held for both noble and non-noble landowners.

'The eighteenth century', as one commentator has noted, 'was remarkable for changing nothing',[29] when it came to the flood of wealth which poured into the purchase of offices and the available forms of proprietary wealth. Indeed, it has been argued that the second half of the eighteenth century saw an increased openness in the channels leading to ennoblement and office-holding.[30] As a purveyor of social advancement and economic security, the absolutist state seemed to offer unlimited opportunities for both bourgeois and noble investors. As François Furet graphically describes the situation:

> Through office-holding, ennoblement and a centralized administration, the state was swallowing up the entire civil society; all of the wealth of the bourgeoisie was ... drawn into its coffers in exchange for ennoblement ... the sales of offices of the *secrétaire de roi* ... rose to new heights in the second half of the eighteenth century with the financial needs of the state. ... The monarchy increasingly pressed by its financial needs, continued to ennoble more *secrétaires de roi*, new members of the *parlements*, and more non-noble military men ... while the old nobility married its sons to the daughters of financiers.[31]

In 1778, Necker estimated that there were no fewer than 51,000 venal offices in the law courts, the municipalities and the financial apparatus of the state with a capital value of some 600 million *livres*. And since these figures excluded offices in the royal household, the military and financial companies as well as less lucrative offices held by guild masters and inspectors of various sorts, the true figures were undoubtedly much higher.[32]

However far removed the immense superstructure of the absolutist state had become from its base through the absorption of ever broader sections of French society into its complex network of venal office-holding, it still remained an inescapable fact that its chief source of revenue – the peasantry – was capable of producing an extremely inelastic and finite social surplus. To the extent that the bourgeoisie had attached itself to the tax/office structures of the absolutist state therefore, it had become a mere appendage of the existing mode of production.

How, then, should the social foundations of absolutist society be characterized? There appears to be little evidence to support the view held by Marx and Engels that absolutism represented a *transitional* form of state midway between feudalism and capitalism.[33] More recent commentators, such as François Furet, have attempted to retain a somewhat similar view, while emptying it of any 'social' or class content. Furet argues that 'the state of the *Ancien Régime* was relatively independent from the nobility and the bourgeoisie.'[34] Furet and others insist on the *political autonomy* of absolutism; they argue that the peculiar autonomy of French absolutism rested on the balance it struck between the preservation of archaic principles of political rule deriving from feudalism and more modern aspects of political organization and government.[35]

What were the *material* roots of the autonomy of the absolutist state? The first point to be made has to do with the definition of feudalism as a mode of production. Prior to the rise of the absolutist state, the process of seigneurial surplus-extraction rested upon what Brenner has described as a '"fusion" ... between "the economic" and "the political" ...'[36] That is, the lord's ability to extract an economic surplus was bound up with his ability to enforce his claim through the application (if necessary) of direct extra-economic or political compulsion. Moreover, it was upon this basic structure of the surplus-extractive relation between lord and peasant that the pre-absolutist state rested; as long as lords took individual responsibility for enforcing their claim to a portion of peasant surplus, feudal political organization could remain decentralized. Thus the early feudal state was characterized by a fragmentation or parcellization of political authority.[37]

The construction of the absolutist state in France, as we saw earlier, was a necessary outgrowth of the challenge to decentralized seigneurial power represented by peasant revolts from below. One consequence of this reconstitution of feudal class power, however, was that the absolutist state to a certain extent competed with the local nobility over the distribution of peasant surplus. Thus, in an important sense, the French state did develop, as Brenner has suggested, as an independent or 'class-like phenomenon' through its arbitrary power to tax the land.[38] This, and not some vague compromise between archaic feudalism and principles of modern government is what constituted the *material* or economic autonomy of the absolutist state in France.

On the other hand, in order to consolidate its power as an independent surplus extractor, the absolutist state had to secure the allegiance of the nobility. It did this, as we have seen, by allowing them to receive remuneration through state-related forms of wealth such as venal office-holding, *rentes* and grants of land. In effect, what this meant was that those whose principal source of wealth was derived from landownership, got back by indirect means a portion of peasant surplus which now fell to the state through taxation. This reconstruction of ruling-class incomes and power was accomplished, in large part, through 'the re-creation of private property in the political sphere'.[39] So complete was this transformation of the old feudal nobility, that by the end of the eighteenth century the distinction between the robe nobility and the sword nobility had virtually disappeared.[40]

In the end, this protracted process was to alter radically the *form* of ruling-class power by fusing it with that of the state. But even as the basic structure of feudal social relations were transformed in the face of peasant revolts at the end of the sixteenth century in France, the essential *content* of the feudal surplus extractive relation remained unchanged. In place of the extra-economic compulsion exercised by individual lords, feudal surplus extraction was now increasingly executed through and mediated by the fiscal apparatus of the absolutist state. In many respects, 'political accumulation'[41] through the tax/office state represented the perfected form – the 'highest stage' – of feudal surplus extraction through extra-economic means.

The autonomy of the French absolutist state then, paradoxically, was merely an expression of its direct role as a vehicle of feudal accumulation. It was in no sense a purely political autonomy *external* to the basic relations of production and surplus appropriation since the latter was only possible on the basis of a fusion of the economic and the political.[42]

To conclude, the autonomy of the absolutist state was of a dual-character: to the extent that it competed with other sections of the feudal ruling-class over the distribution of peasant surplus between rent and taxes, it assumed a class-like role in the relations of production. But to the degree that it won the allegiance of its competitors by absorbing them into its tax/office structure, it came to be seen as the vehicle *par excellence* for social advancement and the accumulation of wealth. Even after the formally proprietary nature of office-holding had been abolished by the revolution, the state continued to be the main pole of attraction for those seeking to enrich themselves through winning control of its immense fiscal apparatus. The French state, in other words, continued to exert a class-like role in society at the same time as it absorbed ever greater layers of the population into its orbit: political accumulation was thus a defining feature of the *ancien régime* state.

Marxists have often described the last years of the *ancien régime* as ones of growing tension between an ascendant capitalist bourgeoisie anxious to shake off the last vestiges of feudalism and a reactionary feudal ruling class intent upon retaining its grip over the economic and political life of France. This view is perhaps most clearly expressed in the works of Albert Soboul. For Soboul, the French Revolution is a prototypical instance of a bourgeois-capitalist revolution; the last decades of the *ancien régime* are described as incipiently capitalist, with imagery invoking 'burgeoning productive forces' pressing against the archaic 'fetters' of feudal-absolutist society. The revolution itself is seen as an eruption in which the old social relations are 'burst asunder' by the developing productive forces to make way for social relations conducive to capitalism:

> the Revolution is to be explained in the last analysis by a contradiction between the social basis of the economy and the character of the productive forces. ... At the end of the eighteenth century, the system of property holding and the organization of agriculture and manufacturing were no longer relevant to the needs of the new burgeoning productive forces and were seen to hamper the productive process. The authors of the *Manifesto* wrote that 'these chains had to be broken'. They were broken.

And further: 'Carried through by the bourgeoisie, the Revolution destroyed the old system of production and the social relationships deriving from it and in so doing destroyed the formerly dominant class, the landed aristocracy.'[43] In a more recent formulation, Soboul has argued that it was not the *haute bourgeoisie* that made the revolution; rather the real motive force of capitalism lay with the '*paysans du type yeoman, laboureur, ou kulak*'.[44]

We have already dealt at length with some of the theoretical problems associated with the traditional Marxist interpretation of the relationship between the forces and relations of production. Soboul's analysis falls squarely within this general framework. Moreover, his attempt to equate the French *laboureur* with the English yeomanry remains unconvincing. Our analysis has attempted to show that there simply was no social or material basis at the end of the eighteenth century for the emergence of a French equivalent to the small-scale capitalist farmer which had emerged in England nearly two centuries earlier. We shall return to this question below, but first it is worthwhile examining in more detail the general constellation of class relations and forms of wealth which prevailed at the end of the *ancien régime*.

As mentioned above, from as early as the seventeenth century, bourgeois fortunes were increasingly funnelled into land and office. Even then, it was possible to witness the beginnings of a process which Boris Porchnev dubbed the 'feudalization of the bourgeoisie'. This tendency only became more pronounced as the absolutist state grew in size and strength. Much bourgeois wealth, though not all, took on essentially the same character as noble fortunes. Proprietary wealth, comprising rents from land and the financial rewards of office made up approximately 80 per cent of all wealth in the late eighteenth century. As George Taylor has written:

there was, between most of the nobility and the proprietary sector of the middle classes, a continuity of investment forms and socio-economic values that made them, economically, a single group. In the relations of production they played a common role. The differentiation between them was not in any sense economic; it was juridical.[45]

If we consider the activities and personnel of both commerce and finance, it becomes clear that not only did nobles and non-nobles participate in both areas on an equal footing, but more importantly, the activities of both groups were firmly embedded within the structures of the old regime; neither can be said to embody a new 'productive force' about to burst through the fabric of feudal society.

Finance and banking – what Taylor has inexactly termed 'court capitalism'[46] – was centred in Paris and largely distinct from the activities of commerce and trade. Paris was the centre of high finance chiefly because of its close proximity to the administration of the absolutist state and affairs of the royal court. It was here that the treasurers, the farmers-general, and receivers-general of finance received the tax revenues which poured in from the provinces. And it was in Paris that the great financiers of France, Switzerland and the Netherlands gathered to reap the profits from the trade in credit and public loans to the French monarchy.

It was literally through 'courting' influence in the royal administration, through intrigue and elaborate networks of contacts, that individual financiers were most likely to succeed in profitable ventures.[47] Speculators engaged in such practices in order to gain lucrative charters granted by the court for privileged joint-stock companies like the Indies Company, the Discount Bank, the Paris Water Company and various insurance schemes which appeared in the 1780s.[48] Monopolies of this sort and the speculative fortunes which they brought their recipients, were inconceivable apart from the activities of the absolutist state: 'the most spectacular operations of old regime capitalism were made possible by royal finance and political manipulation rather than industrial and maritime enterprise.'[49]

Nor was the financial world uniformly bourgeois; as Furet has noted, it was 'the cross-over point *par excellence* on the fateful line dividing noble from non-noble status'.[50] The most common pattern was for successful financiers to acquire noble titles and merge with the nobility.[51] Most of these ennoblements came from benefactors at the royal court; so intense was the trade in titles and the prestige it conferred on those engaged in finance, that it became a virtual necessity if one was going to do business with the Crown.[52]

The speculative boom which gripped the Parisian financial world on the eve of the French Revolution – although it had specific causes, notably the war with England – was at another level merely an expression of a more deep-rooted crisis of *ancien régime* society and the social structures upon which it was founded. Even as the state sank into insolvency, *agioteurs* continued to lend large sums of money to the government hoping to reap huge profits at high rates of interest.[53] That they should have continued to do so is not surprising; their primary goal was to realize a quick profit on speculative terms. To achieve this end, bankers had to look no further than the opportunities offered by a state desperate for funds. Almost by definition then, those engaged in finance were less interested in long-term investment in trade and industry which as yet had an unproven potential, than in forms of investment the limits of which were defined by the existing social and political structures. In this sense the 'finance capitalists' of the eighteenth century were no different than their counterparts of the Renaissance; as Marx insisted, 'the mere presence of monetary wealth ... is in no way sufficient for the dissolution into capital to happen.'[54]

Both domestic and international finance were parasitic on the absolutist state and the 'court capitalism' which it spawned; through influence and intrigue the world of high finance merely adapted itself to the existing social structure. At the same time as it speculated on state loans, credit and shares in government companies, financiers bought into the state at another level through the purchase of office and titles of ennoblement:

> The opportunities they exploited had nothing to do with the capital requirements of industrial technology, but reflected the financial needs of the French state, the abundance of speculative capital at Paris, and the privileges that could be obtained at court. The joint-stock enterprises that they formed contributed less to production, trade, or insurance than to stock-jobbing and price manipulation. ... The boom of the 1780s, in other words, was built on the aristocratic and monarchical institutions of the old order rather than the unborn industrial and financial system of the nineteenth century. It exemplified not the so-called Industrial Revolution but the court capitalism of early modern Europe.[55]

Merchant capital and trade differed from the world of finance in important respects. First of all, merchant capital relied less directly on state-related forms of investment than did Parisian banking. Merchant capital was tied up in trading and overseas ventures, wholesale markets and rural manufactures. Even so, very little of its capital was invested in fixed assets; what little there was tended to be extremely rudimentary and usually made of wood. In the textile industry centred in Lyon, for example, which accounted for two-thirds of industrial production by value, most of the tools were owned directly by the artisans themselves.[56] In the rural industries the situation was much the same; merchant manufacturers provided mainly circulating rather than fixed capital. Their primary interest was in the abundant supplies of cheap rural labour which could be exploited on a putting-out basis rather than investment in large-scale plant and machinery. All that was required was that the merchants themselves control access to raw materials and organization of the work process.[57] Thus, merchants' capital for the most part adapted itself to prevailing methods of production. Moreover, it appears that the dominance of merchant capital over rural industry in France actually served to retard the transition to factory-based production:

> The switch from cottage industry to the factory system does not seem to have taken place in regions where putting-out merchants predominated. Since these merchants engaged in manufacture only within the borders of their commercial horizons, they were not readily inclined to raise their fixed costs substantially. Besides if putters-out wished to assure their domination of the direct producers, they had every interest in maintaining traditional conditions of production.[58]

There were other reasons which help to account for the conservative character of merchant capital. Commerce was by its very nature an extremely unstable form of investment. Disasters at sea, changes in the highly volatile and fickle trade in luxury products, and the vicissitudes of nearly constant warfare, could ruin merchant-capitalist fortunes overnight. Thus, the Comte de Villele expressed a common view when he wrote:

> every man with an acquired fortune who desires only to keep it must keep at a distance from people, of whatever class or profession they be, who strive to make a fortune ... he must avoid all business, all relations with them, because they will not fail to make him their dupe. Furthermore, to each man his *metier*, as the proverb says: look at the proprietor trying to speculate, and at the merchant trying to enter agriculture. ... Never have I participated in the least speculation.[59]

These remarks no doubt reflect the obvious prejudices of the nobility with their disdain for men of 'acquired fortune'. This antipathy for commerce and trade had, however, deeper roots in the social structure. On a society-wide scale, the business of making money through commerce and trade was strictly subordinate to the aristocratic ideal of wealth derived from proprietary forms of investment. It was very often the case, therefore, that wealth accumulated in commerce was converted into proprietary forms of either land, government *rentes* which paid a fixed annuity, or office. The *haute bourgeoisie* which grew in some of the great cities and ports were able to command social respect usually only after noble status had been conferred as a symbol of respectability.

Historians have referred to a general trend towards a ' "decapitation" of the commercial class'[60] in which the stability and prestige of proprietary forms of investment were preferred to the pursuit of commerce and trade. As Colin Lucas has written:

> The consistent pattern of the eighteenth century, as of the seventeenth, was that commercial families placed their capital in land, in government and private annuities [*rentes*], and venal office, all of which gave returns on investment in the order of 2 to 4 per cent, instead of seeking the higher returns on commercial investment. These men were dominated by the social motive not the capitalist motive. They accepted that trade was by definition ignoble and dishonourable. ... Thus in economic terms, nobles and bourgeois resembled each other to the extent that both sought to secure the greater part of their fortune in non-capitalist forms ...[61]

In sum, in all areas of bourgeois investment and business activity – finance, commerce and trade, and the proprietary sector – there is little evidence to suggest that there existed a 'revolutionary bourgeoisie' on the brink of bursting through the 'fetters' of feudal society. Like the nobility, bourgeois fortunes were fully integrated into the structures of existing society. 'Private enterprise', such as it existed, was of a decidedly non-capitalist character.[62] It was based not upon the expanded reproduction of capital through technological innovation, but rather upon the private ownership principally of offices and land which entitled the owner to a share of the wealth extracted from the peasant population.

Having said all of this, it is important not to overstate the case. The *ancien régime* was by no means stagnant economically. Between the 1720s and the outbreak of the revolution, foreign trade grew by 400 per cent, the production of wool cloth and linen by 61 per cent and 80 per cent respectively, iron by 300 per cent and coal production by 700 per cent.[63] Although the economy was growing, it was neither in quantitative nor qualitative terms a comparable match for the rapidly developing capitalist economy of Britain.[64] These two features, growing numbers of bourgeois *parvenus* who inevitably sought advancement through the structures of the *ancien régime*, and the growing economic and military supremacy of Britain over France, were key factors in the outbreak of the revolution of 1789.

One of the central contradictions of absolutism towards the end of the ancien régime was its inability to keep pace with the growing demand for offices by the bourgeoisie. Even though there was a continuity of forms of investment and wealth between the nobility and the bourgeoisie, it would be wrong to conclude that there was no basis for social conflict between the two groups. Indeed, the main source of conflict between the two appears to have arisen from a contraction in the established channels of social advancement – mainly office-holding and titles of ennoblement – towards the end of the *ancien régime*.[65] The upper ranks of the military and other high offices in the state had been traditionally reserved for men of great wealth and old noble families. This exclusivism was only made worse when the monarchy failed to increase the number of available venal offices and acts of ennoblement. Added to this was the fact that the value of lower offices had fallen due to inflation, whereas the value of offices like the *secrétaires du roi* – reserved for only the wealthiest financiers and bankers – appear to have retained their value.[66] Thus, for large sections of the lesser nobility, the bourgeois professions and lower office-holders, the traditional means of social promotion seem to have contracted dramatically in the final years of the *ancien régime*.

The question is: why did this occur? Why was the absolutist state no longer able to co-opt large sections of the bourgeoisie and lesser nobility through the further extension of offices in the state? The fundamental cause was rooted in the general crisis of the state, itself a result of the growing incapacity of the French state to match the competitive onslaught of British capitalism, in both the economic and military spheres. The demand for greater representation by the Third Estate and the lesser nobility, as the precipitating event of the revolution in May 1789, had a deeper cause in the financial ruin of the state and the economy following the Seven Years War and the American War of Independence:

> The French Monarchy lost all of the intra-European wars of the eighteenth century in which it became involved, achieving a victory of sorts only in the far-flung war over American independence; and that victory came at the price of bankruptcy for the state. The humiliation of martial defeats, along with the strain of raising revenues for wars, rendered credible critics' arguments that the country's institutions were in need of basic overhaul.[67]

It might be thought that this explanation places too much emphasis on the *external* causes of the revolution. However, the distinction between 'external' and 'internal' causes is valid only if it is assumed that forces and relations of production could still be, in the late eighteenth century, demarcated in purely local and national terms. Marx saw the eighteenth century as the beginning of what could be genuinely described as world history in which the rise of commerce and a world market dominated by English capitalism, was 'destroying the former natural exclusiveness of separate nations'.[68] The advent of world history also meant that the forces and relations of production of the most advanced countries could have a profound impact on the less advanced:

> Thus all collisions in history have their origin, according to our view, in the contradiction between the productive forces and the form of intercourse.

Incidentally, to lead to collisions in a country, this contradiction need not necessarily have reached its extreme limit in this particular country. The competition with industrially advanced countries, brought about by the expansion of international intercourse, is sufficient to produce a similar contradiction in countries with a more backward industry . . .[69]

Viewed from this perspective, the financial crisis of the French state can be seen as an expression of a more deeply-rooted crisis involving a particular form of surplus-extraction. A central aspect of the dynamic of political accumulation which lay at the heart of absolutism, was the ability of the state to wage war. If this was disrupted, the whole structure of productive relations upon which the state rested was bound to be thrown into severe crisis.

Furthermore, the effects of international competition not only disrupted existing productive relations it helped to *transform* them in the direction of capitalism; social forces had to exist *within* French society which were affected by these 'external' dynamics. This fact has enormous ramifications for how one interprets the events of the revolution in general and the relationship between the bourgeoisie and capitalism in particular. It is true, as we have argued, that the bulk of bourgeois wealth was tied to the *ancien régime* and that the bourgeoisie formed part of the ruling class. But it is also true that sections of French industry and commercial wealth were undergoing considerable growth and transformation in the eighteenth century. Few would now argue that a fully-formed capitalist class existed prior to the revolution. But that sections of the French bourgeoisie were in the process of being transformed into such a class under the impact of international competition seems indisputable. Moreover, as we have seen, there was a connection between the development of industry and commerce and the growing demand for offices by the bourgeoisie which helped to precipitate the revolution. This is not to suggest that there was a direct or conscious relationship between the political demands of the bourgeoisie before or during the revolution and the economic needs of capitalism. But it does suggest that there was *some* relationship between the two.

The important point to stress here is that the counterposition of external and internal causes of the revolution makes little sense. How, for example, does one go about classifying the impact of competition in terms of such a dichotomy? Was competition external to French productive relations or was it internal? It is much more illuminating to view the essential conflict which precipitated the revolution as one between two sets of productive relations. It is possible, therefore, to see the crisis of the absolutist state as part of a long and extremely uneven process in which a new set of capitalist forces and relations of production were coming into sharper and sharper conflict with an older set of productive relations increasingly ill-suited to the competitive pressures of the new international order.

II. Across the Revolutionary Divide

On the eve of the revolution, of course, no one was aware of the historic significance of the crisis facing the French state nor of the events which it would precipitate. Reviewing recent debates on the nature of the French Revolution, Eric Hobsbawm has written:

> it must be accepted that many of the 'revisionist' criticisms of the orthodox interpretation are both factually and conceptually legitimate. There was not, in 1789, a self-conscious bourgeois class representing the new realities of economic power, ready to take into its own hands the destinies of the state, eliminating the declining feudal aristocracy; and insofar as there was in the 1780s, a social revolution was not its object, but rather a reform of the institutions of the kingdom; and in any case its conscious objective was not the construction of an industrial capitalist economy. Nor was this the result of the revolution, which almost certainly had a negative effect on the French economy, both because it severely disrupted it for several years and because it created a large bloc of politically significant citizens – peasants and petits-bourgeois – whose interest it was to slow economic growth.[70]

If the French Revolution was not a revolution carried out by a 'self-conscious bourgeois class' intent on installing a capitalist social order in France, how then should we interpret the events of the revolution itself and its consequences for the long-term development of capitalism in France?[71] Was it, as Taylor has argued, merely 'a political revolution with social consequences and not a social revolution with political consequences'?[72] Or was it, as Furet and other 'revisionist' scholars insist, an even more narrowly defined autonomous political and ideological struggle bereft of virtually any social or economic content?[73]

Any serious Marxist attempt to meet the revisionist challenge must come to terms with a number of questions. Much of the revisionist case seems to rest on the absence of a class-conscious capitalist bourgeoisie in the events of the revolution. We need to ask therefore, whether or not the idea of bourgeois revolution requires the self-conscious intervention of capitalists. Alex Callinicos has argued that the revisionist case is only damaging if we concede that bourgeois revolutions require the existence of such self-conscious actors:

> Responding to the revisionist attacks requires a shift in focus. Bourgeois revolutions must be understood not as revolutions consciously made by capitalists,

but as revolutions which promote capitalism. The emphasis should shift from
the class which makes a bourgeois revolution to the effects of such a revolution
– to the class which benefits from it. More specifically, a bourgeois revolution
is a political transformation – a change in state power, which is the precondition
for large-scale capital accumulation and the establishment of the bourgeoisie
as the dominant class. This definition, then, requires a political change with
certain effects. It says nothing about the social forces which carry through
the transformation.[74]

Central to this formulation is the distinction between conscious agency
and the intended outcome of certain actions, and the consequences of
these actions, which may, in both the short and long term, differ dramatically from the original intentions of the social actors involved. How does
this help to illuminate the events of the revolution?

Let us examine first the question of conscious agency. As the above
survey makes clear, if we were to begin to search in 1789 for evidence
of a class-conscious bourgeoisie with a fully articulated programme for
throwing off the shackles of absolutism and noble privilege and initiating
capitalist development in France, we would not be able to find any. The
revisionists are right at least in the argument that the eighteenth-century
bourgeoisie and nobility were for the most part, though not completely,
indistinguishable as regards their forms of wealth. Indeed, as Elizabeth
and Eugene Genovese argue, the 'entire history of the *ancien régime* ...
militated against the formation of a national class that could be called
bourgeois.'[75] This placed real limits on the development of a distinctively
bourgeois culture. At best, the development of such a culture was a highly
uneven affair:

> Some nobles held beliefs and cherished values that might retrospectively be
> called bourgeois. The bourgeoisie of the *ancien régime* held no monopoly of
> enlightenment thought. Different groups from the second and third estate
> adhered to views compatible with bourgeois ideology, but those views were
> frequently perceived to conflict. ... The bourgeoisie made, and was conscious
> of making, only fragmented contributions to the outbreak of the French Revolu-
> tion.[76]

Thus, it is fair to say that no one, not even those sections of the
bourgeoisie who would play a leading role in the revolution, had a clear
blueprint or programme for carrying through a bourgeois-capitalist revolution. Close study of the *cahiers* fails to reveal anything resembling such
a programme or, for that matter, much in the way of class consciousness.[77]

That this should be so, is hardly surprising. What united the Third
Estate at the beginning of the revolution was a loose set of ideals based

around concepts of 'merit', 'equality' and 'individuality', all of which
had a very specific meaning in the historical context. 'Equality' was never
intended to imply a commitment to equality of all social classes or to
democracy. It was to be the equality of worthy 'professional men'.[78] 'Merit'
and 'individuality' had little to do with commercial or industrial activity,
but were rather defined more in negative terms in opposition to aristocratic
exclusiveness. As Hobsbawm writes:

> there is no sign at all that members of such middle strata, however devoted
> to the ideal of a civil society of equal rights and chances for all, saw themselves
> as a ruling class or as challenging the political structure of old regimes. Indeed,
> one of the ideologically conscious strata of this kind, the German *Burgertum*,
> consisted, until the mid-nineteenth century, largely of a body of men 'bound
> by multiple links to the state of enlightened absolutism and of monarchical-
> bureaucratic constitutionalism' who were, with all their liberalism, mostly loyal
> functionaries of their governments.[79]

What this group demanded was a state which based itself on 'careers
open to talent' which put an end to the narrow exclusivism of the office-
holding elite of the old regime. Such demands in no way implied that
those who populated the revolutionary assemblies rejected either the principle of office-holding or landownership as a criterion of elite status.[80]
It was quite logical, in other words, for the bourgeoisie to begin from
a set of demands which corresponded to their material interests. And
their immediate material interests were closely bound up with those of
the old order and especially with the surplus-extractive powers of the
absolutist state.

That these material interests were crucial in shaping many of the
demands for greater access to state office is beyond dispute. But should
we conclude from this fact, as George Comninel does, that the central
political struggle of the revolution was fundamentally *only* about the achievement of these demands? Comninel writes:

> The French Revolution was essentially an *intra-class* conflict over basic political
> relations that at the same time directly touched on relations of surplus extrac-
> tion. It was a civil war within the ruling class over the essential issues of power
> and surplus extraction. The focus of the struggle was the nature of the state,
> giving the conflict its specifically *political* form, because the fundamental social
> interests at stake were directly tied to state relations.[81]

Comninel does not deny that the victors of the revolution were in the
main bourgeois. Nor does he dispute that under the impact of the popular
revolution the conscious aims of the bourgeoisie were transformed. The
waves of popular rebellion, Comninel suggests, had the effect of forcing

to the forefront of the revolution radical groups which defined their politics 'from within an increasingly well-defined spectrum of liberal ideological positions'.[82] What he does deny is that the bourgeoisie was a capitalist bourgeoisie and that the society and state which it presided over after the revolution was capitalist. 'The Revolution was not fought by capitalists, and it did not produce capitalist society.'[83] On the whole, Comninel concludes, 'there is no evidence to support any aspect of the "theory" of bourgeois revolution except that, in some sense, the leadership of the Revolution came to rest with the bourgeoisie, and that they identified their opponents as the aristocracy.'[84]

Now if all that is meant here is that the bourgeois leaders of the revolution were not capitalists themselves and that they did not fully appreciate the relationship between their political achievements and the development of capitalism in France, there is little room for dispute. That the leaders of the revolution were drawn in the main from the 'middle strata' of lawyers, office-holders, and professions is not particularly surprising. These were the sections of the bourgeoisie which most acutely felt the impact of restrictions on their mobility and talents within the *ancien régime*. 'Professional advocates of causes, keenly aware of the restrictions on "men of talent" like themselves, they were (and still are) natural spokesmen for bourgeois interests.'[85] Moreover, if it is meant that on the morrow of the revolution France was not yet a fully-developed capitalist power there is equally little room for disagreement. But this does not appear to be the gist of Comninel's argument. The thrust of his analysis seems to be that the 'liberal ideological positions' adopted by the bourgeoisie were compatible with the constitutional but non-capitalist state which presided over French society after the revolution. Thus, even though the popular revolution did transform the initial aims of the bourgeoisie, there was nothing that was specifically capitalist about the political programme of the bourgeoisie, before, during and seemingly following the revolution. There is very little in any of this which suggests that there was any relationship between the revolution and the development of capitalism. Where the effects of unintended outcomes are acknowledged at all, these are not associated in any direct way with the emergence of political or economic forms associated with the rise of capitalism.

All of this contrasts with the argument we have been developing. The successive phases of radicalization of the revolution can be seen as instances in which the bourgeoisie was forced by the dual threat of revolt from below and counter-revolution to forge a national programme which entailed, as an 'unintended consequence', the institution of measures which were vital to the long-term development of capitalism in France.

It was against the background of urban unrest and in the wake of

the first major wave of rural revolts among the peasantry, that the Constituent Assembly was compelled to 'abolish feudalism' in the famous
decree of 4 August 1789. In the days that followed, of course, many
of the original decrees were watered down. Since many landowners were
bourgeois, an attempt was made to distinguish between rights which were
'feudal' and those which were considered 'property rights'. Peasants were
declared free, but the land they held was not. They could only gain full
rights to the land by redeeming dues at many times their value. Despite
these reservations, important aspects of feudal privilege had been
abolished:

> Distinctions, privileges, and special local concessions had been abolished. In
> future all Frenchmen had the same rights and owed the same obligations, they
> could enter any profession according to their talents, and they paid the same
> taxes. The territory had a new unity and the multiple divisions of *ancien régime*
> France were ended; local customs and the privileges enjoyed by the provinces
> and towns had also disappeared.[86]

The qualifications which had been placed on the decrees of 4 August
1789, which left in place many of the seigneurial dues, sparked a series
of peasant revolts punctuating the next three years.

The declaration of war in July 1792 gave a further boost to the level
of popular involvement in the revolution. The mobilization of popular
support in defence of the revolution bound huge sections of the mass-
movement to the otherwise limited aims of its leaders. As the revolution
unfolded, it was to become a central feature of the dialectic in which
popular forces were called upon to staunch the tide of counter-revolution,
each time pushing the revolutionary leadership to adopt more radical
measures. As Theda Skocpol writes: 'What "democracy" did come to
mean ... was *popular political mobilization* to secure the virtuous defense
of the revolution against its treasonous, conspiratorial enemies at home
and abroad.'[87]

The masses of 'passive citizens' who flooded into the sections and the
National Guard following the call by the National Assembly in July 1792,
gave a huge boost to those who were pressing for further change. Finally,
the insurrection of 10 August 1792 overthrew the monarchy and forced
the election of the Convention.

> By introducing universal suffrage and arming passive citizens, this second revo-
> lution brought the common people into the political nation and marked the
> coming of democracy in the politics of the Revolution. At the same time the
> social content of that Revolution was becoming very much more dominant.
> After various abortive attempts to stem the tide of change, the former partisans

of a policy of compromise with the aristocracy left the political scene of their own accord.[88]

The successive phases of the revolution followed a similar pattern. Want and economic deprivation among both the urban and rural masses, and fear of counter-revolution by the revolution's external and internal enemies, spurred the Jacobins to institute further changes. After the successful mass insurrection on 2 June 1793, the Jacobins undertook the sale of emigré properties. On 17 July, a decree was passed abolishing all remaining feudal dues without compensation. The Constitution of 1793 declared the right to work, public assistance and education, and enshrined the principle of universal male suffrage in the election of the Legislative Assembly.[89]

A further set of measures were instituted just prior to the final Jacobin assault on the popular movement. Fearing that Danton's *Indulgents* would gain the upper hand, in early 1794, the Jacobins once more sought to win the support of the masses. A new General Maximum on food prices was decreed; seizure of suspects' property was instituted to be distributed among the poor; a pension scheme for mothers and widows was devised as well as a scheme of poor-relief in rural areas. Most spectacularly of all, slavery was abolished outright in the French colonies on 4 February 1794.[90]

When the Jacobins finally settled accounts with the popular movement, arresting and then executing leading figures of the Left and suppressing the popular sections, it also sealed the fate of the most radical phase of the revolution. But, whatever the subsequent phases of the revolution held in store in the way of political reaction, and however contradictory its *consequences* in terms of the future development of capitalism, one thing is certain: despite its conscious aims or design, the French bourgeoisie had, through the pressure of events, been transformed into a conscious class with a national programme for the transformation of France in the image of other bourgeois societies. The pre-revolutionary 'middle classes' would unquestionably have disavowed any foreknowledge of such an outcome. But that is not really the point. As Hobsbawm summarizes:

What the French Revolution did was to transform bodies of such people into self-conscious 'classes' with the ambition to reshape society as 'ruling classes'. In France this happened because in the course of events discoveries were made. First, it became clear that the programme of enlightened reform and progress would not be carried out through the old monarchy but through a new regime – that is, not by reform from above, as men of goodwill had hoped, but by a revolution. Second, it became clear that this programme required a collective struggle of 'the people' or Third Estate against the aristocracy and that, for practical purposes, those who represented the Third Estate and spoke for it – and hence shaped the new France – were the *classes disponsibles* of that estate, men of the middle ranks of society. Finally, it became clear in the course of the revolution that within the former Third Estate 'the people' and the middle stratum had seriously conflicting interests. The makers of the new regime needed protection against the old and the new threats – the nobles and the masses. It is not surprising that they should learn to recognize themselves retrospectively as a middle class and the events of 1789–99 as a class struggle. Outside France it was merely necessary to learn the French lessons and apply them with the required local modifications to make a bourgeois revolution.[91]

That the revolution brought fundamental achievements for capitalism is indisputable. Noble privilege and seigneurialism had been abolished. The system of internal tolls which prevented the formation of a national market was brought to an end. A unified national state based on direct rule had replaced the mediated state of the *ancien régime*. Gone was the system of indirect rule in which the affairs of the absolutist state were handled by local officials drawn from the church and nobility. The construction of a unified national state had a tremendous impact on areas such as taxation, public works, justice and so on, all of which would profoundly shape the character of capitalist development in France in the decades which followed the revolution.

In terms of its immediate economic effects, however, the legacy of the revolution was highly contradictory. France had indeed undergone a political revolution which cleared away much of the old 'feudal rubbish' which hindered the development of capitalism. On the other hand, the revolution had also strengthened the hold of the peasantry over the land, a fact which all but insured the failure of attempts to transplant into the French countryside agrarian capitalist relations like those which existed in England. Secondly, it had created a massive state edifice which continued to represent a powerful pole of attraction for sections of the bourgeoisie seeking social advancement in a state which was now 'open to talent'. This is not to say that nothing had changed as far as the functioning of the state was concerned. It had, but the pull which state employment and economic activities in some way connected with those of the state continued to exert a powerful pole of attraction on bourgeois fortunes and energies. This meant that industrial capitalism was for a long time delayed. There were thus powerful material reasons for those at the top and those at the bottom of French society to resist the full-scale development of capitalism in France following the revolution.

For the peasantry, the revolution brought clear advantages in so far as it strengthened peasant property rights. It is undoubtedly the case that the better-off *laboureurs* and *fermiers* benefited most since it was they, and not the mass of smallholders, who were able to take advantage of the sale of *les biens nationaux* confiscated from the church and emigré nobles after the revolution.[92] In addition, it was this group which appears, somewhat paradoxically, to have resisted *partage* or the break-up of common lands. By doing so, richer peasant farmers deprived poorer peasants of a share in the revolutionary land settlement and in the process contributed to the perpetuation of the traditional pattern of peasant attachment to communal rights in vast areas of France.[93] This contrasts markedly with the actions of yeoman farmers in England in the sixteenth century, who initiated the first enclosure movement by engrossing and consolidating the holdings of their poorer peasant neighbours. In France, moreover, it was this attachment to traditional collective rights which recent scholars have suggested lay behind the resistance in *chouan* areas such as the Sarthe and the Vendée. Middling peasants appear to have strengthened the resilience of peasant communities in *chouan* zones against the encroachments of bourgeois land-buyers.[94]

All of this suggests that the conception of private property within the peasantry differed substantially from the capitalist notion of private property. Peasants were much more concerned with the protection of *customary* rights to property, while preserving individual ownership.[95] Thus, Soboul's claim that the motive force of capitalism lay with the better-off peasantry, looks even more dubious in the light of developments after the revolution. The French *laboureur* was in no sense a comparable social force to the English yeoman farmer; even though the former enjoyed relatively secure tenures, they were still subject to rent squeezing and thus unlikely to engage in agricultural innovation. The trend was towards fragmentation of holdings rather than consolidation. As P.M. Jones notes, 'the revolution strengthened the subsistence sector of the rural economy. Far from nudging French agriculture in a capitalist direction, petty producers practiced auto-consumption as far as possible.'[96] Middling peasants formed only a small minority of the French peasantry, with average holdings at the end of the eighteenth century of around fifty acres. By contrast, the English yeomanry, who as tenants were forced into competition with one another through a system of competitive rents, had held substantially larger holdings – in the area of two hundred acres – and appear to have been more numerous. During the revolution in France, it was the richer peasant farmers who were particularly hard hit by forced requisitions and price controls.[97] By 1826, this middling section of the peasantry represented only 10 per cent of landowners and had not significantly increased the size of their individual holdings over what they had been just prior to the revolution.[98] Overall, this section of the French peasantry appears to have been a rather doubtful candidate for the role of purveyors of capitalism following the revolution.

Of the roughly 80 per cent of the population of France which remained on the land in 1820, 89.3 per cent of this total subsisted on five acres or less.[99] In France then, the *general tendency* in agriculture after the revolution was towards fragmentation of holdings and *morcellement*, roughly the pattern which had existed prior to the revolution. Thus, although the revolution opened up wider opportunities of land ownership, there was no generalized trend towards enclosure and improvement either by the middling peasantry or by large landowners. This situation was only made worse by the inheritance laws of the First Empire; under the Napoleonic Code, *quotite disponible* amounted to one-third of a family's fortune when there were two children, and one-quarter when the number eligible to inherit exceeded three children. The rest had to be divided equally amongst the heirs.[100] In general, these measures are estimated to have increased the number of smallholders by 27 per cent between 1826 and 1858.[101] The prevailing trend throughout the first half of the nineteenth century was towards 'deproletarianization' of urban centres and an increase in the numbers of small cultivators who owned their own land. The overall level of subsistence farming increased by 50 per cent during the century as a whole.[102] Rather than improvement of agriculture through the introduction of labour-saving technology, small peasant proprietors preferred to rely on traditional 'extensive' farming methods such as land clearances to increase cropland and reclamation of wastelands.[103]

Large estates, as well, continued to play a major role in the economy following the revolution, comprising roughly 20 per cent of the land in 1826. In the eighteenth century, large properties were common in the northwest, in Normandy, Picardy and the Ile de France; in the centre, in Nivernais; and in the south, in Languedoc. However, despite their superficial similarity to the capitalist farms of England during the same period, the large estates of France were markedly different in their social structure. First of all, they were surrounded by a mass of semi-landless peasants who sought out leases from the big landowners. In such conditions it made more sense for landlords to increase their revenues through raising rents – since new tenants were readily available – and extending their holdings through the purchase of debt-ridden properties than it did to invest in improvements and fixed capital. Despite their similarity in outward form to the capitalist farms of England, these large estates 'expressed in reality the existence of very different social-productive relations from those which obtained in England.'[104]

Large landowners, with average holdings of 273 acres in 1826, were still dominated by a *rentier* mentality despite the fact that many noble landowners had been replaced by bourgeois owners – though in fewer numbers than is often assumed. In areas where large concentrations of property had been the pattern, peasant land hunger and the persistence of *vain pature* made it feasible for large owners to continue to rely on traditional practices rather than engage in enclosure and improvement. Peasant holdings in these areas were extremely small, averaging around three hectares which was well below the national average of five hectares.[105] This only encouraged reliance on labour-intensive practices rather than their replacement with capital-intensive agriculture, of extending holdings rather than innovating to raise rural productivity.

In other areas of France, where commercial agriculture did not exist, the old practices of *metayage* and tenant farming survived as well. As late as the mid nineteenth century, in the Pyrenees region, it is estimated that sharecroppers were giving over as much as two-thirds of their yield to *rentier* landowners. Seigneurial dues, which had been formally abolished by the revolution, had simply been incorporated into leases.[106] In short, although much land had changed hands during and after the revolution, through the sale of the *biens nationaux* and emigré noble properties, the structure of French agriculture remained much the same as it had been previously.[107]

III. The Post-revolutionary State

One of the main 'political' questions of the revolution centred on the issue of *privileged* access to the levers of 'political accumulation'. During the revolution, the bourgeoisie was forced to recognize that if the channels of social promotion and access to state office, and hence to state-appropriated wealth, were to be 'open to talent', the principle of venality would have to be abolished. This did not mean, however, that careers in the state should offer anything less than they had previously. And, in practice, the post-revolutionary state appeared to offer more. While the revolution had dispensed with the venality of office, fiscal immunities and the special legal privileges of the nobility, office-holding still promised lucrative rewards in the form of the redistributed proceeds of taxation.

In the early years of the revolution, the state bureaucracy expanded at a dramatic pace, partly in response to the events of the revolution itself and the exigencies of warfare. But one of the central aims of the revolution had also been to open up the state apparatus to the legions of lower office-holders of the Third Estate who had been deprived of the preferments of office enjoyed by the wealthy financiers and rich nobles. Between 1792 and 1795, the bureaucracy expanded to five times its size; in 1788, its central administrative core increased by 850 per cent.[108] During the Directory, the bureaucracy as a whole had grown to between 130,000 and 250,000 employees.[109]

While many of those who sought employment by the state did so for the first time, a large number came from the ranks of the *officiers* who held office in the absolutist state. This was in keeping with a pattern which had been established by the revolution itself; a substantial portion – roughly 40 per cent – of the coalition of nobles and non-nobles from the Third Estate which dominated the revolutionary assemblies from 1788 onwards were former office-holders.[110] On the whole, over half of the administrative service during the Directory had been employed since before 1789.[111] Even so, there was still a large influx of people who came into state employment for the first time. As Church notes: 'Administrative posts gave people some assurance of a salary and conditions which were better than those available on the open market. The feeling of making some kind of contribution to the new order was subordinate to this.'[112]

The post-revolutionary state had thus become a strong pole of attraction for large sections of French society. For the lower orders of the administrative corps, however, the degree of mobility within the civil service was strictly limited.[113] The upper reaches of the bureaucracy, on the other hand, functioned much as they had under the old regime, despite the fact that their positions were no longer strictly guaranteed by law. Significantly, the divide which separated the privileges and financial rewards of functionary status and employee status inside the state bureaucracy mirrored the class divisions in society as a whole. The tension between the two was to become even more significant with the passage of time.[114]

The new state elite which emerged during the Consulate and First Empire was composed predominately of *notables* overwhelmingly drawn from the old Third Estate. Napoleon's aim was to create a new hereditary class of dependent state-*notables* which was united within the administrative framework of the state bureaucracy.[115] Over 3,000 noble titles were created by Napoleon between 1808 and 1814, and the majority of these – over 60 per cent – were military.

The centrepiece of the new administrative apparatus was the prefectorial corps. Prefects were responsible for administering the newly created *arrondissements*, which served to undermine local government by granting agents of the central administration greatly enhanced powers over taxation, police, the *biens nationaux*, conscription, communal rights, finances, and so on. Prefects earned substantial salaries, anywhere between 8,000 and 24,000 *francs*. Thus, the prefectorial corps became an attractive means of social advancement for the sons of wealthy bourgeois and nobles.[116]

The state elite which came to prominence under Napoleon did not, it is true, hold their positions through legal or hereditary guarantees as had office-holders under absolutism; rather, 'notability was allied with *capacité*.'[117] Nevertheless, there still existed a strong connection between landownership and office-holding. As Bergeron points out, 'the *fonction-*

naire was also a *propriétaire* . . . an owner of land, or of land and buildings. His impact, therefore, came both from his authority and from the redoubled security of receiving both rents and salary.'[118]

Perhaps the most significant example of this connection between office-holding and landed wealth lay in the connection between military tribute and noble status. Those whose personal fortunes were small, were very often given grants of property from either the imperial domain or from conquered territories acquired through the nearly constant warfare which marked the regime. Napoleon thus

> transformed the practice of accepting personal tribute into an extravagant system of largesse. This generosity towards the marshals and their dependence on foreign sources of revenue gave them a direct material interest in maintaining the frontiers of the empire at their greatest possible extent.[119]

Domestically, the Napoleonic state relied on both direct and indirect forms of taxation to finance its operations. It revived many of the indirect taxes of the *ancien régime*, such as those which were applied to tobacco, playing cards and alcohol. In 1806, the Salt Tax was reintroduced, recalling the *gabelle* of pre-revolutionary times. In total, revenues raised by these various indirect taxes, known as the *droits réunis*, increased by over 50 per cent and constituted roughly one-quarter of government receipts.[120] The burden of this taxation was disproportionately felt by small peasant producers. Even though real estate was taxable and constituted a signifi-cant part of government receipts in direct taxes, it produced in 1813 the same amount as in 1791 when it was created. This was obviously dispro-portionate when set against the expansion of the lands controlled by the Empire and the continuous increase in land values. However, it was consistent with the policies of the regime in that it 'corresponded to the wishes of the *notables*, always opposed to whatever might restrict the free enjoyment of their property.'[121]

In many respects, the fiscal system built up by the Napoleonic state merely perfected the system which had operated only imperfectly under absolutism. Although the system of tax collection still remained more or less 'privatized' as it had been under absolutism when it was overseen by independent tax-farmers, Napoleon attempted to make the receivers-general more accountable by having them sign an obligation at the begin-ning of every month equivalent to the amount they were to receive in taxes. The Treasury accelerated this process by discounting these obliga-tions through private financiers. Gradually, however, the state was able to circumvent the great financiers by issuing bonds in direct proportion to anticipated taxes that no longer had to be discounted.[122] In doing so, the state was able to secure for itself a more efficient flow of wealth into its own coffers and thus more direct control of taxation revenues.

But even these improvements in the fiscal operations of the state proved inadequate. The constant demands of warfare soon sapped the Treasury. By 1812, total state expenditure amounted to 1,000 million *francs*. Somewhere between 60 and 80 per cent of this expenditure was on military needs; in 1813, it is estimated that 817 million *francs* were committed to cover the cost of military campaigns.[123] In other words, the Napoleonic state, despite its attempts to centralize and improve the efficiency of its fiscal operations, still fell victim to a pattern of events commonly repeated under absolutism: the demands of warfare and territorial expansion meant an increasing reliance on indirect and extra-ordinary taxation, a squeezing of the peasantry, and an escalating spiral of indebtedness.

Although the Napoleonic state did represent a fundamental break with the *ancien régime*, we should not lose sight of its contradictory underpinnings. In a situation where capitalism was developing slowly, the formal aspects of the state which favoured capitalism tended as yet to have little impact. It may be one-sided to claim that the regime 'celebrated military, not "bourgeois" mores, rewarding entrepreneurial activities even less than the so-called "feudal" monarchy of Louis XV',[124] but it is true that much of the economic growth that did occur was due to war, economic blockade and the revival of court society.[125] Napoleon attempted to construct a new state notability, stripped of its feudal forms, but still reliant upon the proceeds of office. A contradictory dynamic was being played out in the post-revolutionary state. While the military and legal reforms of the Napoleonic era were indispensable to capitalist development, it would be mistaken to view the actions of the Napoleonic state from this perspective alone. Equally important, and in a sense pulling in just the opposite direction, was the fact that the state continued to serve as a vehicle for private accumulation.

The restoration saw a renewed emphasis on 'patronage, politics and patrimonialism'.[126] Large sections of the bureaucracy – between a quarter and a third – were purged, to be replaced by 'royal reliables'. Most of these were drawn from the ranks of landowners and the old nobility who had considerably recouped their former position during the Empire.[127] Many *fonctionnaire* positions and much of the prefectorial corps merely changed hands. However, with the return of the old nobility to office, the economic gap between the lower orders of the bureaucracy and those who held *fonctionnaire* offices widened still further. It is estimated that one-half of the *fonctionnaires* of the restoration had private fortunes of over 100,000 *francs*, whereas two-thirds of state employees made less than 2,000 *francs* per annum.[128] The widening of the economic divide between the office-holding elite, which controlled the highest offices of the state, and employees at the bottom, only further exacerbated class tensions within the state structure itself. Overall, however, despite the changes in personnel and the economic differences between *fonctionnaire* and employee, the Bourbon regime was marked by a fundamental continuity in social terms with that of the Consulate and Empire. The distinguishing characteristics of office remained intertwined with land-ownership and noble status, rents and salary.

While the revolution of 1830 struck a definitive blow to the aristocratic revival of the restoration, it also reinforced the state bureaucracy's connections with landed over industrial wealth. Secondly, the revolution only increased the already huge 'parasitic body' of professional office-holders dependent on the state for their livelihoods.

Magraw has described the 1830 Revolution as 'a revolution of frustrated careerists'.[129] The aristocrats who had taken over bureaucratic posts after the Bourbon Restoration in 1815, had created a vast pool of jobless bourgeois and notables from the Napoleonic era. One of the chief tasks of the Orléanist regime was thus to attempt to redress the career grievances of this section of the ruling class at the same time as it smashed the wave of popular insurrection unleashed by the July Days. The monarchy moved quickly on both these fronts. Ninety-five per cent of the prefects appointed under the restoration were purged from the administration.[130] Worker and peasant grievances over wine taxes, communal rights, grain prices and unemployment, were dealt with through savage repression.[131]

On the question of who actually controlled the state after 1830, David Pinkney has shown that

> the Revolution did not give the *grande bourgeoisie* any significantly increased hold on public offices ... the number of bankers, manufacturers, and *négociants* in Parliament and the key offices of the state was small, scarcely more than before the Revolution.[132]

The new office-holders and prefects who replaced those who were purged, were in the main drawn from the ranks of the notables who dominated *fonctionnaire* posts under Napoleon.

The Orléanist regime was dominated by the same section of the French ruling class that had controlled the state under the Consulate and the First Empire; that is, landed proprietors, office-holders and professionals mainly drawn from the old Third Estate. Indeed, the largest single group in both the Chamber of Deputies and the administration was composed of professional office-holders.[133] Many posts in the bureaucracy were held in conjunction with a seat in the Chamber of Deputies. On the whole, this meant that the regime was marked by an increased integration of political representatives, landed interests and professional office-holders.

The events of 1830 cast in perhaps the clearest light the contradictory nature of capitalist development in France. The 1789 Revolution had created a new type of state which embodied all of the formal principles necessary for unfettered capitalist development. However, because of its reliance on mass mobilizations to secure most of the major gains of the revolution, the bourgeoisie was forced to make significant concessions to the popular movement, most significantly in the area of peasant property rights. Because of the nature of the revolutionary settlement, the state had no choice but to rely upon peasant surpluses for the bulk of its taxation revenues. Thus, it is no surprise that landed wealth and peasant proprietorship continued to be the twin pillars upon which the post-revolutionary state rested. At the same time, the continued co-existence of large *rentier*-based landed property and small peasant hold-ings, were the chief obstacles to full-blown industrial capitalism. It was the persistence of this 'symbiosis' between landed wealth, peasant property and the state which sustained the gulf between the formally capitalist character of the state and its day-to-day operations which often limited the further advance of capitalism.

But just because there existed significant obstacles in France to the transformation of agrarian relations and the creation of a rural proletariat along the lines of England, does not mean that other forms of capital accumulation were ruled out. It simply means that, at least until the 1840s, it tended to be those sectors of the economy *least* tied to landed property and the state which witnessed the greatest progress of capitalism. In France, older forms of production such as small-scale household, handi-craft and various types of artisanal production, appear to have played a crucial part in this process:

> With population increasing only slowly, with much of the agricultural popula-tion only partially engaged in the cash nexus, and with the national territory divided into only partially integrated regional markets – both for commodities and labour – there were inherent limits to the possibilities of factory production. In these circumstances, it was economically rational for a large part of the nation's capital to be invested in small-scale artisanal production.[134]

It is often assumed that the development of factory-based production in France meant the demise of artisanal workers. However, the most detailed quantitative studies of French industrialization have shown that small-scale household and handicraft production were responsible for the majority of industrial output (nearly 60 per cent) and employed the majority of industrial workers (over 70 per cent) during the middle decades of the nineteenth century.[135] As late as 1876, the industrial population employed in artisanal industries was twice that employed in large-scale industry.[136] The increase in the number of skilled and semi-skilled factory workers went hand in hand with the increase in the numbers of skilled artisans for the simple reason that everything from the building of the factories themselves, to the supply of food and other essentials for the workers, relied upon a range of different forms of artisanal production. Therefore, the first half of the nineteenth century, at least, 'was an era of rise, rather than of decline, for urban artisans'.[137]

The essential feature of capitalist development in France during this period is that it proceeded, in the main, without the dispossession of the immediate producers, or what Marx termed the 'real subsumption' of labour to capital, but rather through the gradual transformation of pre-existing forms, like artisanal and handicraft production. Marx writes:

> the fact is that capital subsumes the labour process as it finds it ... it takes over an *existing labour process*, developed by different and more archaic modes of production. And since that is the case it is evident that capital took over an *available, established labour process*. For example, handicraft, a mode of agriculture corresponding to a small, independent peasant economy. If changes occur in these traditional established *labour processes* after their takeover by capital, these are nothing but the gradual consequences of that subsumption. ... This stands in striking contrast to the development of a *specifically capitalist mode of production* (large-scale industry, etc.); the latter not only transforms the situations of various agents of production, it also *revolutionizes* their actual mode of labour and the real nature of the labour process as a whole. It is in contradistinction to this last that we come to designate as the *formal subsumption of labour under capital* ... the takeover by capital of a mode of labour developed before the emergence of capitalist relations.[138]

Typical of this process was the silk ribbon industry. In the region around St Étienne, near Lyon, silk workers were the largest segment of the working class by 1872, numbering 40,000 to 45,000, compared to 16,700 coal miners and 12,000 workers in heavy metallurgy.[139] Here, the bulk of production was done in urban households. Master weavers typically owned the loom, paid the rent, heat, lighting, but worked on raw materials provided by the merchant capitalist. The merchant capitalist did not hire wage-labour and the organization of production remained in the hands of the master weaver. Because of the uncertainties of the market for silk products, merchant capitalists were content to leave the bulk of fixed capital in the hands of the household producer.[140] The shift to factory-based production came as the result of a number of factors, but chief among them was the pressure of international competition from mechanized production in England and Switzerland.[141] As a result,

> Household production ... underwent important changes during the nineteenth century, changes which altered the balance of class power between merchant

capitalists and master weavers. In particular, power tended to shift towards capitalists due to the growing indebtedness of master weavers, increased merchant control over the preparatory and finishing stages of silk ribbon production, and the introduction of new non-mechanized handloom technologies.[142]

These changes were a common feature of the artisanal industries dominated by merchant capital in the 1830s and 1840s. They brought with them changes in the scale of production, increases in division of labour, dilution of skills and intensified exploitation.[143] The desperation and insecurity which this produced generated the first mass working-class struggles against capitalism and were a critical stage in the development of class-consciousness among urban artisans. Deprived of their old corporate bodies by the legal reforms of the revolution, workers began to turn the rhetoric of the revolution to their own advantage. In publications like *L'Artisan* and *Le Peuple*, the idioms of 'equality' and 'fraternity' were used to express the lack of equality between workers and capitalists. As an article in *L'Artisan* produced in the wake of the 1830 Revolution put it:

> The most numerous and the most useful class of society is, without contradiction, the class of workers. Without it capital has no value; without it no machines, no industry, no commerce. ... Certain journalists shut inside their petty bourgeois aristocracy insist on seeing in the working class nothing but machines producing for their needs alone. ... But we are no longer in a time where the workers were serfs that a master could sell or kill at his ease; we are no longer in that distant epoch where our class counted in society only as the arm of the social body. Three days have sufficed to change our function in the economy of society, and we are now the principal part of that society ...
>
> Our industry, which you have exploited for so long, belongs to us as our own, and the enlightenment of instruction, the blood that we have spilled for liberty has given us the means and the right to free ourselves forever from the servitude in which you hold us.[144]

By turning the language of the French Revolution against the class in whose name it was fought, workers were able to forge a new discourse which redefined much of their old corporate ideology and traditions in terms of the new reality of French society. Workers' corporations were cast in the new idiom of 'fraternal societies' and a 'confraternity of proletarians' united in a single, voluntary 'association' of all trades and occupations. Their opposition to the state, to individualism and private property, to which they counterposed the ideal of a society of associated producers based upon fraternal solidarity, represents the first stages of the creation of a class-conscious working-class movement in France.[145] As Sewell writes:

> The unprecedented workers' agitation of the early 1830s and especially the dramatic uprisings of the workers of Lyons in 1831 and 1834 inaugurated a new political dialectic of class struggle. In the later 1830s and the 1840s, and especially in 1848, all the oppositions . . . tended to coalesce around an overriding opposition between the working class and the bourgeoisie, an opposition between an individualistic, proprietary, liberal vision of the social order identified with a well-to-do class of property holders and a solidary, collectivist, socialist vision identified with a class of propertyless proletarians.[146]

All of these changes, the growth of artisanal and handicraft production alongside factory production, the encroachments of merchants' capital into the sphere of production, the introduction of new productive forces and methods of work, and the emergence of a class-conscious working class out of the ranks of artisanal producers in the 1830s and 1840s, are features of a wider process of capitalist transformation in which capital was forced to adopt alternative strategies of accumulation in circumstances which prevented, at least in the short term, the full-scale dispossession of both rural peasant producers and urban artisans. In the third volume of *Capital*, Marx distinguished between two distinct paths which the transition to capitalism could take:

> The producer becomes merchant and capitalist, in contrast to the natural agricultural economy and the guild-bound handicrafts of the medieval urban industries. This is the really revolutionizing path. Or else, the merchant establishes direct sway over production.[147]

England had followed the 'really revolutionizing path'. There, petty capitalism had emerged out of the ranks of the small producers themselves. Later on, these same producers had fallen victim to the techniques of dispossession and enclosure they themselves had pioneered as landlords began to consolidate large capitalist farms. Only in England, Marx contended, with the emergence of the 'trinity' of landlord, tenant farmer, and rural wage-labour, did the primitive accumulation of capital assume its 'classic form'. Both the English and French revolutions had relied upon coalitions of popular movements from below and bourgeois forces to carry through political revolutions which were vital to the further advance of capitalism in both countries. In England, however, the popular movement was defeated after the great upsurge of urban rebellions which had helped defeat the royalist forces. This defeat, as we shall see later on, was critical in setting the stage for the full-scale dispossession of the English peasantry in the eighteenth century. In France, as we have seen, the petty producers who had allied themselves with the bourgeois revolution, were only partially defeated. The revolutionary land settlement, more than anything else, prevented the French bourgeoisie from following the 'really revolutionizing path' as had England. Rather, French development more closely conforms to Marx's second path in which 'the merchant establishes direct sway over production.'

Marx was fully aware that merchants' capital could not 'by itself contribute to the overthrow of the old mode of production, but tends rather to preserve and retain it as its precondition.'[148] But this did not mean that merchants' capital played no role in the transition to capitalism: 'To what extent it brings about a dissolution of the old mode of production depends on its solidity and internal structure ... on the character of the old mode of production.'[149] In France, as we have seen, the 'solidity and internal structure' of the *ancien régime* was in serious crisis by the end of the eighteenth century. The growth of merchants' capital had contributed to this crisis to the extent that it had increased the numbers of wealthy bourgeois seeking to integrate themselves into the office-holding structures of the absolutist state. The revolution might not have occurred when it did but for the massive increase in commerce and trade which preceded it. But it is important to recall that merchants' capital itself was not the primary cause of the revolution. Without the presence of international competitive pressures emanating chiefly from England, French absolutism might well have been able to accommodate the demands for greater representation by the bourgeoisie. Merchant capitalists became a *political* force for capitalism when their demands for political representation combined with the fiscal crisis of the state and forced them along the path of revolution. They became an *economic* force for capitalism when the pressures of international competitive accumulation forced merchant capitalists further and further into the sphere of production.

The balance of class power between capital and labour was decisively shifted in the 1830s and 1840s in France, not because of an inherent inclination on the part of merchants' capital to revolutionize production relations, but because they had no choice in the matter; the 'formal subsumption of labour' became the 'real subsumption of labour' to capital because the old mode of production was being outstripped by the competitive drive of English capitalism. In an article written in 1850, Marx alluded to the critical influence which international competitive pressures had on the French economy when he noted that 'French relations of production are determined by France's foreign trade, by its position on the world market ...'[150] And who rules the world market? Marx had answered this question in an article a year earlier:

England rules the world market ... The relations of industry and commerce inside every country are ruled by their intercourse with other countries, and are conditioned by their relation on the world market. But England rules the world market, and the bourgeoisie rules England.[151]

In the 1830s and 1840s, France was becoming more and more capitalist. But there were still large sectors of the economy which resisted integration into the capitalist economy. In the late 1840s, even with the beginnings of the railway boom, close to three-quarters of the French population remained on the land, farming at subsistence levels.[152] The number of factory workers was small; there were just over one million factory workers, employed in enterprises averaging ten workers per factory. Much of the economy continued to be governed by a circuit of production controlled by agriculture and not industry; crises of underproduction in agriculture, demographic catastrophe, and famine remained prevalent up to 1850.[153] At the same time, the state bureaucracy had continued to grow both in size and in terms of the resources it consumed. By 1845, the bureaucracy is estimated to have grown as large as 670,000 and to have devoured roughly 20 per cent of the royal budget.[154]

One of the central impediments to further capitalist development continued to revolve around the 'symbiotic' relationship between both large and small landed property and the state. This 'symbiosis' was only finally broken during the Second Empire. Thus, it was during the 1860s that one of the central contradictions of post-revolutionary France was finally overcome. Thereafter, the French state became not merely the *formal* repository of bourgeois rule, but also the *real* motor force of French capitalism.

IV. The Second Empire and the Bonapartist State

In *The Civil War In France*, Marx described the Bonapartist regime as 'the last triumph of a *State* separate of and independent of society'.[155] A consistent theme which runs through Marx's analysis of Bonapartism has to do with the 'parasitic' character of the state. In the immediate aftermath of Louis Bonaparte's assumption of power, Marx wrote that:

In France the executive has at its disposal an army of more than half a million individual officials and therefore it consistently maintains an immense mass of interests and livelihoods in a state of the most unconditional dependence; the state enmeshes, controls, regulates, supervises and regiments civil society from the most all-embracing expressions of its life down to its most insignificant motions, from its most general modes of existence down to the private life of individuals. This parasitic body acquires, through the most extraordinary centralization, an omnipresence, an elasticity and an accelerated rapidity of movement which find their only appropriate complement in the real social body's helpless irresolution and its lack of consistent formation.[156]

Up to 1859, Marx stressed the tendency towards complete autonomization of the state. Moreover, he clearly saw the 'parasitic' character of the state as an impediment to capitalist development. But he believed that such a state power *independent* of the capitalist class could not last for long, since capitalism was growing increasingly stronger and not weaker. For this reason, Marx tended to emphasize the highly unstable and transitory character of the Bonapartist regime. He only modified this view after 1860 when the regime negotiated the Cobden–Chevalier free-trade treaty with England. This event, Marx believed, signified the regime's movement away from complete autonomization and back towards an accommodation with the bourgeoisie.[157] Only after 1860, therefore, is the Bonapartist state portrayed as unambiguously promoting capitalist development in France in Marx's writings.

There are two aspects to Marx's conception of the Bonapartist state worth exploring which help to elucidate these changes in the French state. The first derives from Marx's analysis of the balance of class forces between the bourgeoisie and the working class in the aftermath of the Revolution of 1848. The autonomy of the Bonapartist state, its independence from all classes in society, rested on an equilibrium of class forces: 'the basic condition of modern Bonapartism' wrote Engels, is 'an equilibrium between the bourgeoisie and the proletariat'.[158]

The primary focus of this aspect of Marx and Engels's analysis is on the extent to which the immediate outcome of the class struggle has given rise to a particular form of state with an extremely high degree of independence from the class forces which shape civil society. The autonomization of the state is seen as an abnormal phenomenon resulting from a conjunctural stalemate in the class struggle; the state is not an 'instrument' in the hands of the ruling class even though its form is the result of class society taken as a whole.

The second aspect of Marx's analysis takes up the question of Bonapartist state autonomy from a different angle. His focus shifts from immediate events to the broader historical foundations of the state. He reminds us, in a passage cited earlier, that the parasitism of the French state has its origins

in the time of the absolutist monarchy. ... The seigneurial privileges of land-owners ... were transformed into attributes of the state power, the feudal dignitaries became paid officials, and the variegated medieval pattern of conflicting plenary authorities became the regulated plan of a state authority characterized by a centralization and division of labour reminiscent of a factory. ... All political upheavals perfected this machine instead of smashing it. The parties that strove in turn for mastery regarded the possession of this immense state edifice as the main booty for the victor.[159]

Here Marx is drawing attention to the deeper material roots of the state. The picture which emerges from Marx's writings on France up to 1859, is one in which the state is inexorably pushing its autonomization to the extreme, where it no longer appears to be rooted in or controlled by the existing class forces; the state seems to have broken loose from its moorings in civil society. 'Only under the second Bonaparte,' Marx writes, 'does the state seem to have attained a completely autonomous position. The state machine has established itself so firmly vis-à-vis civil society that the only leader it needs is the head of the Society of 10 December...'[160]

Marx, of course, goes on to say that 'the state power does not hover in mid-air. Bonaparte represents a class, indeed he represents the most numerous class of French society, the *small peasant proprietors*.'[161] But, by saying that the Bonapartist state 'represents' the peasantry, Marx does not mean that the peasantry asserts its class rule through the exercise of state power. On the contrary, because of their isolation, poverty, and lack of political cohesion, the peasantry 'cannot represent themselves; they must be represented. Their representative must appear simultaneously as their master, as an authority over them ... that protects them from the other classes and sends them rain and sunshine from above.'[162]

For the peasantry, the Bonapartist state symbolized the conservative traditions of the past, the protection of peasant property rights and relief from taxation. Marx recognized this fact,[163] and concluded that peasant support of the regime would prove a sad deception; the Bonapartist state – like its absolutist predecessors – would only augment the poverty of the peasants through increased taxation which, in turn, would accelerate their complete dispossession by capitalist interests:

The bourgeois order, which at the beginning of the century made the state do sentry duty over the newly arisen smallholding, and manured it with laurels, has become a vampire that sucks out its blood and brains and throws them into the alchemist's cauldron of capital.[164]

The Bonapartist state, therefore, cannot be said to have 'represented' the class aspirations of the peasantry in the normal sense since the continued existence and growth of the state rested on the exploitation through taxation of precisely that class which it claimed to represent. 'Taxation', Marx writes, is the source of life for the bureaucracy, the army, the priests and the court, in short, it is the source of life for the whole executive apparatus. Strong government and heavy taxes are identical. By its very nature, small peasant property is suitable to serve as the foundation of an all-powerful and innumerable bureaucracy.[165]

This relationship formed the material underpinnings of the 'parasitism' to which Marx so often refers. The 'real material basis of his [Bonaparte's] stock-jobbing regime,' according to Marx, was 'jobs and plunder'; its peculiar economic drive was bound up with the state bureaucracy, the men 'who one way or another, belong to the Administration, that ubiquitous parasite feeding on the vitals of France.'[166]

To the extent that the bourgeoisie tied itself to the maintenance of this 'artificial caste'[167] it undermined its own independent interests. Huge reservoirs of potentially productive capital were poured into speculative investments and 'unproductive' public works projects typified by Haussmann's urban renewal programme in Paris.[168] The main beneficiaries of such schemes were the financial speculators of the Paris Bourse, since the funds had to be raised through the issuing of state securities and bonds. As Marx observed,

In a country such as France ... where government bonds form the most important object of speculation and the Bourse forms the chief market for the investment of capital which is intended to be turned to account productively, in such a country a countless mass of people from all bourgeois or semi-bourgeois classes inevitably have an interest in the national debt, stock-market gambles and finance ...[169]

State-related forms of investment remained a more potent attraction for them than did other more 'productive' forms of investment. Marx himself notes how closely interlinked were the bourgeoisie's *economic* powers of surplus extraction with the *political* power of the Bonapartist state:

the *material interest* of the French bourgeoisie is most intimately imbricated precisely with the maintenance of that extensive and highly ramified state machine. It is that machine which provides its surplus population with jobs, and makes up through state salaries for what it cannot pocket in the form of profits, interest, rents and fees. Its *political interest* equally compelled it daily to increase repression, and therefore increase the resources and personnel of the state power.[170]

Marx was thus acutely aware of the obstacles which the 'parasitism' of the Bonapartist state placed in the path of capitalism. The bureaucracy's continued reliance on peasant-produced surpluses to sustain itself, coupled with the enduring attractions of office and state-related investments over capitalist enterprise for large sections of the bourgeoisie, are both evidence of this. Marx clearly believed that there were strong *anti-capitalist* impulses at work in the Bonapartist state. The question then arises, did he also believe it to be *non-capitalist*? An obvious answer to this question is that since Marx believed that the 1789 revolution was a bourgeois revolution, he would have been contradicting himself to hold that the French state, some sixty years after the revolution was still somehow non-capitalist. Still, Marx sometimes used language which seems to suggest that the Bonapartist state was non-capitalist. In the first edition of 'The Eighteenth Brumaire of Louis Bonaparte', Marx wrote that the

> destruction of the [Bonapartist] state machine will not endanger centralization. Bureaucracy is only the low and brutal form of a centralization still burdened with its opposite, feudalism. In despair and disappointment at the Napoleonic restoration, the French peasant will abandon his faith in his smallholding, the entire state edifice erected on the smallholding will fall to the ground...[171]

For whatever reasons, this passage was expurgated from subsequent editions of his work. Even so, in other passages Marx makes constant references to the parasitic character of the French state which he acknowledges 'arose in the time of absolute monarchy'. Were these allusions intended to convey Marx's belief that the French state of the Second Empire was non-capitalist? Comninel argues, for example, that

> the state-centred surplus extraction which he describes, the centralized rent extracted directly from the peasantry, seems to be a clear example of the 'extra-economic' modes of surplus extraction that Marx associated with *non*-capitalist societies in Volume III of *Capital*. Marx was simply too good an observer of class society to write an analysis of nineteenth-century French society which neatly conformed to his account of bourgeois revolution.[172]

Was Marx so theoretically inconsistent as all this? Let us take first the historical aspects of Marx's treatment of Bonapartism. We have argued that it is possible to distinguish two distinct levels of explanation at work in Marx's account of state autonomy; the first resting on an assessment of the conjunctural balance of class forces between the bourgeoisie and the proletariat in the aftermath of 1848; the second, which takes a longer view, tracing the character of the regime much further back, drawing parallels even with the absolutist state of pre-revolutionary times. But we should not suppose that these two levels of explanation were somehow contradictory. Rather, Marx was attempting to come up with a historically accurate account of the Bonapartist state by examining it from two related, but distinct, angles. Marx was fully aware of the extent to which the 'symbiosis' between the bureaucracy and the smallholding peasantry contained certain anti-capitalist tendencies. On the other hand, he did not conclude from this, that capitalism had not yet implanted itself in France by the 1850s. It was not the ideal-type of English capitalism to be sure, but it was capitalism nonetheless. The mere existence of 'extra-economic' modes of surplus extraction is no more sufficient for judging French society *non-capitalist* than it would be to claim that the presence of wage-labour in the fourteenth century meant that society was already *capitalist*.

The key to Marx's analysis of Bonapartism is that, whatever the historical parallels with absolutism, he did not fall into the trap of analysing state-centred surplus extraction on its own terms, in abstraction from changes in class relations and productive forces beyond the state. In other words, both elements of his analytical framework are essential; Marx, in a sense, shows how the outward form of the state has retained certain 'continuities' with the past, while at the same time its inner character has been altered by the progressive advance of capitalism.

Because of his overriding preoccupation with historical continuities, Comninel can claim that the Bonapartist state is evidence of 'the fundamentally unchanged role of the French state in surplus extraction. . . .'[173] This surely exaggerates and misconstrues the historical facts.[174] Well before the Second Empire, there is clear evidence to suggest that the priorities of the state were beginning to shift towards a more pro-capitalist orientation. Christopher Johnson claims to have detected the beginnings of a rift between sections of the *fonctionnaire* corps who favoured state-sponsored capitalist initiatives and politicians who remained responsive to traditional landed interests in the 1830s:

> There seems to have been throughout the 1830s, a marked difference of orientation on economic questions between politicians . . . and career bureaucrats. The latter, as the regime consolidated itself, generally stood at the forefront of pro-capitalist policies while politicians dragged their heels.[175]

The decisive turning point in the structure of the French economy, however, came with the Second Empire. Between 1852 and 1857, with the rapid extension of rail networks financed through the new credit mechanisms pioneered by the state, France was able for the first time to sustain a rate of growth comparable to that of other industrializing countries. State expenditure rose by 50 per cent as money was poured into rail companies, engineering and metallurgy companies. Mergers were encouraged in all of these sectors; 53 per cent of iron and steel was produced by eight large companies. Industrial production increased by 50 per cent and exports by 150 per cent.[176] The rapid expansion of capitalism was seen as the antidote to endemic class conflict. But a series of 'liberal' social reforms were also necessary to maintain the populist façade of the regime; universal suffrage was restored, press controls eased, strikes were permitted (1864) and public meetings tolerated.[177]

Industrial expansion and economic modernization became the 'religion' of the St Simonian advisors, like Chevalier and the ex-Orléanist Rouher, who surrounded Louis Napoleon. They pioneered a remarkable number of liberal economic policies, which included the use of deficit financing to finance industrial mergers, liberalization of legislation regulating share-marketing and industrial enterprises, and the negotiation of the Cobden–Chevalier free-trade treaty in 1860. 'Bracing winds of international competition would, it was hoped, accelerate technological modernization, and improve productivity.'[178]

Marx himself pointed to the clearly progressive character of state-sponsored credit schemes such as the *Crédit Mobilier*, set up by the St Simonian Pereire brothers. The extension of long-term credit and the establishment of joint-stock enterprises, Marx recognized, were vital to overcoming the barriers to further capitalist development in France. Such innovations would be the 'base of industrial development' opening up 'a new epoch in the economic life of modern nations' by accelerating the concentration of capital and the more rapid disintegration of small-scale petty industry, and hence, the growth of the modern working class. 'At bottom,' Marx observed, 'a *Crédit Mobilier* was possible and necessary only in a country so immobile' as France.[179]

All of these developments indicate that far from being 'fundamentally unchanged', the Bonapartist state's role in French society had changed because French society, and more importantly, the international balance of forces had fundamentally changed. Static comparisons with absolutism which insist that nothing had really changed not only run the risk of discounting the historical importance of revolutions, they also risk transforming historical materialism into a sociology of 'property forms' divorced from any connection to changes in material life.

Comninel unfortunately comes very close to doing precisely this. Indeed the one-sidedness of his historical account follows from his theoretical method. In the name of rescuing historical materialism from technological determinism in which the development of the productive forces always determine the relations of production, he opts for an interpretation in which the productive forces are given virtually no role to play.

Comninel charges Marx and Engels with never having fully shaken off the 'naturalistic materialism' which they inherited from liberal thought. Commenting on a passage from *The German Ideology* he writes for example:

In appropriating the liberal materialism of the stages theory – notwithstanding their critical amendments and Marx's prior recognition of the social character of human material existence – Marx and Engels unfortunately succumbed to its 'technical' and 'naturalistic' conceptions, especially with regard to the social relationship of division of labor. Much as in the liberal conception, the material basis of social development is said to be *increased productivity, the increase of needs, and, what is fundamental to both of these, the increase of population.*[180]

This failure is then connected to the persistence of the 'liberal conception of class'[181] and finally to Marx's uncritical appropriation of the liberal understanding of the French Revolution as a bourgeois revolution. Since the French Revolution did not pit an exploited class against an exploiting class, it cannot be reconciled with Marx's mature conception of historical materialism which gives priority to class relations of exploitation. 'The inherent problem is that the liberal conception of class which originally gave rise to the theory of bourgeois revolution cannot be reconciled to the historical materialist conception of class society.'[182]

This analysis assumes that the 'naturalistic materialism' of Marx and Engels was as flawed as Comninel says it is. What, after all, justifies Marx's claim that social production is the basis for understanding human history? Marx set out his justification for materialism in the *German Ideology* in the following terms.

The premises from which we begin are not arbitrary ones, not dogmas, but real premises from which abstraction can only be made in the imagination. They are the real individuals, their activity and the material conditions under which they live, both those which they find already existing and those produced by their activity.[183]

From this, it follows 'that the first fact to be established is the physical organization of these individuals and their consequent relation to the rest of nature.' Therefore, the 'writing of history must always set out from these natural bases and their modification in the course of history through the action of men.'[184]

This is the essence of Marx and Engels's justification for materialism, and from a philosophical perspective, the only basis from which it is possible to justify a theory of society and history which begins with material production. Marx was not a vulgar materialist because history begins 'from these natural bases and their modification in the course of history through the action of men'. Without this insistence on the way in which nature conditions and determines human existence, there can be no coherent or compelling philosophical basis for prioritizing social production within any theory of society and history.

It is one thing to claim that Marx and Engels overstated the role of the division of labour and the increase of population in some of their early formulations of historical materialism. It is quite another to assert that Marx and Engels remained mired in 'naturalistic materialism' because they continued to believe that social relationships are no more than reflections of fundamentally natural forces. This is to confuse Marx and Engels's purpose in insisting on the natural and physical basis of production as the starting point of historical materialism. They were attempting to provide a philosophical justification for a materialist understanding of history; they were not, as Marx's criticisms of vulgar materialism make clear, asserting that history was the product of natural forces.

Comninel's failure to appreciate the purpose of Marx and Engels's argument leads him to play down the role of the productive forces in his interpretation of historical materialism. After criticizing Marxists who assign priority to the productive forces in historical change, Comninel commits the opposite error by asserting that 'Any conception of historical development which is rooted in "nature" or "material existence" reveals an underlying liberal ideological orientation which displaces class exploitation as the central fact of history.'[185]

This is a serious distortion of Marx and Engels's conception of historical materialism. For Marx, production is simultaneously material and social. Moreover, the relation between the material and the social is not one of simple cause and effect; they are rather internally or dialectically related. That Marx continued to insist on this meaning of historical materialism is made abundantly clear in the third volume of *Capital*:

> It is always the direct relationship of the owners of production to the direct producers – a relation which always corresponds to a definite stage in the development of the methods of labour and thereby its social productivity – which reveals the innermost secret, the hidden basis of the entire social structure, and with it the political form of the relation of sovereignty and dependence, in short, the corresponding form of state.[186]

Marx's assertion that the relations of production 'correspond to a definite stage in the development of the methods of labour', his insistence on the *unity* of the social and material aspects of production are treated as 'something of an aside' and further evidence of 'Marx's inclination to associate historical materialism with liberal scientific materialism – a tendency even more notable in Engels. ...' Once these shortcomings are recognized, Comninel concludes, 'the "direction" of this correspondence can be reversed from what is usually understood and priority can instead be given to the *exploitive relationship*, as it relates to "the development of the methods of labour".'[187]

Why this insistence on separating class exploitation from the material base? The answer seems to lie in a desire to deny that the forms of economic activity in which the bourgeoisie were engaged both before and after the revolution had anything to do with the long-term transformation of French society in the direction of capitalism. Having separated the material base from class relations in a thoroughly dualistic way, the French Revolution resolves itself into an 'intra-class conflict'; Bonapartism becomes simply one of a succession of pre-capitalist state forms which persisted after the revolution. By expunging developments in the productive forces from historical materialism, what we are left with is the mere sociological description of class with no account of how incremental changes at the 'base' of society affect social classes themselves.

Comninel would, no doubt, claim that his redefinition of historical materialism and abandonment of the concept of bourgeois revolution is a small price to pay if it can provide a coherent Marxist response to the more serious dualism of the revisionists who seek to sever any connection between class and politics. We need to ask, however, whether this is a genuine or a false alternative. Looked at from a different angle, it is arguably Comninel's decoupling of class relations from the forces of production which opens the door to those, inspired by the revisionists, who want to go a step further and decouple class and politics.

This can best be illustrated by examining perhaps the most sophisticated and, in some ways most fruitful development of the revisionist thesis, which is to be found in the work of Theda Skocpol. Drawing on the work of revisionist historians, Skocpol, like Comninel, rejects the crude Marxist view of the French Revolution: 'France provides poor material indeed for substantiating the notion of a bourgeois revolution that supposedly suddenly breaks the fetters on capitalist development.'[188] The society which succeeded the revolution was in no way dominated either politically or economically by an enterprising industrial-capitalist bourgeoisie. Rather, the post-revolutionary state was based on

a symbiotic coexistence of a centralized, professional bureaucracy with a society dominated by some moderately large and many medium and small owners of private property. In this New Regime, the state was not oriented to promoting further social structural change.[189]

Skocpol does not completely deny any connection between the revolution and capitalism. She agrees that the simplification of property rights, the destruction of corporate and provincial barriers in favour of a unified national economy and the creation of single unified state, were all essential to the development of capitalism in nineteenth-century France.[190] However, the revolutionary crisis of 1789 was not, she argues, principally about transforming the class structure but rather about changing 'the structure of government'.[191] The main defect of classical Marxism, accord-

ing to Skocpol, is its failure to take seriously the independence of the
state from the structure of class relations. Because of this, she argues,

> Max Weber is a better and more infallible guide to revolutionary outcomes.
> . . . Classical Marxism failed to foresee or adequately explain the autonomous
> power . . . of states as administrative and coercive machineries embedded in
> a militarized state system.[192]

Like the revisionist historians, then, Skocpol sees the events of the revolution principally as a *political* struggle between sections of the dominant
class over forms of political representation within the state.[193] The group
which came to power following the overthrow of the absolutist monarchy
was not a new ruling class but rather consisted of 'radical political elites,
men who were marginal to the old landed-commercial dominant class
and primarily oriented to self- and national advancement through state-
building activities.'[194] In the end, 'the French Revolution was as much
or more a bureaucratic . . . and state-strengthening revolution as it was
(in any sense) a bourgeois revolution.'[195]

There is much, of course, that Comninel and Skocpol agree on. Both
reject, with some qualifications on Skocpol's part, the interpretation of
the French Revolution as a bourgeois revolution. Both see the revolution
as essentially a political struggle between elites over control of the state
apparatus. And both agree that the outcome of the revolution did little
to foster the development of capitalism. However, where they differ is
equally significant. Comninel, whose analysis focuses exclusively on the
internal structure of French society, attempts to rescue a class interpretation of the revolution by centring on the surplus extractive role of the
state. This is what drives him to the conclusion that the post-revolutionary
state was essentially still pre-capitalist. Skocpol's great strength is that
she attempts to show how internal social and political dynamics are shaped
by international military, political and economic competition. Unfortunately, she associates the latter with 'autonomous' political dynamics
which are somehow thought to be independent of changes in social-
productive relations. To treat them otherwise, she argues, would be to
lapse into economic reductionism.[196]

Skocpol seems intent on erecting a 'dual-systems' approach which
asserts that the state system and the process of capital accumulation
conform to two distinct and separate logics.[197] This is highly debatable
no matter what historical period is being discussed, but it surely misses
what is essential about the period under discussion. It was through state
military competition that the backwardness of French productive relations
was initially, and disastrously, demonstrated. The coercive force of
England's more advanced system of social relations was experienced by

France in a succession of military defeats and the ultimate bankruptcy of the absolutist state. But, military defeat was only the most spectacular expression of the changes which capitalism wrought as it destroyed, as Marx put it, 'the former natural exclusiveness of separate nations'. It also fundamentally *internationalized* a new set of forces and relations of production which had a specific impact on class structures in less advanced countries like France. The French Revolution was not *experienced* as a 'contradiction between the forces and relations of production' but that its underlying causes and outcome were tied to such a process is beyond doubt.

The point which needs to be emphasized is that neither of the dualistic approaches we have examined is capable of explaining how this contradictory process unfolded. In the end, both perspectives share an odd symmetry. Comninel's separation of class relations from the material base leads him to ignore how social classes themselves are shaped by the development of new productive forces, both nationally and internationally. It is arguably also this dualism, with its privileging of systems of 'property forms', which is at the root of Comninel's fixation on internal class relations. Once historical development is reduced to the simple struggle between the propertied and the propertyless, then the focus of historical explanation is bound to be exclusively centred on the national terrain. The tasks of historical analysis dissolve into the typology of national property forms; historical materialism is replaced by 'historical sociology'.[198] Skocpol, herself a proponent of historical sociology, despite the methodological superiority of her analysis, fails because she too wishes to separate historical change from real transformations in the material relations of society. By driving a wedge between the economic and the political she is incapable of showing how different systems of productive relations generated different competitive responses on the part of rival states within the international system.

Historical materialism was never intended by its founders to exempt Marxists from the study of real historical events. Rather, it was conceived as a *method* which was grounded in a *holistic* view of society and social change. Marx insisted on the unity of material and social life; of politics and economics. Obviously, there is much to debate about the precise nature of the relation of the material base to the social, of the economic to the political. But unless their fundamental unity is taken as the starting point of historical analysis, historical materialism quickly loses its meaning.

The analysis of French development presented in this chapter has attempted to apply the basic principles of historical materialism to well-trodden historical terrain. The French Revolution, we have argued, was a bourgeois revolution not because on the morrow of the revolution it gave birth to a fully-formed industrial capitalist society. It was a bourgeois revolution in the specific sense that in the course of the struggle, and often against its immediately perceived aims, a section of the bourgeoisie was forced to articulate a programme which reshaped society in their interests. The dynamics of the revolutionary struggle made the bourgeoisie just as much as the bourgeoisie made the revolution. But the political revolution should not be confused with the development of capitalism which was a much longer and tortuous process. What the former did was to clear away much of the 'medieval rubbish' which stood in the way of capitalism. The bourgeois revolution thesis, therefore, does not require the prior existence of a class-conscious bourgeoisie separate in its ideology and forms of wealth from the nobility, waiting in the wings for its moment to smash the fetters of feudalism. The point is rather that the crisis of absolutism, rooted in the collision of two quite contradic-tory sets of productive relations, left the bourgeoisie with only one way forward: the abolition of seigneurialism, the creation of legal equality and guaranteed property rights, and the unification of France into a single economic market – all of which were central to capitalist development.

The nature of the revolutionary settlement, however, was such that real obstacles still lay in the path of capitalism. This was nowhere more evident than in the contradictory role played by the post-revolutionary state. While formally enshrining a legal framework for capitalism, the 'parasitic' character of the state especially on the agricultural economy, meant that for at least the first three decades after the revolution, the most dynamic sectors of the economy were those least tied to the orbit of the state and landed property. French capitalist development did not follow the 'really revolutionizing path' outlined by Marx, but rather the much slower path involving the gradual transformation of older forms of merchant capitalist production. Under the pressure of competitive accumulation, capital was forced to follow the paths open to it. This was by no means a smooth or linear process; factory production often grew up alongside merchant capitalist enterprises which still retained many of their pre-capitalist characteristics; artisanal producers and handi-craft workers continued to grow in numbers alongside and increasingly, as part of the modern proletariat.

The 1850s, and more so the 1860s, represented a crucial turning point in the development of French capitalism. The pressures of international competition meant that even the most backward states in the world economy were forced to take a much more active role in fostering capitalist growth. But to succeed in the scramble to catch up to the more advanced, a high degree of centralization was required. Here, France was in a fortu-nate position. The massive 'parasitic' state edifice, which had for so long stood as an obstacle to capitalist development, now became the only vehicle through which the rapid advance of capitalism could be effected. Thus, in France, there was no neat separation of the economic and the political as capitalism advanced. On the contrary, the relative economic backwardness of private capital meant that the state increasingly became, in Engels's phrase, 'the personification of the total national capital'.[199]

Notes

1. Karl Marx, 'The Eighteenth Brumaire of Louis Bonaparte', in David Fernbach, ed., *Surveys From Exile* (Harmondsworth: Penguin Books, 1977) pp. 237–8.

2. Ibid., p. 143.

3. Ibid., p. 144.

4. Nicos Poulantzas, *Political Power and Social Classes* (London: Verso, 1978), p. 258.

5. Ibid., pp. 29, 260–61.

6. Theda Skocpol, *States and Social Revolutions* (Cambridge: Cambridge University Press, 1979), pp. 3–43.

7. J.H.M. Salmon, *Society in Crisis, France in the Sixteenth Century* (London: Methuen, 1975), p. 34.

8. Marc Bloch, *French Rural History*, trans. Janet Sondheimer, (London: Routledge & Kegan Paul, 1966), pp. 117–20.

9. Salmon, *Society In Crisis*, p. 215.

10. C. Lis and H. Soly, *Poverty and Capitalism in Pre-Industrial Europe* (Atlantic Highlands: Humanities Press, 1979), pp. 58–9.

11. Salmon, *Society in Crisis*, pp. 287–90.

12. Ibid., pp. 291–2.

13. Perry Anderson, *Lineages of the Absolutist State* (London: Verso, 1974), pp. 18–19.

14. Lis and Soly, *Poverty and Capitalism*, p. 55.

15. Anderson, *Lineages*, p. 98.

16. David Parker, *The Making of French Absolutism* (London: Edward Arnold, 1983), p. 64.

17. Lis and Soly, *Poverty and Capitalism*, p. 99.

18. Ibid., p. 100.

19. Victor Kiernan, *State and Society in Europe 1550–1650* (New York: St Martin's Press, 1980), p. 6.

20. Parker, *Making of French Absolutism*, p. 63. This combination of powers of surplus-extraction and military office was not fortuitous. The ability to collect taxes was often contingent on the amount of force which could be brought to bear on the peasantry and local nobles who assisted them in resisting royal tax-collectors.

Perry Anderson has commented on the general role of warfare under feudalism: '... it can be argued that war was possibly the most rational and rapid single mode of expansion of surplus extraction available for any given ruling class under feudalism. ... It was thus logical that the social definition of the feudal ruling class was military. The economic rationality of war in such a social formation is a specific one: it is a maximization of wealth whose role cannot be compared to that which it plays in the developed forms of the successor mode of production, dominated by the basic rhythm of the accumulation of capital and the "restless and universal change" (Marx) of the economic foundations of every social formation.' Anderson, *Lineages*, p. 31.

21. Parker, *Making of French Absolutism*, p. 106.

22. Barrington Moore, *The Social Origins of Dictatorship and Democracy* (Boston: Beacon Press, 1966), p. 19.

23. Parker, *Making of French Absolutism*, pp. 110–12. See also: Boris Porchnev, *Les soulevements populaires en France de 1623 à 1648*. Sections of this work are contained

in Isser Woloch, ed., *The Peasantry In the Old Regime* (New York: Robert Krieger Publishing, 1977); Roland Mousnier, "Conjuncture and Circumstance in Popular Uprisings", in Woloch. For an account of the debate between Boris Porchnev and Roland Mousnier over the nature of peasant revolts in the seventeenth century, see J.H.M. Salmon, 'Venality of Office and Popular Sedition in Seventeenth Century France', *Past and Present* no. 37 (July, 1967); Robert Mandrou, 'Porchnev, Mousnier and the Significance of Popular Uprisings', trans. by Linda Kimmel and Isser Woloch, in Isser Woloch, ed., *The Peasantry*. Mandrou, like Parker, argues that there is little evidence for the view held by Porchnev, that these revolts could have spilled over into full-scale revolution against the absolutist state. See also Pierre Goubert, 'The French Peasantry in the Seventeenth Century: A Regional Example', in Woloch. Goubert contrasts the condition of the French labourer with that of the English yeoman.

24. Parker, *Making of French Absolutism*, p. 64.

25. William Doyle, 'Was There An Aristocratic Reaction in Pre-Revolutionary France?', in Douglas Johnson, ed., *French Society and the Revolution* (Cambridge: Cambridge University Press, 1976), p. 22.

26. Lis and Soly, *Poverty and Capitalism*, p. 137.

27. Pierre Goubert, 'Seventeenth Century Peasantry', *The Ancien Régime*, trans. Steve Cox (London: Weidenfeld and Nicolson, 1973), esp. ch. 5.

28. Lis and Soly, *Poverty and Capitalism*, p. 136.

29. Doyle, 'Was There an Aristocratic Reaction?', p. 7.

30. Ibid., p. 14.

31. François Furet, *Interpreting the French Revolution* (Cambridge: Cambridge University Press, 1979), pp. 103–6.

32. George V. Taylor, 'Non-Capitalist Wealth and the Origins of the French Revolution', *American Historical Review* vol. 72, no. 2 (1967), p. 477.

33. This was the view most consistently expounded by Engels. He writes: 'By way of exception, however, periods occur in which the warring classes balance each other so nearly that the state power, as ostensible mediator, acquires for the moment, a certain degree of independence of both. Such was the absolute monarchy of the seventeenth and eighteenth centuries, which held the balance between the nobility and the class of burgers; such was the Bonapartism of the First and still more the Second Empire ...' *The Origins of the Family, Private Property and the State* (Moscow: Progress Publishers, 1977), p. 168. Marx and Engels's various writings on the absolutist state are admirably summarized in Hal Draper, *Karl Marx's Theory of Revolution: State and Bureaucracy* vol. 1 (New York: Monthly Review Press, 1977), esp. pp. 475–96. Anderson has effectively criticized the ambiguities and conceptual 'slippage' found in Marx and Engels's various formulations on the nature of absolutism; See Anderson, *Lineages*, pp. 15–16.

34. Furet, *Interpreting the French Revolution*, p. 102.

35. Ibid., pp. 109–10.

36. Robert Brenner, 'The Agrarian Roots of European Capitalism', in T.H. Aston and C.H.E. Philpin, eds., *The Brenner Debate* (Cambridge: Cambridge University Press, 1987), p. 227.

37. 'Feudalism as a mode of production', Perry Anderson writes, 'was originally defined by an organic unity of economy and polity, paradoxically distributed in a chain of parcellized sovereignties throughout the social formation. The institution of serfdom as a mechanism of surplus extraction fused economic exploitation and politico-legal coercion at the molecular level of the village. The lord in his turn typically owed liege-loyalty and knight service to a seigneurial overlord, who claimed the land as his ultimate domain.' *Lineages*, p. 19. See also; Ellen Wood, 'The Separation of the Economic and the Political in Capitalism', *New Left Review* 127 (May–June, 1981), pp. 86–9.

38. Brenner, 'Agrarian Class Structure and Economic Development', *Brenner Debate*, p. 55.

39. Brenner, 'Agrarian Roots', *Brenner Debate*, p. 290.

40. Colin Lucas, 'Nobles, Bourgeois and the Origins of the French Revolution', *Past and Present* 60 (August 1973), p. 98.

41. Brenner, 'Agrarian Roots', *Brenner Debate*, pp. 236–42. Our usage of the term

'political accumulation' here and elsewhere varies slightly from Brenner's. His usage is generally restricted to the accumulation of the powers which made extra-economic surplus extraction possible in the first place. While it may be useful to distinguish between the two processes, our definition refers not to the former process but to the latter, that is, accumulation of 'economic' surpluses by 'political' means.

42. As Brenner notes, '... those historians who have stressed the heavily "political" nature of feudal dynamics have tended sometimes to forget that much of feudal government, feudal "state" building was about "economics" – the extraction, circulation, redistribution and consumption of peasant produced wealth.' Ibid., p. 240.

43. Albert Soboul, *The French Revolution 1787–1799*, trans. Alan Forrest and Colin Jones (New York: Vintage Books, 1974), pp. 21–2, 553.

44. Albert Soboul, 'Du feodalisme au capitalisme: la Revolution française et la problematique des voies de passage', *La Pensée* no. 196 (1977), p. 64.

45. George V. Taylor, 'Non-Capitalist Wealth', pp. 487–8.

46. George V. Taylor, 'Types of Capitalism in Eighteenth Century France', *English Historical Review* vol. 79 (July, 1964), p. 479.

47. George V. Taylor, 'The Paris Bourse on the Eve of the Revolution, 1781–1789', *American Historical Review* vol. 67, no. 3 (April, 1962), p. 959.

48. Taylor, 'Types of Capitalism', p. 488.

49. Taylor, 'Types of Capitalism', p. 491. Taylor's usage of the term 'capitalism' to describe such activities is highly misleading. As will become clear later, the fact that such activities were fully integrated into a circuit of production which ultimately rested on 'extra-economic' coercion indicates that they have much more in common with *feudal* relations of production than with capitalism.

For an analysis more consistent with this line of argument see: Tom Kemp, *Economic Forces in French History* (London: Dobson Books, 1971), pp. 54–5.

50. Furet, *Interpreting the French Revolution*, p. 101; Taylor, 'Paris Bourse', p. 954.

51. Kemp, *Economic Forces*, p. 56.

52. Taylor cites the case of one such non-noble, who wrote to his son that he was 'virtually compelled to become a farmer-general and a noble'. Taylor, 'Types of Capitalism', p. 490.

53. Taylor, 'Paris Bourse', p. 963.

54. Karl Marx, *Grundrisse* (Harmondsworth: Penguin, 1973), p. 506.

55. Taylor, 'Paris Bourse', p. 977.

56. Taylor, 'Non-Capitalist Wealth', p. 483.

57. Kemp, *Economic Forces*, p. 35.

58. Lis and Soly, *Poverty and Capitalism*, p. 155.

59. Quoted in Robert Forster, *The Nobility of Toulouse* (Baltimore: Johns Hopkins Press, 1960), p. 118.

60. Ibid., p. 102.

61. Lucas, 'Nobles, Bourgeois', p. 92.

62. J. F. Bosher, *French Finances, 1770–1795: From Business to Bureaucracy* (Cambridge: Cambridge University Press, 1970), p. 286.

63. Paul McGarr, 'The Great French Revolution', *International Socialism* no. 43 (June, 1989), p. 23.

64. 'In 1789, Britain had over 20,000 spinning jennies, 9,000 of the newer mule jennies, and 200 Arkwright mills. The equivalent figures for France were: fewer than a thousand, none and eight!' McGarr, 'Great French Revolution', p. 27.

65. Lucas, 'Nobles, Bourgeois', p. 103.

66. The resentment of lower office-holders, whose offices were becoming worthless, toward upper office-holders such as *secrétaires du roi*, helps to explain the vociferous denunciations of financiers which were common in the revolutionary assemblies.

67. Theda Skocpol, 'Reconsidering the French Revolution in World-Historical Perspective', *Social Research* vol. 56, no. 1 (Spring, 1989), p. 60.

68. Karl Marx, in C. J. Arthur, ed., *The German Ideology* (New York: International Publishers, 1974), p. 78.

69. Ibid., p. 89.

70. Eric Hobsbawm, 'The Making of a "Bourgeois Revolution"', *Social Research* vol. 56, no. 1 (Spring, 1989), p. 18.

71. For Immanuel Wallerstein the 'revisionist' attack on the orthodox interpretation of the revolution is something of a non-issue since, by definition, France was already capitalist by 1789. 'The French Revolution could not have been a "bourgeois revolution" since the capitalist world-economy within which France was located was already one in which the dominant class strata were "capitalists" in their economic behaviour.' Immanuel Wallerstein, 'The French Revolution as a World-Historical Event', *Social Research* vol. 56, no. 1 (Spring 1989), p. 36.

72. Taylor, 'Non-Capitalist Wealth', p. 491.

73. Furet, *Interpreting the French Revolution*, p. 104. For a useful summary of 'revisionist' writings on the revolution, see William Doyle, *Origins of the French Revolution* (New York: Oxford University Press, 1980), esp. ch. 1.

74. Alex Callinicos, 'Bourgeois Revolutions and Historical Materialism', *International Socialism* no. 43 (June, 1989), p. 143. This is similar to the argument developed by Geoff Eley referred to earlier. Eley and Blackbourn, *Peculiarities*, pp. 82–3.

75. Elizabeth Fox-Genovese and Eugene D. Genovese, *The Fruits of Merchant Capital* (New York: Monthly Review Press, 1983), p. 225.

76. Ibid., p. 226.

77. Fox-Genovese and Genovese, *Merchant Capital*, p. 221.

78. This point was made abundantly clear in the Abbé Sieyes's famous pamphlet on the Third Estate. Hobsbawm, 'A Bourgeois Revolution', p. 22.

79. Hobsbawm, 'A Bourgeois Revolution', p. 24.

80. Lucas, 'Nobles, Bourgeois', p. 126.

81. George C. Comninel, *Rethinking The French Revolution: Marxism and the Revisionist Challenge* (London: Verso, 1987), p. 200.

82. Ibid., p. 114.

83. Ibid., p. 202.

84. Ibid., p. 182.

85. McGarr, 'Great French Revolution', n. 83, p. 103.

86. Soboul, *French Revolution*, p. 150.

87. Ibid., p. 61.

88. Ibid., p. 251.

89. Ibid., pp. 315–16.

90. McGarr, 'Great French Revolution', p. 71.

91. Hobsbawm, 'A Bourgeois Revolution', pp. 24–5.

92. Kemp, *Economic Forces*, p. 86.

93. David Hunt, 'Peasant Politics in the French Revolution', *Social History* vol. 9, no. 3 (October, 1984), p. 297.

94. Hunt, 'Peasant Politics'; Paul Bois, *Paysans de l'Ouest* (Paris, Mouton, 1960); T.J.A. Le Goff, *Vannes and its Region: A Study of Town and Country in Eighteenth Century France* (Oxford: Oxford University Press, 1981); Donald Sutherland, *The Chouans: The Social Origins of Popular Counter-Revolution in Upper Brittany* (Oxford: Oxford University Press, 1982).

95. Theda Skocpol, *States and Social Revolutions*, p. 126.

96. P.M. Jones, *The Peasantry in the French Revolution* (Cambridge: Cambridge University Press, 1988), p. 254.

97. Moore, *Social Origins*, p. 88.

98. Roger Price, *The Economic Modernization of France 1730–1880* (London: Croom Helm, 1975), p. 54. The average holding of the richer peasantry averaged about sixty acres, a marginal increase over the eighteenth-century norm.

99. Ibid., p. 55. In England at the same time only 35 per cent of the population still remained on the land. See Lis and Soly, *Poverty and Capitalism*, p. 140.

100. Kemp, *Economic Forces*, p. 88; Robert Forster, 'Survival of the Nobility During the French Revolution', in Johnson, *French Society and the Revolution*, p. 144.

101. Georges Dupeux, *French Society 1789–1970*, trans. Peter Wait (London: Methuen 1976) p. 109.

102. Ibid., p. 112.

103. Dupeux, *French Society*, p. 113; Hugh D. Clout, *The Land of France 1815–1914* (London: George Allen and Unwin, 1983), p. 18.

104. Brenner, 'Agrarian Roots', *Brenner Debate*, p. 312.

105. Clout, *The Land of France*, p. 33.

106. Price, *Economic Modernization*, p. 55.

107. Jones emphasizes the inherently 'conservative character of the revolutionary land settlement'. Jones, *Peasantry*, pp. 254–5.

108. Clive Church, *Revolution and Red Tape, The French Ministerial Bureaucracy 1770–1850* (Oxford: Clarendon Press, 1981), p. 72.

109. Ibid., p. 150.

110. D.M.G. Sutherland, *France 1789–1815, Revolution and Counter-revolution* (London: Fontana, 1985), p. 40.

111. Church, *Revolution and Red Tape*, p. 82.

112. Ibid., p. 100.

113. Ibid., p. 186.

114. Ibid., p. 311.

115. Ibid., p. 258.

116. Sutherland, *France 1789–1815*, pp. 344–5; Louis Bergeron, *France Under Napoleon*, trans. R.R. Palmer (Princeton: Princeton University Press, 1981), pp. 27–31.

117. Sutherland, *France 1789–1815*, p. 258.

118. Bergeron, *France Under Napoleon*, p. 138. Napoleon was quite explicit on this point when he stated: 'I will employ only people who have fifty thousand livres a year in landed rents.' Bergeron, p. 152.

119. Sutherland, *France 1789–1815*, pp. 367–8.

120. Ibid., p. 380; Bergeron, *France Under Napoleon*, pp. 38–9.

121. Bergeron, *France Under Napoleon*, p. 38.

122. Ibid., pp. 41–51.

123. Ibid., pp. 39–40.

124. Sutherland, *France 1789–1815*, p. 438.

125. Ibid, p. 382.

126. Church, *Revolution and Red Tape*, p. 287.

127. Sutherland, *France 1789–1815*, p. 387.

128. Ibid., p. 293.

129. Roger Magraw, *France 1815–1914: The Bourgeois Century* (London: Fontana Books, 1983), p. 42.

130. Church, *Revolution and Red Tape*, p. 296.

131. Magraw, *France 1815–1914*, p. 296.

132. David Pinkney, 'The Myth of the Revolution of 1830', *A Festschrift for Frederick B. Artz* (Durham: Duke University Press, 1964), p. 54; *The French Revolution of 1830* (Princeton: Princeton University Press, 1972), ch. 2.

133. Ibid., p. 58.

134. William H. Sewell, *Work and Revolution in France 1789–1848* (Cambridge: Cambridge University Press, 1980), p. 153.

135. Figures quoted in Ronald Aminzade, 'Reinterpreting Capitalist Industrialization: A Study of Nineteenth-century France', *Social History* vol. 9, no. 3 (October, 1984), p. 330.

136. Sewell, *Work and Revolution*, p. 154.

137. Ibid., p. 157.

138. Karl Marx, *Capital* vol. 1 (New York: Vintage Books, 1977), p. 1021.

139. Aminzade, 'Capitalist Industrialization', p. 335.

140. Ibid., pp. 336–8.

141. Ibid., p. 341.

142. Ibid., p. 339.

143. Sewell, *Work and Revolution*, p. 158.

144. Quoted in Sewell, *Work and Revolution*, p. 198.

145. Ibid., p. 282.

146. Ibid., p. 282.

147. Marx, *Capital* vol. 3, p. 334.

148. Ibid., p. 334.

149. Ibid., p. 332.

150. Marx, 'The Class Struggles in France', in *Surveys from Exile*, ed. David Fernbach (Harmondsworth: Penguin Books, 1977), p. 45.

151. Karl Marx, quoted in Hal Draper, *Karl Marx's Theory of Revolution, vol. 2: The Politics of Social Classes* (New York: Monthly Review Press, 1978), pp. 243–4.

152. Price, *Economic Modernization*, p. 167.

153. Ibid., pp. 61–71, 136–40; Church, *Europe In 1830*, pp. 179–80; Hobsbawm, *Age of Revolution*, pp.189, 200–01, 207–8; Guy Palmade, *French Capitalism in the Nineteenth Century* (Newton Abbot: David and Charles, 1972), ch. 2; Kemp, *Economic Forces*, ch. 6.

154. Church, *Revolution and Red Tape*, p. 298.

155. Karl Marx, quoted in Draper, *Marx's Theory of Revolution*, vol. 1, p. 463.

156. Marx, 'The Eighteenth Brumaire', p. 186.

157. Draper, *Marx's Theory of Revolution* vol. 1, pp. 460–61.

158. Engels, quoted in Draper, *Marx's Theory of Revolution* vol. 1, p. 482.

159. Marx, 'Eighteenth Brumaire', pp. 237–8.

160. Ibid., p. 238.

161. Ibid, p. 238.

162. Ibid., p. 239.

163. Karl Marx, 'The Class Struggles in France', pp. 72, 76–7.

164. Marx, 'Eighteenth Brumaire', p. 242.

165. Ibid., p. 243.

166. Karl Marx, quoted in Draper, *Marx's Theory of Revolution* vol. 1, p. 455.

167. Ibid., p. 243.

168. Ibid., p. 457.

169. Marx, 'Class Struggles in France', pp. 110–11.

170. Marx, 'The Eighteenth Brumaire', p. 186.

171. Ibid., p. 243.

172. Comninel, *Rethinking*, p. 203.

173. Ibid., p. 202.

174. This point is also remarked upon by Robin Blackburn in *The Overthrow of Colonial Slavery* (London: Verso, 1988), n. 4, pp. 549–50.

175. Christopher Johnson, 'The Revolution of 1830 in French Economic History', in John M. Merriman, ed., *1830 in France* (New York: New Viewpoints, 1975), p. 160.

176. Magraw, *France 1815–1914*, pp. 159–60.

177. Ibid., p. 164.

178. Ibid., p. 162.

179. Marx, 'The Eighteenth Brumaire', pp. 244–5.

180. Comninel, *Rethinking*, p. 148.

181. Ibid., p. 150.

182. Ibid., p. 152.

183. Karl Marx, *German Ideology* (New York: International Publishers, 1974), p. 42.

184. Ibid., p. 42.

185. Comninel, *Rethinking*, p. 159.

186. Marx, *Capital* vol. 3, p. 791.

187. Comninel, *Rethinking*, p. 169.

188. Skocpol, *States and Social Revolutions*, p. 177.

189. Ibid., p. 204.

190. Ibid., p. 179.

191. Ibid., p. 66.

192. Ibid., pp. 286–92.

193. Ibid., p. 67.

194. Ibid., p. 185.

195. Ibid., p. 179.

196. Ibid., pp. 24–33.

197. Skocpol's dualism only makes sense if class relations and politics are defined in the most restrictive fashion. Colin Barker usefully reminds us, however, that 'Capitalism ... is a world system of states, and the form that the capitalist state takes is the nation-state form. Any discussion, therefore, of the capitalist state form must take account of the state both as an apparatus of class domination and as an apparatus of competition between segments of the bourgeoisie.' Colin Barker, 'A Note on the Theory of Capitalist States', *Capital and Class* (1978), p. 118.

For a useful critique of Skocpol's 'dual-systems' perspective see Christopher Chase-Dunn, 'Interstate System and Capitalist World-Economy: One Logic or Two?', *International Studies Quarterly* vol. 25, no. 1 (March, 1981).

198. Comninel, *Rethinking*, p. 77.

199. Frederick Engels, *Anti-Dühring* (Moscow: Progress Publishers, 1969), p. 330.

3

Germany:
Prussian Absolutism to Bismarck

The course of German history, just as much as that of France, has often been enlisted to confirm broad historical judgements about the contrasting 'paths to modernity' followed by each country. Where the history of the latter, from the *ancien régime* to the fall of Louis Napoleon, is most often seen as the gradual consolidation of political institutions conducive to the requirements of modern industrial capitalism, the former has been portrayed as a case of failed or partial 'modernization', the ultimate consequence of which was horrifically demonstrated by the Nazi regime in the first half of this century. Where France is said to have produced a triumphant bourgeoisie in 1789, Germany ostensibly produced a supine and weak bourgeoisie, incapable of conquering state power for itself and thus predisposed to accommodate itself to 'pre-industrial' elites who were openly hostile to Parliamentary democracy and liberal capitalism.

Thus the pattern of development from the beginnings of Prussian absolutism to the consolidation of the Reich under Bismarck has been seen not only as a deviation from general European trends but as a prelude to twentieth-century Fascist regimes. In the words of Hans Rosenberg, 'the conservative heirs of the absolute monarchy share the responsibility for the rise and victory of mass dictatorships and twentieth-century totalitarianism.'[1] Theodore Hamerow goes so far as to claim that 'the mistakes of 1848 had to be paid for not in 1849, but in 1918, 1933 and 1945.'[2] Ralf Dahrendorf has described Imperial Germany as a form of 'industrial feudal society' which evolved on the basis of a 'formalized status hierarchy of a system of social stratification modelled on military or bureaucratic orders of rank.' As a result of this tradition,

> Germany could – and possibly had to – step on the path to National Socialist dictatorship because her society bore many traits that resisted the constitution of liberty. ... Neither in the sense of a society of citizens nor in that of one dominated by a confident bourgeoisie did a modern society emerge.[3]

Similarly, Barrington Moore has singled out German development as an instance of 'conservative modernization' in which the political realm continued to be dominated by 'pre-industrial' elites predisposed to authoritarian forms of rule, due to the absence of a revolutionary breakthrough by an urban-based bourgeoisie in conjunction with peasant allies in the countryside.[4]

This emphasis on the 'peculiarities' of German development finds some echo in the works of Marx and Engels as well. Thus for example, where Marx sees French absolutism as playing an essentially progressive role by 'preparing the class rule of the bourgeoisie', his characterization of Hohenzollern absolutism is far less flattering.[5] In correspondence with Engels, Marx describes the rise of Prussian absolutism as the result of 'Petty thieving, bribery, direct purchase, underhand dealings to capture inheritances, and so on – all this shabby business is what the history of Prussia amounts to.'[6]

Of the German bourgeoisie's role in 1848, Engels described it as 'infinitely more faint hearted than the English or French ...'[7] Marx's assessment of the bourgeoisie is no less withering: 'In France it won out, in order to humble the people. In Germany it humbled itself, in order to keep the people from winning. All history shows nothing more *ignominious and mean-spirited* than the *German bourgeoisie.*'[8]

For Marx and Engels it was the bourgeoisie's political backwardness combined with the continued hegemony of the feudal aristocracy which gave the nineteenth-century German state its unique character. Thus Engels draws a direct link between 'what the bourgeoisie itself had been too cowardly to carry through from 1848 to 1850' and what the Bismarckian state was forced to do in 1871 – namely, abolish the last vestiges of feudalism through a unified state.[9] In a celebrated passage, Marx described the Bismarckian state as 'nothing but a military despotism, embellished with Parliamentary forms, alloyed with a feudal admixture, already influenced by the bourgeoisie, furnished by the bureaucracy and protected by the police'.[10]

This 'agglutination of epithets',[11] as Perry Anderson has described it, was never developed much further by Marx and Engels. Engels came closest to developing a general theoretical perspective on the phenomenon of revolution from above when he described it as 'the real religion of the modern bourgeoisie'.[12] Although some of Engels's formulations regarding Bismarck are somewhat overdrawn, the general thrust of his analysis was accurate. The path of bourgeois revolution from above followed by Germany, although based on certain peculiarities of German development, should also be seen in the context of wider historical developments. The phenomenon of revolution from above became the 'religion of the modern bourgeoisie' not out of any conscious design. It was rather something which was forced on countries at a specific stage in the development of world capitalism. The price of admission into the ranks of capitalist nation-states by the 1860s increasingly required that individual states undertake the rapid transformation of their economies. If their native bourgeoisies were insufficiently developed to carry through this task, then other social forces could be called upon to accomplish what was required. Cast against the backdrop of the English and French revolutions, events in Germany may appear unique. Viewed from the perspective of contemporary and future developments, they take on a different meaning. The 1860s saw a host of similar revolutions from above in countries as diverse as Japan, Italy and the United States.[13] From this perspective, there may be very little that is particularly special about Germany's *Sonderweg*.

However, from the standpoint of its prior history, there were certain features of German development which had a profound impact in shaping the specific form of Bismarck's revolution from above. Prussian absolutism has often been characterized as one of the most backward in Europe. And yet, it also proved to be one of the most tenacious, undergoing in the course of the eighteenth and nineteenth centuries a remarkable number of transformations. Although its bureaucracy never swelled to the size of the French absolutist state, Prussian absolutism proved far more adept at avoiding disastrous challenges to its authority from both the aristocracy and the bourgeoisie. In order to understand why this was so, we need to turn first to an examination of the historical roots of Prussian absolutism.

I. The Rise of German Absolutism

Although the consolidation of Hohenzollern absolutism in Prussia occurred comparatively late following the Thirty Years War, many of the social ingredients which were to give it its distinctive character were established much earlier, in the period stretching from the Europe-wide agrarian crisis of the late fourteenth and early fifteenth centuries up to and including the epoch of the price revolution and agrarian upturn of the sixteenth century.

By the middle of the fifteenth century, the peasantry in the southern and western areas of Germany had achieved a degree of autonomy unheard of in most other parts of Germany. Although serfdom (*Leibeigen-*

schaft) still dominated rural social relations, the jurisdictional controls of the nobility over the peasantry had become severely strained. Through a combination of peasant resistance and migration, the ability of individual lords to exact two or three days' labour on their demesnes had broken down. The fragmentation of jurisdictions which resulted from peasant migrations meant that individual peasants could owe dues to a number of different lords. Even so, such conditions were far less burdensome on the peasantry than the system of labour services had been.[14]

From the twelfth to the fifteenth centuries, the conditions of the east-Elbian peasantry were markedly better than those west of the Elbe. Here too, serfdom prevailed but the terms which peasants had received from the colonizers of the Teutonic Order were generally favourable. In many instances, village charters (*Handfeste*) were granted which stipulated the customary rents, dues and labour services, defined communal rights which were to be paid (usually modest) and set out conditions of peasant mobility (usually minimal).[15] The terms of these agreements were overseen by the village community (*Gemeinde*) under the tutelage of the village *Schulz* – who functioned more or less as a mediator between the peasant community and the seigneurial authority.[16]

Thus, for a period of time at least, the east-Elbian peasantry were in a fairly strong position, one made even stronger by the chronic labour shortages which plagued the region. Added to this was the fact that the fortunes of the nobility had suffered greatly during the agrarian crisis which carried on into the fifteenth century.

The beginning of the sixteenth century marked a crucial turning point for both the east and west Elbian peasantry. The German Peasants' Revolt of 1525 brought to an end nearly a century of sporadic peasant revolt – and gradual peasant gains. The revolt itself was centred mainly in the southwest, although it did have significant reverberations in the northwest and in limited areas east of the Elbe, particularly in the densely populated area of Samland in the northern part of East Prussia.[17] In the West, the revolt seems to have centred around two inextricably connected issues. On the one hand, the lords wanted to increase the amount of dues they received by reasserting their jurisdictional control over the peasantry and attempting to undermine customary rights of pasturage and access to common lands. In the words of one commentator, reassertion of jurisdictional control was necessary 'in order to convert the fragmented bonds of personal lordship – where one serf might be subject to three or four different lords – into the more coherent and financially rewarding bonds of *land* lordship and territorial rule'.[18] The lords appealed to their former feudal rights of physical control in order to increase the dues which they could collect from a peasantry which now enjoyed hereditary rights over their holdings.[19]

The level of resistance which these assaults instigated among the peasantry was mainly due to the highly developed character of the peasant village community (*Gemeinde*). In the words of one historian, there could be 'no rebellion without the *Gemeinde*'.[20] In virtually all areas of revolt, village organization had taken on a political character which significantly weakened the powers of local lords and undermined their legitimacy in the eyes of the peasants:

> According to rural legal sources ... every member of the *Gemeinde* was obliged to support armed intervention; a jury composed of peasants exercised a judicial function. Administrative functions such as the supervision of the meadow and common land, fixing of the sowing and harvesting times, control of the village streets and commercial concerns were undertaken by peasants elected by the village. The mayor ... provided the link with the higher authorities. He came from the village community but was usually appointed by the lord. With the *Gemeinde*, which flourished in the late Middle Ages, a social organizational framework developed within which the peasant ... was co-responsible for the political order. ... The other side of the process of emancipation was the loss of legitimacy by those lords who were no longer able to afford more protection than the community could provide for itself.[21]

In the celebrated *Twelve Articles* drawn up by two urban-based supporters of the Peasants' Revolt, the demand was made to establish the peasant *Gemeinde* as an equal working partner with the landlords. The intent of the document was to keep the lords from encroaching further on peasant surpluses by clearly circumscribing the 'extra-economic' institutional powers of landlordship.[22]

Although it is difficult to assess the extent to which such a programme reflected the aspirations of the majority of peasants involved in the uprisings, it did have a profound impact on the nobility:

> Confronted with a peasantry who were apparently united behind a common programme ... the greater and lesser landlords and territorial rulers forgot their own internal differences (which had surfaced in the Knights War of 1522–3) and organized armies like those of the Swabian League which defeated peasant armies at the battles of Frankenhausen (12 May 1525) and at Bablinigen, Zebern and elsewhere.[23]

Although the peasantry was decisively defeated on the battlefield – between 50,000 and 130,000 are estimated to have perished – peasant demands were incorporated into the constitutions of the dynastic rulers who constructed the mini-absolutist states of the succeeding period.[24]

Not only can the Peasants' Revolt of 1525 be linked directly to the rise of dynastic absolutism in western Germany, it also defined its character to a significant extent. The fact that, as Robert Brenner has insisted, the mini-absolutisms developed as 'archetypal' instances where the state assumed the role of a 'class-like surplus-extractor', was connected to the need to protect the peasantry against overly harsh exploitation. These states thus became pioneers of the practice of *Bauernschutz*.[25]

The form which this took in various regions and principalities varied greatly. In some regions, such as Voralberg and Tyrol, serfdom was abolished outright. In others where serfdom survived, the serfs generally enjoyed the best conditions of tenure, whereas formally free peasants had to make do with holdings in poorer areas of scrub, marshes and wasteland. As Benecke has observed, 'at least for West Germany, the best lands and tenures went to unfree, serf families. The common countryman who was a freeman was not an enviable person. The rich serf-peasant in the village *Esch* was, however, enviable indeed.'[26] Thus, paradoxically, in a number of regions in the northwest and particularly in the ecclesiastical territories, serfdom (*Leibeigenschaft*) survived in a form which provided the peasantry with increasing rights and privileges at the same time as it tied the peasant more firmly to the land.[27]

The form and degree of 'protection' afforded the peasantry could depend upon a number of things. For example, if the peasantry were fortunate enough to be subject to a local law-court controlled by a territorial ruler or ecclesiastical authority different from their immediate landlord, they could exploit landlord–ruler competition, often to their own advantage. If, on the other hand, the local courts were controlled by the local lord their situation could be much worse, since no authority was likely to intercede on their behalf to protect them – even if for purely self-interested reasons – from intemperate exploitation by the local lord. In general though, in the small states which made up the loose federal system of western Germany prior to the ascendancy of Prussia, the territorial ruler tended to assume the role of 'protector' of peasant rights since their own revenues depended on a viable peasant economy. For example, in the ecclesiastical territory of Paderborn in the northwest, the bishops, as territorial rulers, often acted on behalf of the peasantry:

The bishops of Paderborn had an interest in all peasants because they paid the largest share of the extraordinary taxes which were needed to keep the territory from bankruptcy. In this they had to see that the peasants were not so exploited or so badly mismanaged by any of their landlords that they would be in no position to pay the ruler. ... The ruler thus took an active part in the problems arising out of tenant–landlord relations. He was also, of course, the most prominent landlord himself. He empowered his local judge to make laws by precedent as each particular case presented itself. As each legal problem came up it was dealt with in question-and-answer form and then preserved in writing as a local custom, a *Landesurteil* or *Weistum*.[28]

Overall, such measures tended to improve the conditions of the peasantry, even if the majority in western Germany remained servile. Servile peasants could own land or at least hold their lands in hereditary tenures. And in general, the system of overlapping jurisdiction so common in southwest Germany, worked to the advantage of the peasantry.[29] In addition, the *Bauernschutz* practised by territorial rulers tended to shield the peasantry against the worst excesses of seigneurial exploitation. It needs to be stressed, however, that the degree of inter-class competition between lords and rulers over peasant surplus never reached the levels it had in France. In both the lay and ecclesiastical territories of northwest Germany from the sixteenth century onwards, there was a growing level of co-operation between territorial rulers and landlords; conflicts over the distribution of peasant surpluses between rent and taxes were resolved to their mutual advantage and to the disadvantage of the immediate producers.[30]

It is generally agreed that the conditions of the east Elbian peasantry were worse than those who lived west of the Elbe after the mid sixteenth century. The favourable conditions of tenure which had been granted the east Elbian peasantry as an enticement for settlement by the Teutonic Order, had allowed for a significant development of the peasant economy. Throughout the fifteenth century, peasants were able to increase their surpluses by responding to growing market demand for grain. Their situation was made even better by the fact that rents in kind had been converted into customary money rents, often as a condition of settlement.[31]

Stable rents in conditions of rising prices worked to the disadvantage of the landlord. The devaluation of the lords' income from fixed money rents, and the perception that profits from the growing market in grain increasingly fell not to themselves but to their peasant tenants, forced lords at the beginning of the sixteenth century to look for new ways to increase their incomes.

The solution, in the majority of cases, was to press for the substitution of labour services for fixed money rents. Through a series of ordinances passed by the local estates in the early part of the sixteenth century, the nobility attempted to deprive the peasantry of their autonomy. Ordinances were passed which allowed lords to dispossess peasants of their holdings and to deprive the latter of any legal safeguards against their lords. In 1540, peasant inheritance rights were severely curtailed and lords reserved the right to have their tenants' children serve as menials. Overall, the legal status of the peasantry rapidly deteriorated.[32]

Over the course of the century, the east Elbian peasantry was forced to adjust their production to the requirements of the *Gutsherrschaft* system (manorial jurisdiction). In the second half of the eleventh century, lords began to demand much heavier labour services as they plunged themselves into extensive demesne farming in an effort to take advantage of rising prices and the growing demand for corn. As Carsten succinctly put it: 'Heavier labour services and the tying of the peasant to the soil were the corollary of extensive demesne farming which depended on peasant labour.'[33] Few would deny that the general conditions of the east Elbian peasantry deteriorated in the eleventh century. Moreover, few would question that the peasantry were unable to evade heightened labour services.

The reason that east-Elbian peasantry could not ultimately resist the imposition of labour services was related to two factors. First, by accident or design, the eastern lords had established compact peasant settlements which facilitated their domination and control. This avoided the fragmented pattern of jurisdictional control between lordship and village so common in the west which, as Robert Brenner points out, 'led to divided authority and gave the western peasants certain potentials for manoeuvre apparently unavailable to their eastern counterparts'.[34] Second, the level of village organization, although in some cases very high, was less effective as a means of resisting lordly power owing to the fact that the *formal* privileges and rights enjoyed by the peasantry (which were often greater than their western German counterparts) were not, in the main, the product of peasant struggles organized through the *Gemeinde*. Rather as Brenner has stressed,

> these conditions were *granted* by the lords (for their own reasons), ... the peasants *received* them from the lords. This was a very different process from that which occurred in the west, where the peasants often *extracted* their gains from the lords by means of successful resistance requiring the self-organization of the community over the very long run. In consequence, the peasants of the east were at a disadvantage when the lords changed their policy in the direction of greater exactions and controls, in order to deal with their problems of labour scarcity.[35]

The question which remains to be answered is, what *was* the extent of this 'disadvantage' for the peasantry and what implication did it have for their ability to resist their lords? And how did the potential for peasant resistance affect the character of lordly self-organization and political power?

A number of historians have begun to question just how seriously the introduction of extensive labour services actually undermined the peasant economy. On a broader scale, it has been suggested that the traditional division drawn between the conditions and capacities for resistance between the east Elbian and west Elbian peasantry has been greatly exaggerated. The immediate importance of this debate, for our purposes, is that it significantly alters conventional estimations of the balance of class forces throughout Germany. On the one hand, it raises serious questions about the extent of the extra-economic powers enjoyed by the east Elbian *Junkers* over the peasants they ruled. Secondly, and perhaps more importantly for the future development of Prussian absolutism, it suggests that the balance of power between the central political authority and the local landlords was less weighted in favour of the latter than previously thought. In this respect, the debate bears directly on the nature of the conditions which eventually gave rise to the Prussian absolutist state. For example, William Hagen argues that:

> the great expansion of noble demesne farming in central and eastern Europe during the sixteenth century cannot bear the weight of the fateful significance the historical literature assigns it. By throwing themselves into manorial production the landed nobility rescued and even greatly magnified their fortunes. But this required neither the economic subversion of the peasantry nor the rise of an absolutist state guaranteeing by the force of princely arms the landlords' fleecing of their peasant subjects ... to exaggerate the *Junkers'* dominance is to diminish without warrant the peasantry's powers of resistance. The *Junkers'* success in the sixteenth century did not predetermine the rise of Prussian absolutism, nor did it cause the social structure of Brandenburg to diverge ominously from the western European pattern, in which the powers and income of noble landlords also loomed exceedingly large.[36]

The core of Hagen's argument questions not so much whether the lords possessed the requisite extra-economic powers to enserf the east Elbian peasantry, but rather the degree and balance of these powers with respect to the subject peasantry. His data, based on studies of the Priegnitz region of Brandenburg, suggests that in the sixteenth century, 'the peasantry submitted to heightened labour-service, on conditions that held the total burden of rent weighing upon their farms within tolerable limits'.[37] That is, the imposition of labour services as a heightened and obviously less preferred form of rent increase on peasant farms often entailed either a freeze or a reduction in previously existing cash rents or rents in kind.[38] The implication is that traditional assessments of the imposition of serfdom have exaggerated the coercive powers of eastern lords and played down the capacity of the peasantry to bargain for more tolerable conditions *even if* their overall ability to resist the imposition of heightened labour-service was strictly limited.

This line of argument has further ramifications with regard to the extent of extra-economic political powers of the lords manifest at the local and national levels. The form taken by lordly political power in the east, as expressed in the rise of the estates system, provided for the nobility's direct control over their lands and the peasantry and ensured that its administrative costs were kept to a minimum.[39] However, the actual effectiveness of the legal statutes and ordinances passed in the *Junker-*

dominated assemblies was perhaps less than is often assumed to have been the case. For example, in Brandenburg, the statutes empowering lords to engross peasant holdings into their demesnes, often did not amount to much in practice. In the Middle Mark region only about 7 per cent of peasant farms (*Hufen*) were incorporated into noble estates by the mid seventeenth century.[40] Statutes allowing for unlimited labour services were in practice 'finally defined in a customary routine expressing the local balance of power between lord and peasants.'[41] Moreover, in those areas where strong *Gemeinde* existed, as in the nucleated village settlements, the extent of manorial services had to be negotiated and fixed at a precise level. If these were violated by the lord, peasants often engaged in rent and labour strikes. 'The villagers' defenses rested on their communal solidarity, typically very strong, and on their hereditary tenures, which made eviction of obdurate farmers difficult, especially when they acted collectively.'[42]

It seems, therefore, that however effective the extra-economic powers of the *Junkers* might have been when compared to western European landlords in the sixteenth century, they were still insufficient to break the back of east Elbian peasant resistance.[43] The much more circumscribed character of lordly powers may indeed have had much to do with shaping the conditions under which Hohenzollern absolutism arose.[44] First, it suggests that over the long term the threat of peasant revolt – though less of a phenomenon than in the west – was a factor the *Junkers* had to be wary of, all the more so given the decentralized character of noble political organization which made it more vulnerable to such threats than in a centralized state.[45] In one sense, the *Junkers* needed the absolutist state much more than the state needed the *Junkers*. Therefore, the ascendancy of the Hohenzollern dynasty over the estates may have been more an expression of the weakness of the 'mighty *Junkers*' than it was a social arrangement between an economically powerful ruling class and its political representative – the absolutist state. All of this indicates that the absolutist state itself grew up on a much more *autonomous* footing as a class-like *competitor* of the aristocracy than most accounts which stress the *Junker* dominance of the state would lead us to expect.

II. The Consolidation of Hohenzollern Absolutism

It would be absurd to deny that Hohenzollern absolutism rested on essentially aristocratic foundations. The basic structure of the Prussian polity was unquestionably, as Hans Rosenberg insists, 'sustained by a compromise between bureaucratized monarchical autocracy and the *Junker* aristocracy which further consolidated the local bases of its power'.[46] But it is precisely the exaggerated character of this dualism under Prussian absolutism – the persistence of rural noble political power and centralized administration – which highlights the intense competition which existed between the centralized state, intent upon cultivating its own independent sources of revenue, and the aristocracy, equally as committed to holding on to its residual powers. Moreover, once the myth of the rural omnipotence of the *Junker* aristocracy is placed in proper perspective, it becomes possible to make greater sense of the 'compromises' which various Hohenzollern monarchs were prepared to make with the nobility and to see just how contradictory the interests of state and the interests of the nobility actually became over the long term.

Perhaps more than anywhere else in Europe, the German states were ravaged by feudal warfare as the various dynasties of the early modern period sought to extend their territorial, and hence economic, power. One of the bloodiest of these conflicts – the Thirty Years War – was fought largely on German territories. The combination of war deaths and epidemics related to the devastation caused by war is estimated to have claimed 40 per cent of the rural population and 33 per cent of the urban population between 1618 and 1648.[47] Of the roughly three hundred principalities which emerged after the Treaty of Westphalia which ended the Thirty Years War, no single German state had as yet demonstrated the capacity to assert its hegemony over other states in the region. The pre-history of Hohenzollern absolutism very much rested on a balance of power between the states which made up the Holy Roman Empire. Most of these states, because of their small size and limited resources, remained economically and politically vulnerable. This was the basis for the loose but relatively stable federalism which characterized the Holy Roman Empire during this period.[48]

Brandenburg, the seat of the Hohenzollern dynasty, had been a relatively weak princely power during the agrarian revival of the sixteenth century. It 'formed a sleepy provincial backwater' with a feeble nobility which was much poorer than feudal lords in other parts of Germany.[49] The economic downturn of the Thirty Years' War and population losses of nearly 50 per cent in Brandenburg left them weaker still. Under such conditions, it was relatively easy for Frederick William (the Great Elector) to assert control over the noble estates. By degrees, the estates were stripped of their independent powers to set taxes and even their rights to organized opposition through the *Lantage* – the local *Diet*.[50] Frederick William's decisive achievements involved securing control over foreign policy without consent of the estates, and the maintenance of a permanent standing army.

It is true that these measures were achieved through a series of compromises with the aristocracy which insured that the powers of the absolutist state 'stopped short outside the private estates'.[51] At the famous Recess of 1653, the estates conceded a subsidy of a half million *thalers* only after receiving confirmation of their seigneurial jurisdictions and immunity from taxation. In addition, the system of *Leibeigenschaft* was to remain in force wherever it was customary; peasants were assumed to be *Leibeigen* serfs unless they could prove otherwise.[52] Again in the 1660s and 1670s, concessions were made to the nobility especially in areas of taxation. In 1680, the excise tax was imposed on the electoral towns while both the eastern and western nobility remained exempt.[53]

It would be easy to see in these measures a situation in which 'the Estates got the better of the bargain'.[54] In the short term, they undoubtedly did benefit greatly. At the same time, these were necessary concessions for the time which arose from the relative weakness of Prussia. The Thirty Years War had demonstrated to the Hohenzollerns that only territorial expansion could possibly deliver them from the mercy of other feudal states. Territorial weakness translated itself into fiscal weakness, which in turn meant that the estates remained relatively free to assert their will against the interests of the central state. It was thus necessary to grant concessions to the nobility so long as the military machinery required for territorial aggrandizement had yet to be constructed. As Anderson comments: 'the immediate preoccupation of the Elector was ... to secure a stable financial basis with which to create a permanent military apparatus for the defense and integration of his realms.'[55]

The role of the military reveals perhaps most clearly the underlying contradictions of Prussian absolutism and the basis for the concessions which the state was forced to make to the nobility. Territorial warfare was a prime means of feudal accumulation and one particularly suited to providing the state with independent sources of revenue, since defeated territories were unlikely to harbour recalcitrant nobles. But in order to achieve such territorial acquisitions, rulers had to rely upon a loyal and efficient army. And in Prussia, as elsewhere, where wealth continued to be based on the extra-economic exploitation of landed property, it was still necessary 'to make costly fiscal and economic concessions to those who were the backbone of military strength'.[56]

It was out of the imperative of territorial expansion – so central to the feudal dynamic of surplus accumulation – that the Prussian tradition of the service nobility was born. The development of a service nobility, as a means of merging the material interests of the landed nobility with those of the absolutist state was, in important respects, 'the Eastern correlate of sales of office in the West'.[57] But it would be a mistake to see it as something peculiarly Prussian. The relative absence in Prussia of venal office-holding, cannot be ascribed principally, as Perry Anderson insists, to the absence of a commercial and mercantile bourgeoisie.'[58]

In France, the purchase of office was by no means restricted to bourgeois interests. For the state, sales of office had a twofold purpose: first, it provided a mechanism through which feudal landowners – whether bourgeois or noble in origin – were compensated for the loss of income they suffered when the state intervened to protect peasant rights and to rake off its share of peasant surplus through taxation. It was thus a device for binding the private interests of the nobility and the bourgeoisie to the 'public' sphere of the state. And secondly, sales of office provided an easy and seemingly inexhaustible source of revenues for a state which was chronically indebted due to warfare.

In Prussia, the balance of forces between the nobility and the state in the early years of absolutism was not propitious to the large-scale development of sales of office on the French model. As we have seen, the 'settlement' between Crown and nobility secured by Frederick William never allowed the state to encroach as far as it might have liked on lordly jurisdictions, to the point where it could have 'protected' peasant property rights – and thus its own independent source of revenue – to the extent that was possible in France. In addition, state indebtedness was never as compelling in Prussia as it was in France. There was no deficit until the nineteenth century. In general, the necessity of compensating the nobility through the preferments of office was not as pressing as it was in France. Indeed, it could even be argued that because this option was unavailable to it, the policy of territorial expansion through warfare became the *only* means through which the absolutist state could satisfy its need for independent sources of revenue at the same time as it gave the nobility 'a cut of the take' by granting them privileged status in the army.

At any rate, the device of noble service to the Crown should not be seen as evidence of the backwardness of the Prussian absolutism. In an important sense it was a sign of just the opposite. For it accomplished at a single stroke what the sale of offices by the French state was only able to do imperfectly: it served both to bind the nobility to the fortunes of the state and to unify with a remarkable degree of efficiency the fiscal and military requirements of the state. In France, the office of tax-farmer and later, intendancies, combined military and fiscal functions as well. But, because such offices were often considered the private patrimony of those who purchased them, in fiscal terms they were only about half as efficient as the military commissars who performed an equivalent role in Germany.[59]

In France, war finance inevitably placed great strain on state revenues; and this was only aggravated further by the system of venal office-holding which placed the private interests of tax-collectors above the fiscal needs of the state. In Prussia by contrast, the relative efficiency of the fiscal system which was overseen by 'professional' officials, meant that war finance never produced the cycle of state indebtedness which periodically crippled the French treasury. And this arguably *lessened* the pressure on the absolutist state to make costly concessions to nobility, thereby enhancing its 'relative autonomy'.[60] If the device of service to the state is to be seen, as Perry Anderson would have it, as a sign of Prussian backwardness, then it had the paradoxical effect of fostering a system of bureaucratic efficiency far in advance of other absolutist states of the time.

The institutional foundations of this state were firmly laid in the last decades of the Great Elector's reign. The ascent of the General War Commissariat (*General KriegKommissariat*) in the 1670s marked the first phase of the subordination of the state and society to military imperatives. Taxation became a function of the military apparatus, since expenditure on the army had to be paid for out of tax revenues. Sufficient tax revenues in turn required the maintenance of a healthy tax base. Over the decade, the *General KriegKommmissariat* extended its control over immigration policy and the settlement of Huguenot refugees from France to build up the number of taxable producers on the land. It took control of the guild system, set up naval and colonial enterprises and supervised trade and manufactures. As Carsten observed:

> In this way the *General KriegKommissariat* lost its subordinate position and developed into a central authority directly under the ruler; and 'the maintenance, victualling, and enlargement of the army more and more became the central point of all state activity.' The *General KriegKommissariat* became the most important and the most typical authority of the nascent Hohenzollern state . . .[61]

By the time of his death in 1688, Frederick William had more than trebled the revenues of the state with a *per capita* yield nearly twice that of France. In addition, an army which stood at a mere 4,000 troops at his accession had been built into a permanent standing army of 30,000 soldiers led by a noble officer corps imbued with a growing loyalty to the Crown.[62] Still comparatively small – with a population just over 1.5 million – when compared with France with its twenty million inhabitants, the state fashioned by Frederick William had, nevertheless, established 'the beginnings of an institutional framework capable of initiating and carrying out reform from above and thus preventing revolution from below'.[63]

The reign of Frederick I did little to disturb the basic foundations of the emerging absolutist state, although the quarter-century of his rule was significant for reversing his father's policy of guaranteeing noble domination of the officer corps.[64] The influx of Huguenots from France after the repeal of the Edict of Nantes brought a significant percentage of foreigners into the officer corps. In addition, Frederick's practice of promoting commoners to commissioned rank restricted the access of the *Junker* nobility. This was part of a more general phenomenon which saw the creation of 1,700 royal titles between 1688 and 1713.[65]

But Frederick I also won an important victory over what remained of noble estates power (*Standestaat*). The institutional stronghold of *Junker* opposition to the absolute monarchy was the *Regierungen*, the supreme law courts. These were crucial for enforcing noble legal rights over the peasantry at the local level.[66] Frederick dealt an important blow to these rights by establishing legal control over law suits which came to the Supreme Appeal Court.[67] Measures such as these were gradually undermining the authority of the nobility, an authority hitherto firmly enshrined in a legal edifice of extra-economic powers. The continuing battle for dominance between the system of private law so dear to the nobility and the rise of public law under the tutelage of the absolutist state was an indication of the growing competition between two rival centres of political power.[68] At a deeper level, of course, it was also an expression of the fundamental dynamics of absolutist society: since the process of surplus-extraction in the form of rent or taxes rested upon the application of extra-economic coercion, competition within the ruling class over the distribution of economic surplus was bound to take on a heavily political and legal character. The extension of administrative law by the Prussian state was above all 'a means to develop economic statism' and fiscal centralism.[69] In short, it was a means of refining and developing further the mechanisms of *political accumulation*.

Further advances in this realm were made by Frederick William I, who strictly curtailed the jurisdiction and administrative status of the *Regierung*. He restricted the estates to implementing only the ordinances of the Crown and, in a truly decisive step, reserved for himself the right to appoint his own officials at all levels of the administrative hierarchy of the state. As Koch observes, 'in that step really lay the origin of the Prussian civil service.'[70]

Moreover, Frederick William 'professionalized' the state bureaucracy to a much greater degree than it had been previously by greatly reducing – though not eliminating entirely – the direct purchase of offices. This was accomplished through the novel device of having prospective office-holders make a financial contribution to the recruitment fund (*Rekruten-kasse*) set up to increase recruitment levels in the army.[71] This was, to be sure, a form of venality, but one which reflected the degree to which the priorities of the state had achieved ascendancy over the private interests of those who attained office through such contributions.

But it was also an expression of the lessening importance of noble rank and privilege, as a criterion for attaining offices in the state bureaucracy. The principle of 'careers open to talent' was gradually superseding the ancient principles of social rank based on landownership and inherited privilege.

> The new service rank order was determined by office, function, and the will of the autocratic prince. In government employment, official position as a fountain of social esteem and self-respect competed with rank derived from exalted birth. Men of poor extraction frequently became the supervisory or commanding officers of old-established aristocrats. . . . Their organizational status, relative to hereditary prestige, gained vastly in significance as a social ranking device with the rise of the modern bureaucratic state.[72]

This was not simply an expression of royal patronage coming to replace 'the old spoils system', as Hans Rosenberg contends.[73] The growing dominance of the 'merit system' in state service was also a sign of the growing autonomy of the absolutist state as it secured more independent sources of revenue and power. This was not merely a process of 'rationalization' for administrative and fiscal reasons. Centralization of extra-economic power and the opening-up of bureaucratic office to wider layers of society were two sides of the same coin; as the state secured for itself the undisputed right to extract surplus from the direct producers, it also sanctioned on an ever-widening scale, the *private appropriation* of these surpluses, albeit through the exercise of 'public' office. It was above all an illustration of the increasingly pronounced class-like character of Prussian absolutism. This was nowhere more clearly revealed than in Frederick William I's attitude towards the relationship between the bureaucracy, the nobility and the Crown. As Koch comments:

> if among other things the bureaucracy was to check the nobility, the danger of the bureaucracy becoming too independent could, according to Frederick William, only be met by recruiting the bureaucracy from the aristocracy as well as from the educated middle class. This would foster rivalry between the two social classes, now side by side within one institution, and prevent an alliance between the two against the Crown.[74]

The bureaucracy was quickly becoming, in social terms, a significant counterweight to the nobility. That is, the extra-economic powers of the absolutist state were coming to rival those of the nobility, as the former established its own position as an appropriator of surplus in the relations of production. Equally important was Frederick William's recognition that unless measures were taken to avoid such an outcome, the independent social power of the bureaucracy could one day easily dispense with the formality of a sovereign head of state.

The latter possibility, at least for the time being, was not the principal threat. Firmly entrenching the fiscal independence of the state was still the order of the day. Throughout his reign, virtually every major achievement of Frederick William I was directed towards this goal. The army was doubled in size to 78,000 troops. Far from kow-towing to the nobility, the Crown 'virtually compelled the native nobility to serve as officers in the Prussian Army.'[75] Trade and manufacture were geared to military needs under General Superior Finance, War and Domains. In fiscal matters and questions of taxation, the participation of the estates was completely abolished. The multitude of dues and taxes was replaced with one general Land Tax payable by the nobility, free peasants and heritable peasants alike.[76] In addition, the king attempted to rebuild the royal domains by buying up the estates of indebted nobles such that by the end of his reign nearly one-third of all arable lands was controlled directly by the Crown. In 1713, the royal domains were declared indivisible and unalienable.[77]

In this way, nearly half of all crown revenues was raised directly from taxes levied on the royal domains. Frederick William recognized the extent to which the fortunes of the state and particularly its military ambitions were tied to the health of the peasantry. The peasantry, after all, was not only a source of rent and taxation revenues, it also formed the bulk of the army. And since warfare was one of the main engines of feudal accumulation, it was also one of the quickest ways to enhance the fiscal autonomy of the state still further. To further this process, Frederick William took steps to ameliorate the condition of the peasantry. Beating of peasants was prohibited and peasant services were reduced to, on average, three days a week, or replaced with money payments. The latter, however, was only fully established on crown domains – a not inconsiderable portion of the rural economy. By and large though, the nobility resisted the extension of these reforms to their estates.[78]

At the end of his reign, Frederick William had achieved much of what he had set out to accomplish. The state treasury – which under Frederick I had gone severely into debt – registered a surplus of eight million *thalers*.[79] The population of Prussia had increased by 40 per cent to some two and a quarter million. Perhaps most importantly, he had managed to lay firm foundations for the fiscal autonomy of the state. To be sure, the administrative reforms introduced by Frederick William I were still imperfect; the absolutist state continued to co-exist in an uneasy alliance with the nobility. But the concessions made to the latter should not be allowed to mask the extent to which a class-like rivalry conditioned the relationship between state and nobility.[80]

The inordinate role of warfare and militarism in shaping the entire structure of Hohenzollern absolutism has been emphasized by many commentators.[81] The most perceptive have stressed the extent to which military rivalry between states arose from the imperatives of the feudal system itself – that territorial warfare was an *externally* imposed necessity. Few, however, have grasped the degree to which militarism and external warfare were the product of the *internal* balance of forces between the absolutist state and the landed nobility. The militarization of Prussian society so single-mindedly pursued by Frederick William I was arguably just as much the product of his desire to free the state from noble domination as it was a response to the threat of domination by other states. For the nobility continued to exercise direct jurisdiction over the peasantry and thus retained significant extra-economic powers of surplus extraction. The state's direct access to peasant surplus was still circumscribed by the manorial powers of the landowner. The *Landrat*, which exercised fiscal and military powers at the local level on behalf of the central state, was drawn from the local nobility; taxes were collected directly by the lords.[82] In other words, it was largely because the residual extra-economic powers of the nobility set definite limits on the *internal* surplus-extractive powers of the state, that the enlargement of the royal domains through *external* warfare took on the immense proportions it did under Prussian absolutism.

III. The Frederickan State: Professionalism and Agrarian Reform

Frederick the Great, perhaps more than any other of the Hohenzollern rulers, grasped the nature of the structural constraints which shaped the power of the absolutist state. This is summed up best in his declaration that 'there is no art so beautiful or so useful as war when it is practised by honest men.'[83] The 'usefulness' of warfare, as Frederick acutely recognized, was that it provided a sure means of increasing state revenues in accordance with the cameralist teaching that the growth of the state was inseparable from the *extensive* growth of the economy.[84]

Under feudal conditions such growth was inseparable from territorial expansion, even though, as Frederick and his advisers were aware, 'the strength of the state depends not on the length of its frontiers but on the size of its population.'[85] That is, the amount of revenues raised by the state through taxation depended upon the number of rural producers at the state's disposal. Considerations such as these lay behind Frederick's carefully drawn plans for the annexation of Silesia and East Friesland in the 1740s and for the colonization of eastern Prussia.[86]

The 'honest men' Frederick relied on to achieve his territorial ambitions continued to be drawn from the nobility. Over 6,000 nobles manned the Prussian officer corps.[87] But for Frederick, 'honesty' was synonymous with loyalty to the state and, above all, to the king; the independent interests of individuals or classes were strictly subordinate to those of the state. Although the nobility retained important privileges and control over their estates, they were, in many ways, subjected to harsher treatment than their counterparts in France. For one thing, since the introduction of the uniform Land Tax (*General Hufenschoss*) by Frederick William I, the nobility had been subject to taxation along with the peasantry. Frederick II demanded even more through the *Kontribution*.[88] In addition, 'high civilian officials from the nobility could be thrown into prison, and kept there indefinitely, for offences which were sometimes never disclosed or of which they were later proved innocent'.[89] More than anything else, the bulk of the nobility who found their way into state service did so out of economic necessity:

It was less the threats and prohibitions which prevailed on them to do so than something approaching a career structure. However restricting it was, and however ill paid in the early years, the service of the King had the great merit of relieving a nobleman of his most pressing problem: how to provide for his children.[90]

The administrative structure of Prussian absolutism was increasingly defined by an ethos of 'professionalism' and merit as opposed to privilege and birth. It is true that noble titles continued to be conferred upon non-noble bureaucrats.[91] By the end of the eighteenth century, in fact, 'nothing of significance, except for the accident of birth, separated ... the social position of the top bureaucrats of old noble lineage from the bureaucratic nobles of ascent.'[92] But it would be incorrect to conclude that the top ranks of the administrative bureaucracy had become an exclusively noble preserve:

The social balance which Frederick William I had established was, in fact, maintained by his successors. Bureaucrats were selected from the highest bourgeois and noble groups, but not often from the penurious aristocracy or the petty bourgeoisie. Peasants found their way into the civil service at the lowest level through intermediate service in the army.[93]

In other words, just as in France of the late eighteenth century, the social lines of differentiation were increasingly becoming blurred as *both* nobles and bourgeois sought out service in the state. For the increasingly impoverished nobility, state service provided a ready means of economic survival. For the bourgeoisie, it became a chief source of economic and social advancement. Frederick the Great's councillors of state remained predominantly bourgeois and the courts of justice were almost exclusively bourgeois in composition. Even the officer corps was becoming infiltrated by non-nobles. Overall, as Behrens observes:

> the bourgeois civil servants enjoyed privileges which set them apart from other, inferior, bourgeois and placed them in many important respects on a footing of equality with nobles. ... The state service in Prussia ... provided a means, and for a long time the only one, by which the barriers between nobles and bourgeois could be breached.[94]

While those of bourgeois origin employed by the state remained officially part of the *Burgerstaand*, the question of their origins was now less important than the social role they had come to play as part of the absolutist state. By virtue of their offices, they had become, along with their noble associates, part of an apparatus which repaid their services with revenues gained by increasingly *independent* forms of surplus extraction and plunder. In short, it was not so much the social origins of civil servants which determined the nature of the state; rather, it was the role played by the state in the relations of production which determined the character of the state bureaucracy.

This 'homogenization' of the bureaucracy was enhanced by a series of administrative reforms initiated during Frederick's reign. From 1769 onwards, it was specified that only 'qualified nobles' and 'outstandingly intelligent burghers' could be appointed to the upper posts of the General Directory. This body was responsible for overseeing the work of the War and Domains chambers which constituted the provincial governments under Prussian control.[95] Frederick had decreed examinations and practical training for prospective civil servants on a number of occasions in the 1740s. As one of the administrative reforms of 1770, civil service examinations were made virtually compulsory throughout the state bureaucracy.[96]

Cocceji's legal reforms of the 1740s had further undermined the traditional powers of the nobility by making professional competence a prerequisite of holding a judgeship. Previously, nobles had been guaranteed at least half of such offices. As a result, 'patrimonial jurisdiction was restricted in that it became obligatory for estate owners, as well as for domain lease holders, to have legal matters in their courts dealt with by qualified lawyers.'[97] The ultimate aim of such reforms, though they remained hedged about with concessions to the nobility for some time, was to bring the administration of justice under the control of the central state. Such aims eventually found expression in the *Allgemeine Landrecht* (General Common Law) published after Frederick II's death in 1791. This law, in turn, was to become the basis upon which the generation of reformers after

1806 acted to severely curtail the powers of the king, and to install 'a liberalized pattern of absolutist government' with the bureaucracy at its centre.[98]

Frederick II had hoped to forestall such a development by preserving some of the estates' powers as a counterweight to the growing powers of the bureaucracy. In his Instruction of 1766, Frederick attempted to overhaul substantially the role of both the *Steurrat* (which was responsible for urban economic affairs) and the rural *Landrat* system. The *Landrat* was chiefly responsible for military affairs in their regions such as garrisoning and provisioning of the army. In addition, he oversaw the collection of rural taxes (*Kontribution*) and encouraged those under his jurisdiction to work hard since 'these people have to earn all the provincial, local and service taxes with the sweat of their brow and they must also provide for the state's necessities.'[99] Frederick reintroduced the procedure of having the regional *Landrat* elected by the nobility (though chosen by the king), thus cementing the link between the local nobility and the Crown while at the same time countering those central administrators who wanted to dispense with the provincial estates and country deputies entirely.[100]

Frederick's second major innovation, also designed to offset the powers of the central bureaucracy, was the establishment of the *Regie* (General Excise Administration) as a counter-weight to the fiscal authority of the General Directory.[101] The *Regie* was essentially a consortium of French tax officials, hired by Frederick to root out corruption and graft from the tax system and to raise overall tax revenues which had fallen from 17.3 to 11.8 million *thalers* as a result of the Seven Years War.[102] Employing some 2,000 officials of which 175 to 200 were French, the *Regie* took over nearly complete control of the administration and collection of the *Akzise* – the principal urban excise tax on goods. As well, the *Regie* set up a number of enterprises, such as the General Tobacco Administration, which functioned more or less as state-run monopolies. Coffee, flour and a host of other commodities were brought under its control as well. In all, the *Regie* managed to produce a surplus of 23 million *thalers*.[103]

But if the principal aim in establishing the *Regie* had been to strike a blow against the Prussian bureaucracy, it ultimately backfired. For the resentment generated by the encroachment of the *Regie* on the traditional preserves of the core bureaucracy only hastened the process whereby the bureaucracy consolidated its own powers against those of the Crown: 'Nothing united so many potential enemies more than the sudden appearance of a formidable outside threat'.[104]

Frederick had hoped to use part of the funds raised by the *Regie* to finance a series of agricultural reforms, some of which had been undertaken prior to the Seven Years War. Like many Enlightenment thinkers

Frederick was caught on the horns of a dilemma when it came to the reform of agriculture. Like the French, Prussian state administrators were understandably highly impressed by the achievements of English agriculture at the end of the eighteenth century and anxious to duplicate its successes. Frederick even sent officials to England to study agrarian developments there and English agronomists were invited to Prussia to manage royal and private estates. The problem, for Frederick, as for most practitioners of enlightened absolutism, was that had they truly understood what lay behind the English agricultural revolution they would have recoiled in horror. For the transformation of social relations entailed by the rise of agrarian capitalism in England was completely incompatible with the social foundations upon which the Frederickan state rested.

The interest displayed in agrarian reform by Frederick and his officials sprang from an essentially anti-capitalist interest. It was rooted in finding new sources of revenue for the Royal Treasury derived from the taxation of peasant surpluses. The Frederickan agrarian reforms of the 1760s and 1770s therefore must be seen, despite their 'modern' appearance, as grounded in the tradition of *Bauernschutz* (protection of the peasantry) in the sense that a stable and prosperous peasantry was the precondition for a stable and prosperous Treasury. The greater the degree to which the state was capable of asserting control over peasant surpluses, the greater would be its autonomy and the lesser the likelihood it would have to make costly concessions to the nobility. As Jerome Blum has observed of the agrarian reforms:

> One factor ... seems to have been of constant and crucial significance: the preservation, or strengthening of the power and authority of the sovereign. In nearly all of the servile lands, the efforts of the central powers to ameliorate the condition, and elevate the status, of the peasantry had been a critically important facet of the struggle for supremacy between the absolute monarchs and their nobility. The final reforms that freed the peasants from their servility ... were the last great triumph of royal absolutism over nobility – and, in truth, its last great achievement.[105]

Protection of the peasantry had always been a cornerstone of Frederickan policy.[106] Following the end of the Seven Years War in 1763, Frederick laid down strict instructions to the General Directory to reduce the burdens and dues of the peasantry on the royal domains in order to increase their productivity and hence the amount of taxable surplus. So intense was the preoccupation with peasant productivity and taxation, it is estimated that approximately 80 per cent of the time available to civil servants was taken up with such matters. It appears that such time was well spent, since the Prussian state became the most efficient collector of taxes in eighteenth-century Europe.[107]

Frederick himself never tired of placing the stamp of virtue on what was in fact a necessity of royal finance. Of the peasantry, he wrote, in his *Political Testament* of 1752:

> I have relaxed (on the royal domain) the services which the peasants used to perform; instead of six days service a week, they now have to work only three. This has provoked the nobles' peasants, and in several places they have resisted their lords. The sovereign should hold the balance evenly between the peasant and the gentleman, so they do not ruin one another. In Silesia the peasants, outside Upper Silesia, are very well placed; in Upper Silesia they were serfs. One will have to try to free them in due course. I have set the example on my own crown lands, where I have begun putting them on the same footing as the Lower Silesians. One should further prevent peasants from buying nobles' lands, or nobles' peasants', because peasants cannot serve as officers in the army, and if nobles convert peasant holdings into demesne farms, they diminish the number of inhabitants and cultivators.[108]

And in his instructions to de Launay whom he had placed in charge of the *Regie* in 1766, he wrote, 'Take only from those who can pay. These I hand over to you. ... I well know', he commented, 'that the rich have many advocates, but the poor have only one, and that is I.'[109]

Overall, the agrarian reforms undertaken by Frederick the Great affected the peasantry unevenly, and in some instances, in quite contradictory ways owing to the often vast differences in their conditions. In East Prussia, roughly 26 per cent of the peasants were free peasants (*Kolmer*). These peasants had enjoyed special status since they had colonized the region under the tutelage of the Teutonic Knights. *Kolmer* were personally free from servitude, paid only modest dues, and enjoyed property rights over their holdings. The majority of peasants, however, were subject to some form of personal servitude. In general, where peasants had managed to gain some property rights – as in Mark Brandenburg, Prignitz, east of the Elbe, Lower Silesia and parts of Neumarck – hereditary serfdom did not gain a footing. By contrast, in central and in northeast Brandenburg, Pomerania, most of East Prussia, and Upper Silesia, no freehold peasant property developed to any great extent. Here, the majority of peasants were *Lassiten*, personally free but with restricted legal rights, and under certain conditions, heritable and bound to the soil.[110]

In East Prussia and Pomerania, peasants might be forced to work five to six days a week on the lord's estate. In the whole of east Elbia, the *Gutsherrschaft* system is estimated to have encompassed 50 to 70 per cent of the cultivable land at the end of the eighteenth century. In areas where peasants had acquired some property rights, labour services tended to be much lower, averaging about two or three days a week. Not surprisingly, it was in those areas where the peasantry had something to protect that peasant revolts and uprisings became particularly threatening to the local nobility. In the southwest of Germany, where strong traditions of peasant self-organization and resistance persisted from the revolt of 1525, uprisings continued into the nineteenth century. East of the Elbe, in both Silesia and Bohemia, serious peasant revolts occurred between the end of the Seven Years War in 1763 and the turn of the nineteenth century. In Saxony, areas of Brandenburg, and Pomerania, peasants continued to resist the demands of their lords in a variety of ways, by mounting lawsuits against them, – there were 392 in Saxony in 1792 alone – through open revolt, to perhaps the oldest method of peasant resistance of all – flight.

Indeed, it was fear of spreading peasant revolts at the end of the eighteenth century which pushed many *Junkers* towards accepting the inevitability of some sort of peasant reform. As the Prussian chancellor, Heinrich von Goldbeck, observed in 1799: 'many thoughtful proprietors in Silesia and other royal provinces at every opportunity say that it is better to give up something voluntarily than be forced to sacrifice everything.'[111]

Peasant recalcitrance seems to have been one of the chief factors persuading some estate owners that paid labour was both a cheaper and more manageable form of labour control. The growth and effectiveness of peasant resistance towards the end of the eighteenth century was not accidental. Measures taken by the absolutist state to protect peasant rights, such as Frederick II's *Urbarium* (registers) of 1783, which set peasant rents and *Junker* obligations in each seigneurial jurisdiction, tended to strengthen peasant property rights. This, in turn, increased the level of peasant autonomy by allowing enterprising peasants greater access to the market. Despite their substantial burdens in dues, there is strong evidence to suggest that full peasants owning between 20 and 70 hectares were able to take advantage of the upswing in the grain export market between 1766–75. Around Berlin, for example, marketable surpluses could average approximately two to four tons per annum.[112] As peasant incomes rose and property rights were strengthened under the tutelage of the state, 'the lords had to resort to paid labour, whether they liked it or not. ... The conversion of the traditional feudal estate into a modern estate based on wage-labour thus became economically justifiable.'[113]

How 'modern' these *Junker* estates were is a matter of some debate. They certainly had the *appearance* of being based on the same organizational principles which governed agrarian relations in England. However, it is important to bear in mind how agrarian capitalist relations in England differed from the apparently similar conditions in Prussia at the end of the eighteenth century. In England, the consolidation of large capitalist farms was facilitated by the unchallenged control of the state by the landed interest following the English Revolution. Parliament had become a 'committee of landlords' which permitted acts of enclosure of peasant holdings and common lands, enshrined the rights of private property and punished its violaters with a battery of new and brutal statutes, regulated wages, and outlawed combinations among the rural proletariat. By decisively defeating attempts to construct a viable absolutism in the seventeenth century, the English landowners were left with no serious competitor in the appropriation of wealth. The fact that the English lords enjoyed full control of the state at both the national and the local level virtually insured the untrammelled 'primitive accumulation' of capital – despite the bitter and heroic resistance of the English peasantry. 'And this history,' Marx observed, 'the history of their expropriation, is written in the annals of mankind in letters of blood and fire.'[114]

In Prussia, by contrast, the *Junkers* were not – despite the mythology which surrounds them – an omnipotent force in Prussian society. The most obvious index of this was the fact that an absolutist state *did* exist and *did* compete with the nobility over the distribution of peasant surplus. By protecting the peasantry and building up its own domains, the state had succeeded in securing for itself a high degree of independence, and thereby, weakening the extra-economic powers of the *Junkers*. Therefore, it is ironic that Frederick the Great's own officials lamented the relative weakness of Prussian landlords as one of the main reasons why English-style agriculture had not yet taken hold in Prussia. As one adviser, whom Frederick II had sent to England, reported:

> the power of the English landlords was much greater than that of the landlords in the Absolute monarchies where the old agricultural practices prevailed; for the English landowners dominated Parliament and in the period when enclosures were most frequent, they were introduced by law.[115]

Despite the fact that the Prussian nobility was able to retain significant jurisdictional controls over the peasantry, these do not appear to have been enough for them to retain their traditional position within Prussian society. In East Prussia, the *Junkers* were forced to commute labour services into cash rents, not because they wanted to, but because peasants had been able to establish fixed labour rents which had not changed in over a century.[116] The turn to cash rents and to wage-labour was largely the product of *Junker* class weakness and not of its strength – perhaps the most striking contrast with English lords. At any rate, only a small portion of Prussian nobles actually lived and worked on their estates at the beginning of the nineteenth century. In Kurmarck, only 27 per cent lived on the land; 42 per cent came back after long periods in the royal service;[117] 29 per cent lived in towns either fulfilling some government-related post or receiving a pension, usually for military service. As Sagara summarizes:

In general ... the overall picture of life in the first Prussian estate at the end
of the eighteenth century excited concern rather than envy among contemporaries. For all its privileged status, the Prussian nobility had neither freedom from
financial care, nor the leisure to enjoy it. Its dual function, to defend and
represent the state and to create the basis of an existence befitting its position
by cultivating hereditary lands proved a burden too heavy to bear.[118]

While it is undeniably the case that a profound agrarian transformation
based on enclosed estates employing wage-labour emerged in east Elbian
Prussia at the beginning of the nineteenth century, its character was quite
different from the agrarian capitalism which had emerged in England.
The weakness of Prussian agrarian capitalism – it was never able to exert
a determining influence over the national economy – had much to do
with the conditions under which relations on the land were transformed.
Commutation of labour services and the resort to wage-labour were
changes foisted on the landlords which they took up as a defensive measure
and not a set of reforms which they imposed on the peasantry from a
position of strength. In short, the emergence of a labour-repressive form
of agrarian capitalism in the countryside must be assessed in terms of
the overall pattern of Prussian social relations. Unlike the English case,
the *compulsion* for the landed classes to submit to a capitalist logic was
still relatively weak. As Hussain and Tribe have persuasively argued:

neither the dispossession of large numbers of serfs, nor the granting of freedom
to serfs to migrate or sell their labour power, by themselves revolutionized
the conditions in the east Elbian countryside; they only started to have effects
later when the German cities, as a result of capitalist development, and the
open spaces of the US started to suck labour from the countryside ... for
those who remained in the countryside the conditions of employment ...
retained in some ways a striking resemblance to serfdom.[119]

In general, however, despite the protection afforded peasant property
by the state, the German peasantry did not fare that well when compared
with the peasantry of France. Only peasants on the royal domains achieved
anything resembling the kind of property rights which the French peasantry won during and following the French Revolution. The vast majority
were left subject to a host of dues and services which persisted until
1850.[120] The state continued to play a role in easing peasant burdens
by instituting redemption programmes whereby the state paid the cost
of redeeming peasant dues and rents and set up credit banks to help
peasants buy their freedom. In Prussia, peasants were allowed to pay
back these loans at a rate of 5 per cent interest over forty-one and a
half years.[121] Even so, the terms of the legislation abolishing serfdom
were far from favourable. Two categories were designated for hereditary

and non-hereditary tenures. In order to attain ownership in the first cate-
gory, one-third of the peasant's holding had to be given over to the lord.
For those with non-hereditary tenures – which constituted the vast majority of peasant holdings in Germany – half the holding had to be given
over to the landlord in payment.[122]

Once the threat of Napoleon's armies had been dealt with in the 'War
of Liberation' in 1813, there was a marked retreat from reform.[123] The
edict of 1816 made the provisions for emancipation even more stringent:

> only those peasants who had holdings large enough to support them, whose
> labour services included the use of draft animals, whose holdings were entered
> in provincial tax rolls as peasant land and not seigneurial land, and who could
> prove that their holding had been held by peasants at a fixed rate that ranged
> from 1749 to 1774, depending upon the province, could redeem their land
> and their obligations.[124]

Most had to await the law of 1850 which allowed all peasants to redeem
their land and obligations.

The era of agrarian reform thus continued a trend which had been
evident for some time. In Saxony, for example, the number of peasant
holdings large enough to support a family had fallen to 25 per cent in
1750; by 1843, it was only 14 per cent. In the same period, the number
of landless peasants rose from 38 per cent to 52 per cent respectively.[125]
A similar trend is evident in other areas. In the Prignitz region of Brandenburg, between 1725 and 1801, the number of landless labourers increased
sixfold, while the number of peasant holdings remained more or less constant.[126] Overall, therefore, even if the impulse of agrarian capitalism
remained weak, a vast pool of landless labour was being created which
would be vital to fulfilling the needs of industrial capital later in the
century.

IV. The Emergence of Bureaucratic Absolutism

In the short term, however, the agrarian reforms did have the indirect
effect of strengthening the hand of the state against the nobility. Although
the reforms had not produced for the state an independent source of
extractable surplus based on a stable property-owning peasantry, they
had severely undermined the seigneurial powers of the nobility. This diminished further the obstacles standing in the way of state control over
local government.[127] Such changes were part of the broad package of
reforms marking the transition from 'personal' to 'bureaucratic' absolutism.[128] While some commentators have correctly stressed the *continuity* between the two periods, their accounts have often become overly

preoccupied with the question of the class composition and social background of the state bureaucracy before and after the reforms. Rosenberg
has argued, for example, that because the bureaucracy continued to be
dominated by '*Junkers* and neo-*Junkers*',[129] the overall effect of the
administrative reforms limiting monarchical authority was to increase
the authority and social pre-eminence of the landed nobility:

> The strengthening of the authoritarian rule of both the bureaucratic elite and
> the landed aristocracy turned out to be the outstanding result of the substitution
> of bureaucratic absolutism for monarchical autocracy in the pre-industrial
> society of Prussia ... the reformers fought a battle not against but for the
> landed aristocracy by removing deterrents to the further growth of large agricul-
> tural enterprise, by emphasizing 'the career open to talent,' and by invoking
> the spirit of *noblesse oblige* in public life.[130]

According to this view, the frictions which arose between the state
bureaucracy and the nobility in 1806–7 and again in the 1850s were due
to a handful of reformers whose overall social weight was slight. From
this perspective, the social character of the state is dependent on whichever
class is numerically dominant within its ranks and offices. The notion
that the bureaucratic state itself could lay claim to a set of distinct social
and economic interests, deriving from its own independent sources of
economic surplus, is completely foreign to this view.

Eckart Kehr developed a somewhat different perspective. For Kehr,
struggles such as that between the judiciary and the administration after
1807, are seen as political manifestations of battles being fought between
the bourgeoisie and the aristocracy *outside* the boundaries of the state.
According to Kehr, the judiciary, because of its preoccupation with developing a system of normative law, was the leading edge of pro-capitalist
reform within the state bureaucracy. Only the judiciary kept alive the
ideal of a *Rechstaat* based on principles of 'legal formalism': it 'thereby
satisfied the interests of the bourgeoisie diverting it from its preoccupation
with politics.'[131] Here the state is seen as a mediator or arbiter between
the dominant classes; bureaucratic *autonomy* after 1806, according to
Kehr, was rooted in the fact that the bureaucracy

> was able to retain power by playing the aristocracy off against the bourgeoisie
> at a time when these two classes were their only dangerous opponents and,
> since the eighties, by playing both the classes off against the new adversary,
> the proletariat.[132]

These two perspectives – the one which endeavours to derive the class
character of the state from the numerical predominance of the aristocracy
within the state administration, and the other which sees the state as

a political *arbiter* of economic class struggles originating *outside* the state – have tended to dominate most discussions of the nature of the Prussian state bureaucracy. Both views were developed in reaction against the conservative tradition of German historiography which emphasized what one commentator has labelled 'the imaginary universality of particular interests' within the Prussian civil service (*Beamtenstand*). That is, for thinkers like Otto Hintze and Max Weber, following in the tradition of Hegel, ideological considerations such as the supposed commitment of the bureaucracy to a shared concept of the state 'outbid the divisiveness of particular interests, and endowed the bureaucracy with the institutional capacity to guarantee the existence of the state itself.'[133] Thus a conservative writer such as Hintze could forthrightly deny that the bureaucracy was motivated by anything so base as economic interest:

The quite unique spiritual constitution of the civil service is the effect of a long process of education as an estate ... and indeed of familial cultivation. This effect could not have been achieved through the free play of economic forces. The status of private officials might at a pinch be described in purely economic terms, though even here a relationship of trust and moral elements in general play a considerable role which cannot be adequately defined as economic; but in the case of public officials, it is quite evidently impossible to see them as an institution governed by economic factors. It is rather a political institution, which bears within it the unmistakeable and ineradicable sovereign character of the state as such (*Staatswesen*) and whose rather archaic structures and motivation are evidence of a long past. It is very hard to construct either a judicial or economic concept of this status. There is in it something unique, something irrational, which can only be grasped in terms of history.[134]

The one thing that can be said for this kind of view is that it attempted to uncover the internal mechanisms of the state. Its great weakness, however, is that it attempted to do so in profoundly idealist terms. On what basis is it possible to demarcate economic interests from the 'ineradicable sovereign' political character of the state? Was not the entire fiscal apparatus of the state, from which the bureaucracy derived its economic life-blood, based upon the coercive extraction of peasant and artisan surpluses through political means? Only the most restrictive definition of 'the political' could fail to take note of the connection between the class-like interests of the *Beamtenstand* and the manner in which its *private* material (economic) interests set the tone of the constitutional (political) and ideological struggles which dominated German political life throughout the first two-thirds of the nineteenth century.

In his critique of Hegel's *Philosophy of Right*, Marx emphasized precisely the class-like character of the state bureaucracy. He did not set out to disprove the Hegelian proposition that the bureaucracy was a class;

he sought only to show that it was not a universal class as Hegel believed, but a particularistic one based on definite material interests. Marx notes that the bureaucracy holds 'the essence of the state ... in its possession; it is its *private property*.' Marx writes: 'Class in the medieval sense remained only within the bureaucracy itself, where civil status and political status are directly identical.'[135] In other words, state power for the bureaucracy plays the same role in terms of its material interests (posts, career advancement, and so on) as private property does for the propertied classes. Stated another way, for Marx, the fusion of economic and political powers which characterized the general form of feudal surplus-extraction relations, holds true only for the state bureaucracy; only here is its economic position directly tied to its political position.

The emphasis of these passages is important in constructing a comprehensive analysis of the roots of state autonomy in the post-reform era. Kehr's account, which traces the autonomy of the state to its role as a 'social arbiter' between the nobility and the bourgeoisie, captures only part of the picture. Marx's formulation also calls attention to the internal basis of this autonomy by seeking to show how the surplus extractive needs of the state set it at odds with private exploiters to the degree that it competed with them over economic surpluses. In addition, by insisting on the fusion of the economic and the political as the material basis of bureaucratic power, Marx's formulation repudiates the Hegelian conception of bureaucratic autonomy, later taken up by Hintze and others, which sees the state as a purely 'political institution' standing above the fray of competing economic interests. What this meant concretely was that the extra-economic character of the fiscal system tended to pervade virtually every aspect of economic and social life. Direct coercion still formed what one commentator has described as 'the hard core of state domination' well into the nineteenth century.[136]

In the two areas most directly associated with state-coercive activities – the police and the military – pre-capitalist practices and forms of organization tended to predominate up to 1850, if not beyond. Ludtke emphasizes the persistence of 'traditional cameralistic maxims of action' among the police force at both the local and national levels as late as the 1880s:

The 'servants of the state', as they were labelled in the *Allgemeine Landrecht*, had not only pushed ahead with a frequently violent 'policing' of the subjects in connection with the development of the fiscal and military state establishment. ... In particular, the 'assassination' of property was to be prevented or deterred all the more decisively the more the importance of property grew, which it did in two respects: as the basis of expansion of production, i.e. as a legal title to dispose of resources and 'productive energy'; and as the real foundation of legitimate rule. The functional requirements of increased economic mobilization, above all for fiscal purposes, mingled with and strengthened counter-revolutionary protection of the status-quo. The protection of property thus represents a common interest even for the *Junkers* who despised the 'state machine' and its bureaucracy.[137]

The coercive intervention of the police in the process of surplus-extraction at the behest of state administrators, was in addition to the still considerable police powers exercised at the local level by landowners – though the two cannot be assumed to be completely complementary. After the defeat of the 1848 revolution, the police powers of the nobility were abolished as part of a broad package of agrarian reforms introduced by the Prussian state to secure peasant loyalty.[138]

Perhaps more significant was the role played by the military in the process of surplus extraction. 'Citadel practice', which Ludtke defines as 'the ponderous use of military force in the sphere of state administrative action' continued to be a central aspect of state fiscal activity.[139] Into the 1850s, nearly 50 per cent of town-dwellers lived in garrison towns housing between eighteen and one hundred men. The presence of such 'citadels' pervaded nearly every aspect of town life: gates to the town were locked and unlocked by soldiers, firing ranges took up much of the land in the immediate vicinity, which not only deprived the local population of traditional hunting grounds and living space, but also impeded the construction of roads and railways. And for those civilians inside the town ramparts, there was the constant inconvenience and expense of billeting soldiers.[140]

Braun has admirably summarized the connection between the surplus-extractive requirements of the state and the predominance of military and police powers in Prussian society:

> The excessive growth of the police apparatus during the mercantilist-cameralist era was mainly caused by its fiscal functions. ... The fiscal system and fiscal situation of Brandenburg Prussia required the linkage of the extraction apparatus with the police apparatus and the military organization.[141]

Although he stresses the extent to which the prominence of the military presence prepared the way for the later advance of capitalism, Ludtke is equally aware of the historical continuities with the use of military force under feudalism:

> The extensive power of the military to determine civil and administrative daily life was not at all unusual, stemming as it did from the tradition of the *ancien régime*. The increased independence of the bureaucracy and the civil service

since the end of the eighteenth century, organizationally and legally confirmed during the state reforms after 1807, corresponded to only a brief period of uncertainty with regard to the traditional competences of the military. The normative guarantee of the right of intervention in 1818–20 then served to confirm the largely unchanged practice, i.e., that 'military participation in (almost) all police affairs' . . . was still very extensive.[142]

Germany still expressed many of the contradictions of a society in which, as Engels put it in his assessment of early modern absolutism, 'the political order remained feudal, while society became more and more bourgeois.'[143] Although the state was increasingly forced to introduce measures which had the effect of undermining the old order, it strove at the same time to preserve those aspects of the old society which were vital to its own independent sources of economic surplus. Indeed, it often did the two things at once: agrarian reform, for example, was intended to create an independent peasantry which would provide a constant source of taxation revenue. Its overall effect, however, was to hasten the dispossession of the peasantry.

The same contradictory impulses could be seen at work within the bourgeoisie itself. Those sections of the petty bourgeoisie who were engaged in small-scale capitalist production, as well as the smaller number of big capitalists, were more or less content with the legal changes of the reform era. The slow accumulation of capital among petty producers, although not as spectacular as the industrial boom later in the century, was nonetheless evidence of 'a "silent victory" for the German bourgeoisie'.[144] On the other hand, for those sections of the professional bourgeoisie whose fortunes were tied to the state bureaucracy, the commitment to capitalism was considerably more ambiguous.

V. German Liberalism and the Bureaucratic State

This raises an important set of questions regarding the nature of German liberalism. Traditionally, the term 'liberalism', as applied to German political development, has been used rather indiscriminately. At its most general, it has been invoked to describe the correlation between liberal political aims – judicial equality of citizens before the law, an emphasis on talent over birth, and a commitment to some form of representative government – and the economic aims of a capitalist bourgeoisie – the dismantling of pre-capitalist obstacles to private enterprise, a free market in land, labour and all other commodities. Theodore Hamerow describes the German liberal movement up to 1848 as being led 'by middle-class leaders inspired by a dream of Parliamentary government and industrial might'. Liberalism sought

the creation of a new civic order based on talent and wealth. Behind their blueprints of federal union and individual freedom rose the vision of a land of factories, banks, railroads and steamships in which political and economic liberty were one.[145]

In recent years, there has been a growing recognition of both the complexity of social forces in Germany which identified themselves, at different times and in different historical contexts, with liberalism, and of the difficulties involved in any straightforward identification of liberalism with the class interests of a capitalist bourgeoisie. It is now widely acknowledged that the leadership of the liberal Parliamentary movement was drawn not from the *grande bourgeoisie* of industry and finance, such as they existed prior to 1848, but rather from the ranks of professionals and intellectuals. By far its largest number of members and the most important spokesmen in Parliament, came from the state bureaucracy. Moreover, just as in France, it was frustration over access to office and control over the state budget – more than a desire to free individual economic initiative from the shackles of feudalism – which provided the impetus for liberal demands favouring 'careers open to talent' and limited Parliamentary representation. As James Sheehan has written: 'For men whose occupations were closely tied to the state in one way or another, career frustrations almost inevitably became political frustrations.'[146] Sheehan argues that it is impossible to draw any direct correlation between liberalism and capitalist economic interests; only a few liberals were unambiguous supporters of capitalist industry and economic liberalism. On the whole, he concludes, most 'lived in a pre-industrial world of state service, artisanal production and small enterprise'.[147]

Similarly, Geoff Eley has questioned 'whether liberalism can reasonably be regarded – however shorthand or convenient the formulation – as straightforwardly "bourgeois" at all.'[148] According to Eley, one of the first conditions for making sense of German economic and political development in the nineteenth century, must be 'to break this identity between liberalism as a political movement and an unmediated and unitary notion of the bourgeoisie's interests as a class.'[149]

This raises the question of the bourgeoisie's role in the revolution of 1848. First of all, as Eley notes, the *grande bourgeoisie* was an extremely reluctant participant in the events of 1848. The political reforms they supported were minimal and fell far short of anything resembling liberal democracy on the British model.[150] Moreover, we are left with the problem of explaining how an ostensibly 'bourgeois revolution' came to be dominated by avowedly non-bourgeois, and in some cases, explicitly anti-capitalist groups such as artisans, state-employees, peasants and students. We can begin to make sense of this 'paradox', Eley contends:

> by carefully separating the content of the popular revolutionary struggles in 1848 (or 1789) from the actual changes they ultimately helped to confirm, or at least failed to obstruct. Abstractly this means distinguishing between two levels of determination and significance – between the revolution as a specific crisis of the state, involving widespread popular mobilization and a reconstitution of political relationships, and on the other hand the deeper processes of structural change, involving the increasing predominance of the capitalist mode of production, the potential obsolescence of many existing practices and institutions and the uneven transformation of social relations.[151]

Eley's solution, in other words, is to redefine the concept of 'bourgeois revolution' by freeing it from any direct equation with the immediate aims of class actors, or necessary association with liberal-democratic forms of political rule. Eley argues for a broad definition of bourgeois revolution, 'to mean the "inauguration of the bourgeois epoch" i.e. "the successful installation of a legal and political framework for the unfettered development of industrial capitalism"'.[152] Eley equates the concept of 'bourgeois revolution' in this epochal sense, with the long period of upheaval spanning roughly the Prussian reform era, the 1848 revolutions, and the decade of unification up to 1871.[153]

Eley's arguments are an important corrective to the long-standing identification of the bourgeoisie with liberal politics. However, he concludes, that 'to the extent that the stress on "bourgeois revolution" in the epochal sense involves a retreat from the problem of causality, it amounts to an important weakness.'[154] But this is true only if we confuse the long-term consequences of bourgeois revolutions, that is, the gradual development of capitalism over an extended period of time, with the process of revolution which is a much shorter and more compact *political* rupture. Eley at points seems to collapse the two processes together. Much more satisfactory is his definition of 'revolution from above' which he describes as an event occurring in a 'concentrated space and time and through a radical process of political innovation . . . [which] delivered the legal and political conditions for a society in which the capitalist mode of production could be dominant.'[155]

To extend this process over virtually the entire nineteenth century in Germany is to go too far. Prior to Bismarck, neither the reform era nor the 1848 revolution represented a decisive political transformation of the old order. Unlike France in 1789, the 1848 revolution failed to bring about a thorough-going 'reconstitution of political relationships'. Indeed, the state emerged from the revolution with a new lease on life. Here, the question of the *kind* of liberalism which prevailed among sections of the bourgeoisie in 1848 does become important. It is certainly reasonable to argue that part of the reason for the failure of the 1848 revolution had to do with the widening gap between the infant working class and petty producers of various sorts, and sections of the liberal bourgeoisie. Because of this process of differentiation, it was much more difficult to forge the kind of revolutionary coalition between small producers and the bourgeoisie that existed in the French and English revolutions. In the most advanced areas of Germany, the working class had already begun to develop its own independent organizations. This set the industrial bourgeoisie against the working class. As Marx quickly recognized, this meant that 'the gentlemen of the bourgeoisie [would] try as much as possible to change absolute monarchy into a bourgeois monarchy in an amiable way without revolution.'[156]

At any rate, the industrial bourgeoisie formed only a small fraction of the leadership of the 1848 revolution. By far the majority of the delegates to the Frankfurt Parliament were petty officials and bureaucrats. In and of itself this is hardly surprising; the bulk of those who populated the revolutionary assemblies during the French Revolution were drawn from similar backgrounds. But the Frankfurt Parliament contained few Jacobins or radical republicans spurred on by the momentum of popular insurrection. The disjunction between the popular movement and the leadership of the revolution ultimately meant that the proposals for reform which did get put forward were quite conservative. The inherent conservatism of the most numerous section of the 'liberal' bourgeoisie in the Frankfurt Parliament derived ultimately from the contradictory nature of their position within the state bureaucracy. What many desired was simply more control over state-appropriated surpluses and greater access to strategic offices in the state. To this extent, there was no necessary connection between such 'liberal' demands and the encouragement of capitalism.

Many German liberals were caught in a peculiar dilemma. On the one hand, they desired a more liberal political order which would guarantee an open and secure career structure within the state and greater control over its fiscal apparatus. Moreover, the language used to express these demands – much of it, no doubt, borrowed from the fervently anti-absolutist English tradition – often had the appearance of representing a fundamental challenge to the old order. And yet, since their *material* interests were often tied to the preservation of a bureaucratic apparatus which still rested on pre-capitalist foundations, they were forced to defend those elements of the old order from which they derived their livelihood. In essence, that meant defending those extra-economic powers of the state tied to the process of surplus extraction, at the same time as they attempted to 'modernize' and 'democratize' its structures. This predicament

produced in many liberals an ambivalent attitude towards the state. As
James Sheehan observes:

> Liberal attitudes toward the state ... were the product of two conflicting sets
> of pressures. On the one side was the antistatist impulse of Western European
> liberal thought and the frustrations caused by the repressive realities of bureau-
> cratic absolutism. On the other side, however, was the record of progressive
> reforms sponsored by the state and, equally important, the conviction shared
> by many liberals that the state remained an indispensable ally in a society
> as culturally, religiously, and economically backward as their own. Most Ger-
> man liberals did not want to limit or destroy the power of the state but rather
> to purge it of abuses and turn its power toward liberal aims.[157]

At one level, of course, these conflicting pressures were only apparent,
since few liberals harboured any aspirations of overturning the foundations of German society. In the constitutional debates of 1848, therefore,
it is difficult to find anything resembling a liberal-capitalist blueprint for
the transformation of German economic and political life. On the contrary, the constitutional proposals put forward in the Frankfurt Parliament, by the bureaucratic and professional men who formed the majority
of its delegates, were remarkable for their lack of temerity:

> They wanted the new constitution to remove the abuses of the existing political
> system but they were content to leave monarchical authority and states more
> or less intact. This cast of mind informed the constitutional draft prepared
> in April by Friedrich Dahlman. ... In the forward of his proposals, Dahlman
> left no doubt where he felt the center of political power should continue to
> reside: 'To our princely houses belong not only the old habits of obedience
> ... in truth they are the only possibility to lead gradually this multi-faceted
> and divine Germany into a unified state.[158]

Marxists have often accused the liberal bourgeoisie of betraying
its historic mission by accommodating itself to *Junker* 'backwardness'
in the political sphere. This would be to assume that the forces of liberalism
were striving for capitalist reforms in the first place, and not, as appears
more likely, some modified form of 'bureaucratic absolutism' resting on
essentially the same social foundations as before. The German liberals
of 1848 did not 'betray' the historic tasks of the bourgeoisie, since their
goals were of an entirely different order than those which are normally
associated with the 'liberal-capitalist' political model based on the English
experience.

It was precisely the inherent conservatism of their political demands
which allowed German liberals to be so easily outflanked by the diehard
supporters of personal absolutism grouped around Frederick William
IV. Indeed, the royal constitution, promulgated in December 1848 after

the defeat of the Frankfurt Parliament, had simply taken over much of the liberal programme. As one commentator has noted, 'the liberal aspects of the constitution astounded contemporaries. It seemed a Prussian King in the moment of victory had enshrined the principle of democracy.'[159] On one of the most important issues – control of the budget – the Crown retained *de facto* command because the wording concerning budgetary control remained vague and virtually meaningless. In addition, the king's constitution contained guarantees regarding civil rights, freedom of the individual, of movement, religion, assembly and association as well as providing for an independent judiciary.[160] In short, many of the basic ingredients of the liberal conception of the rule of law were contained in the 'absolutist' constitution of Frederick William IV.

For the peasantry, the new constitution was just as 'anti-feudal' as anything offered by the Frankfurt liberals. The royal constitution

promised the prompt enactment of measures dealing with the commutation of manorial dues, the annulment of feudal privileges and the elimination of tax exemptions. Article XXXVIII of the constitution prohibited the establishment of new entailments, while Article XL put an end to the police powers of the nobility.[161]

It is certainly possible to interpret the actions of conservative reformers as purely a series of shrewd tactical manoeuvres designed to forge, at nearly any cost, an alliance with the peasantry against the liberals. This helps to explain why manhood suffrage held so little terror for progressive conservatives – sometimes less than it did for liberals.[162] But, at a deeper level, it reveals how little the distance separating the supposed forces of feudal reaction and purveyors of capitalism really was. In truth, both conservatives *and* liberals had a common interest in preserving the peasantry, both as a basis of support and as an independent source of revenue for the state. That is, because both groups were vying for control of peasant-appropriated surplus through control of the state, it was essentially a struggle not over *how* these surpluses could be secured, but of *who* was to control their appropriation.

From the standpoint of the peasantry, the 'who' of it did not matter so long as the 'how' of it provided for greater security of tenure:

... the peasant saw in the counterrevolution only the executor of a policy of rural reform. Since neither the bourgeoisie nor the aristocracy was prepared to satisfy his most cherished ambition, the achievement of free proprietorship through the expropriation of the landlords, he settled for a compensated emancipation, and thereafter his interest in the struggle between constitutionalism and absolutism waned.[163]

The victory of the counter-revolution, then, was more than merely a 'political' event. It was a reaffirmation of the symbiosis between the peasantry and the state which formed the core social-productive relation upon which both royal and bureaucratic absolutism rested. The state protected peasant property rights only in so far as such guarantees provided it with a secure and, above all, independent source of surplus. The structural importance of this relationship cannot be over-stressed. The reinvigorated autonomy of the Prussian state after 1850 was what allowed it to steer a course which was largely unconstrained by either aristocratic or non-aristocratic forces. This reality is not adequately captured by accounts which attempt to read off the social nature of the state from the class backgrounds of those who inhabited its offices. The counter-revolution, for example, did not automatically translate itself into greater influence for the *Junkers*:

> It is a common error to think that the conservative ministers acted in close alliance with the *Junkers*. They no more wished for the *Junkers* to exert political power than that the liberals should enjoy any. The *Junkers* had not been permitted to show any signs of political independence since the days of the Great Elector.[164]

The Prussian state after 1850 did not become more 'feudal' because it attempted to replace liberal administrators and those in high bureaucratic posts with 'royal reliables'.[165] Such purges were not unimportant, but it would be mistaken to ascribe their social significance to some sort of victory by 'feudalism' over the interests of a nascent 'bourgeoisie' inside the state bureaucracy. Ekhart Kehr's contention that the *judiciary* represented the stronghold of bourgeois-liberal interests as against the 'neo-feudal' *Junkers* who dominated the state administration under the arch-reactionary Puttkamer, has been shown to be false.[166] As Gillis has shown, 'the significant difference was not between the two branches but within the ranks of each.'[167] However, even if we accept that internal strife within the bureaucracy during this period was more evenly spread throughout different sections of the state – and that no coherent 'bourgeois-liberal' interest had coalesced around the judiciary – it does not follow, as Gillis seems to imply, that these struggles were *not* 'essentially social' in character.[168]

They were social in two vital ways. First, they reflected the continuing struggle between upper and lower office-holders over the fruits of state-appropriated surpluses. Secondly, they demonstrated how the advance of capitalism in German society as a whole was producing sharper and sharper conflicts within the state bureaucracy, albeit along lines that did not neatly conform to divisions between bourgeois and aristocratic office holders. At one level, these quite contradictory impulses dovetailed into one another. In the attempt to reinvigorate the social foundations of royal absolutism, those who controlled the state were increasingly forced to adopt policies which were quite compatible with the further growth of capitalism. While the conscious aim of the royal constitution was to resurrect the old order, its effect was to prepare the way for the new.

VI. Bismarck and Bourgeois Revolution from Above

This same contradictory dynamic between conscious aims and outcome lies at the heart of the decisive political transformation which occurred under Bismarck's direction between 1862 and 1879. But to understand fully why this dynamic expressed itself in the form of a radical alteration of the state from above, it is insufficient to consider internal developments in isolation from changes in the world economy. As Geoff Eley has insisted, in order to make sense of Bismarck's revolution from above, 'we need something like the classical Marxist concept of "uneven and combined development".'[169] That is, we can only fully appreciate why Bismarck's violent reordering of the state was an imperative forced upon the Prussian state, and not the product of some sort of historical omniscience on Bismarck's part, if we understand that the competitive compulsions of the world market and military competition between states set definite limits on ruling-class choices. By the 1860s, less advanced countries such as Germany could only compete and catch up with the more advanced capitalist powers through rapid transformation of existing social and political structures. As Eley notes,

> German and Italian unifications occupied a distinct temporality when compared with the earlier sequence of the Dutch, British, American, and French Revolutions. Where the latter occurred before the global victory of capitalist relations on a European, let alone world, scale – the former actively presupposed the triumph of capitalism ...[170]

Only by placing the phenomenon of 'bourgeois revolution from above' in the broader context of European developments, therefore, can we hope to make sense of its historic significance.

We still need to explore, however, how and through what processes the internal dynamics of the imperial state prepared the way for capitalism. Two main lines of argument have emerged among Marxist theorists. The first, drawing on Engels's pioneering analysis, sees the Bismarckian state as an essentially backward political structure dominated by the *Junker* nobility. Due to the domination of the state by 'pre-industrial elites', the German state is thought to have only imperfectly represented capitalist interests. Eley and Blackbourn have challenged this view by insisting on the progressive character of the state and its compatibility with capitalism. Let us take each in turn.

Engels saw the 'blood and iron' phase of Bismarck's rule, which ended in Prussia's domination of the German federation, as 'the fulfilment of the national aspirations of the bourgeoisie....' It was a bourgeois 'revolution ... that he was prepared to carry ... through by revolutionary means.'[171] Nevertheless, Engels still considered that Bismarck's actions were part of a desperate attempt to cheat both the bourgeoisie and the working class of power 'for the benefit of the decadent Prussian cabbage-*Junkers*'.[172]

Drawing on Engels and the work of Eckart Kehr, Hans-Ulrich Wehler, in a widely influential work has revived the 'Bonapartist' interpretation of Bismarckian Germany. 'Bonapartism', Wehler writes:

> is best understood as an authoritarian form of government which first appeared in a relatively early phase of industrialization when the pre-industrial elites were still able to demonstrate their strength; the bourgeoisie was making rapid advances while simultaneously threatened from below by the workers' movement – foreshadowed by the 'red spectre' of the revolutionary years of 1848 to 1849. ... Bismarck balanced traditional and modern elements in a combination that was typical of Bonapartism. For example, he combined an absolutist-style military policy with state interventionism on behalf of vested interests and underpinned it by plebiscitary approval. Through a policy of war up to 1871 and later in the 1880s, of social and economic imperialism, he sought to stifle internal problems by diverting attention to the sphere of external affairs. Through it all he lived off an undeniable and heightened charisma derived from his role in the founding of the German Empire, his foreign policy and his successful mediation over a long period between the two dominant classes...[173]

Wehler sees 'Bonapartism' as symptomatic of a certain phase of industrial development. Like Engels, he stresses the political 'backwardness' of the social forces which held political sway. According to Wehler, the 'autocratic, semi-absolutist sham constitutionalism' of the Bismarckian state derived from the 'cartel of dominant conservative forces' or 'pre-industrial elites' which dominated the state up to 1879.[174] The balance between the bourgeoisie and the *Junker* aristocracy clearly favoured the latter – a fact which was to have profound implications for Germany's future development:

> In terms of its social effects, this rearguard action meant – in the short term in other countries, but in Germany in the long term – a socially conservative, anti-emancipatory obstruction of modernization throughout German society, allowing for no more than partial change.[175]

For Wehler, it is the disjunction between these two aspects of Bismarckian 'Bonapartism' – its progressive economic role and the backward and conservative character of its polity – which determined the crisis-prone character of the imperial state:

> At the root of all the major problems of Imperial policy lay the central dilemma of a tension that could not be overcome: a tension between a rapid economic and social development towards an industrial society on the one hand, and its inherited, petrified political structure on the other.[176]

Eley and Blackbourn have challenged this latter judgement on the grounds that it exaggerates the extent to which the 'non-correspondence' between the state and the economy was inimical to a stable and functional form of bourgeois rule. They argue that 'both the Bismarckian state and an authoritarian mode of politics were perfectly effective in securing specifically "bourgeois" interests, if these are strictly defined in relation to the fundamental processes of class formation and capitalist industrialization.'[177] In other words, they reverse the emphasis of Wehler's account by rejecting the claim that the imperial state was biased in favour of non-capitalist interests.

> ... the Imperial state showed itself reasonably adaptable ... to the tasks which a capitalist state is called upon to perform – securing the conditions of capitalist reproduction, doing the work of legitimation ... , organizing the unity of the dominant classes, mobilizing the consent of the people. In fact, I would suggest ... that the strictly reactionary elements were considerably more isolated in the political system, that the Constitution was considerably more flexible, and that 'modernizing' forces had achieved considerably more penetration – indeed that the 'traditional' elements were considerably less 'traditional' – than recent historians have tended to believe.[178]

Both Eley and Blackbourn rightly acknowledge the extent to which the large-scale collision of social forces allowed the Prussian state executive the degree of autonomy required to execute its revolutionary policies during the 1860s: 'It is this theoretical content of the idea of Bonapartism – the creative independence of the state executive, inside the limits imposed by the political dynamic of capitalist social development, in the context of a general social and political crisis – that defines its value....'[179] The emphasis of their argument is clearly on the capitalist character of the 'Bonapartist' regime; the 'relative autonomy' of the Bismarckian state – despite the residual power of 'pre-capitalist' forces in the state executive – is interpreted as a capitalist phenomenon.[180]

It may be that both of the interpretations examined above capture essential aspects of the Bismarckian state. After all, what was involved was a process in which one of the most reactionary forces in Prussian society was called upon to carry through a 'revolution from above' in the interests of capitalism. The question is *how* this process unfolded; how did a state forged under conditions of feudalism become transmuted into a bourgeois state? One answer would be to insist that it was *despite* its pre-capitalist character that the state did eventually promote the development of capitalism in the pursuit, as it were, of its pre-capitalist interests and logic. What we are arguing, then, is that the imperial state still contained strong anti-capitalist impulses *and* that, in conditions of 'uneven and combined development' where capitalism was imposing its own logic on society, the state became a force for the development of capitalism.[181]

Therefore, in analysing the actions of the Bismarckian state it is necessary to distinguish between its immediate goals, motivated by the logic of 'political accumulation', and its increasing inability to do so as capitalism gained the upper hand. A useful model for understanding the *contradictory* nature of this process, is to see it as an instance of what Robert Brenner has termed an '*unintended consequence*' of the rationally self-interested actions of pre-capitalist actors.[182] That is to say, the actions taken by the Bismarckian state to consolidate new sources of surplus compelled it to pursue policies which had the effect of strengthening capitalism, even though the intended outcome was to reinforce pre-capitalist social relations.

This account, at least, avoids turning Bismarck 'into the supreme manipulator of German history, miraculously aware of what the true interests of bourgeoisie and aristocracy were and implementing them against the wishes of both.'[183] Bismarck was by no means a passive agent in the transformation of Germany. But his policies were driven by a more mundane pragmatism than by any super-historical vision of the future requirements of capitalism. Bismarck's desperate attempts to appease both the bourgeoisie and the aristocracy was part of a general strategy to reconstruct a stratum of dependent state notables in conditions which were rapidly eroding the economic basis for the maintenance of such a class. As Alan Mitchell writes:

> The operative fact can be described not as the winning or losing by certain political or social factions but an amalgamation of the foremost property-owning strata: *les notables*. It was the primacy of an expanded notability which ... Bismarck sought to anchor in the political institutions ... This required mutual concessions of aristocracy and upper bourgeoisie, governmental inducements to both, and an attempt to repress or assuage any popular opposition to such a restricted realignment of privilege.[184]

The same tensions were evident in debates over the state budget. In the constitutional conflicts which re-emerged in the 1860s we find the same set of preoccupations which characterized the earlier debates. At their centre, loomed the question of who, ultimately, would exercise control over state-appropriated surpluses. As Sheehan comments:

> Throughout the sixties they [liberals] continued to demand what they had wanted since the new era; not the right to dominate the government, but control over the budget, legal guarantees, and the right to present their views to the nation in Parliament.[185]

After the liberal electoral victories of 1858, a dispute erupted over the amount of time conscripts had to serve in the army. Liberal members in the lower chamber of the Prussian Parliament argued that two years was sufficient service, while William I insisted on three years. Even within this seemingly arcane debate could be glimpsed the continuing dispute over which group would control the fiscal apparatus of the state.

> Behind the complex technical issues of how many years a Prussian should serve in the regiments of the line and how many in the reserve, and how many new regiments should be raised, was the fundamental question of whether Parliament should retain financial control over army expenditure and so in effect control over the budget.[186]

When it is recalled that the army represented not just a symbol of state power but also one of the chief means – aside from taxation – by which the state was able to expand the available economic surplus at its disposal, the constitutional crisis which this debate produced, begins to make greater sense.

Warfare, from the time of the Great Elector onwards, lay at the heart of absolutist policy. It was, after all, one of the primary ways absolutist rulers had managed to extricate themselves from the grip of *Junkerdom* and secure an independent basis for 'political accumulation'. Bismarck's wars of unification certainly had crucial *consequences* for capitalism. Unification secured 'the conditions of existence of the emergent capitalist mode of production, the institutional consolidation of the national market, and a German-wide process of industrialization. ...'[187] In terms of their conscious aim, however, the wars of unification may be seen as an expression of more traditional dynastic rivalries, fuelled by the dynamic of 'political accumulation' whereby territorial expansion was one of the most efficient ways of expanding the revenues of the state.[188] Territorial aggrandizement, in Bismarck's thinking, may have been seen as the means through which the material requirements for the reconstitution of a dependent state notability could be met.

However, the 'uneven and combined' character of capitalist development meant that the social basis for such an endeavour was fast disappearing. The rapid advance of urban-based capitalism coupled with changes in the world grain market forced the *Junkers* to begin farming on capitalist principles.[189] Long resistant to the penetration of capital, *Junker*-dominated agriculture finally succumbed to the logic of capital.

> The estate agriculture of East Elbia at the end of the nineteenth century came under pressure from two different sources – the international grain market and the domestic labour market, in particular the urban labour market catering for the needs of industry. The pressure on *Junker* agriculture to change therefore came more from events outside agriculture in German cities than from internal competition within German agriculture. ... This cannot be too heavily emphasized, since it means that it is not at all legitimate to talk of autonomous dynamics of capitalism in German agriculture.[190]

With the advance of capitalist relations in the countryside, the *Junker* capitalists became less dependent on the state for a livelihood and, therefore, less likely to be attracted into the ranks of the state notability or, indeed, to see their interests as necessarily corresponding to those of the state. With the expansion of their fortunes through privately appropriated surpluses, they were less likely to be compelled by economic circumstances to rely upon incomes derived from state-appropriated surpluses.[191]

For the bourgeoisie, the attractions of state service had even less appeal. In the 1870s, a new kind of 'notable politics' was emerging which, in many respects, made a virtue out of its exclusion from political affairs.

> The form of notable politics ... which crystallized in the decades between 1850 and 1870 owed its existence to the establishment of a national communications network through railway, telegraph, and press. It was predicated on important changes, ... equality before the law, rights of association, the creation, in short, of a public sphere where 'opinion' could be formed.[192]

The new notable politics which took root, for the most part, outside the orbit of the state in 'civil society', presupposed the 'silent victory' of capitalist social relations. In the end, therefore, it was the growing capitalist character of both town and country life – the 'unintended' by-product of the state's own initiatives – which doomed Bismarck's attempts to create a stable state notability of the old type.

By the 1880s, Prussian absolutism had indeed been, in Perry Anderson's words, 'transmuted into *another* type of state'.[193] The 'theoretical *conditions of possibility* of this "transmutation"'[194] however, were more than simply the product of Germany's *geographical* proximity to the West, as Anderson seems to suggest; they were, above all, a response to compelling pressures emanating from a world economy now dominated by capitalism.

The spread of capitalist social relations in German industry and the gradual incorporation of rural production into the circuits of international capitalism had ultimately eroded the social relations on which the extraeconomic surplus extraction depended. The necessary substratum upon which political accumulation rested had, as it were, been pulled from beneath the elaborate superstructure of the pre-capitalist state once and for all. Henceforth, the immense resources of the German state were deployed unequivocally in the service of capital.

Notes

1. Hans Rosenberg, *Bureaucracy, Aristocracy and Autocracy: The Prussian Experience 1660–1815* (Boston: Beacon Press, 1966), p. viii.

2. Theodore Hamerow, *Restoration, Revolution and Reaction* (Princeton: Princeton University Press, 1958), p. viii.

3. Ralf Dahrendorf, *Society and Democracy in Germany* (New York: Anchor, 1969), pp. 58, 376.

4. Barrington Moore, *Social Origins of Dictatorship and Democracy* (Boston: Beacon Press, 1966), pp. 433–52.

A recent survey of this literature in English is provided in: Richard J. Evans, 'The Myth of Germany's Missing Revolution', *New Left Review* no. 149 (January–February, 1985) pp. 67–95; also, Richard J. Evans, 'Introduction: Wilhelm II's Germany and the Historians', in R.J. Evans, ed., *Society and Politics in Wilhelmine Germany* (London: Croom Helm, 1980).

The so-called 'structural continuity thesis' has been most strongly attacked by two non-German historians. See David Blackbourn and Geoff Eley, *The Peculiarities of German History* (Oxford University Press, 1984).

Blackbourn and Eley's work, in turn, has generated a barrage of criticism and debate which is summarized for the English reader in three useful articles: Roger Fletcher, 'Recent Developments in West German Historiography: The Bielefeld School and Its Critics', *German Studies Review* vol. 7, no. 3 (October, 1984); Robert G. Moeller, 'The Kaiserreich Recast? Continuity and Change in Modern German Historiography', *Journal of Social History* (Summer, 1984); 'Social History with a Vengeance? Some Reactions to H.-U. Wehler's "Das Deutsche Kaiserreich"', *German Studies Review* vol. 7, no. 3 (October, 1984).

5. Karl Marx, 'The Eighteenth Brumaire of Louis Bonaparte' in *Surveys from Exile*, ed. David Fernbach (Harmondsworth: Penguin Books, 1977), p. 238.

6. Marx, quoted in Perry Anderson, *Lineages of the Absolutist State* (London: Verso, 1974), n. 1, p. 237.

7. Frederick Engels, quoted in Hal Draper, *Karl Marx's Theory of Revolution, vol. 2: The Politics of Social Classes* (New York: Monthly Review Press, 1978), p. 223.

8. Marx, quoted in Hal Draper, *Karl Marx's Theory of Revolution*, vol. 2, p. 225.

9. Engels, quoted in Hal Draper, *Karl Marx's Theory of Revolution*, vol. 1, p. 418.

10. Marx, quoted in Anderson, *Lineages*, p. 277.

11. Ibid., p. 277.

12. Engels, quoted in Draper, *Marx's Theory of Revolution*, vol. 1, p. 413.

13. Blackbourn and Eley, *Peculiarities*, p. 84; See Alex Callinicos, 'Bourgeois Revolutions and Historical Materialism', *International Socialism* no. 43 (June, 1989) for a more developed overview of these cases.

14. Sheldon Watts, *A Social History of Western Europe, 1450–1720* (London: Hutchinson, 1984), p. 133.

15. F. L. Carsten, *The Origins of Prussia* (Oxford: Oxford University Press, 1954), p. 63.

16. Heide Wunder, 'Peasant Organization and Class Conflict in East and West Germany', *Past and Present* no. 78 (February, 1978), p. 49.

17. For differing assessments, see Wunder, 'Peasant Organization', p. 51; Carsten, *Origins*, p. 150.

18. Watts, *Social History*, p. 147.

19. Peter Blickle, 'Peasant Revolts in the German Empire in the Late Middle Ages', *Social History* vol.4, no. 1 (May, 1979), pp. 233–5.

20. Ibid., p. 235; Eda Sagara, *A Social History of Germany* (London: Methuen, 1977), p. 150.

21. Blickle, 'Peasant Revolts', p. 235.

22. Ibid., p. 239; Watts, *Social History*, p. 149.

23. Watts, *Social History*, p. 149. The general effect of the revolt was to strengthen the self-organization of feudal lords throughout Germany: 'In the rest of the German lands, 1525 was the end of a century and more of rural violence against law and order of ruling princes and municipalities.' G. Benecke, *Society and Politics in Germany 1500–1750* (Toronto: University of Toronto Press, 1974), p. 10.

24. Blickle, 'Peasant Revolts', pp. 238–9.

25. Robert Brenner, 'Agrarian Class Structure and Economic Development in Pre-Industrial Europe', in T. H. Aston and C.H.E. Philpin, eds., *The Brenner Debate* (Cambridge: Cambridge University Press, 1987), p. 56.

26. Benecke, *Society and Politics*, p. 19.

27. Ibid., p. 76.

28. Ibid., pp. 77–8.

29. Anderson, *Lineages*, p. 223; Sagara, *Social History*, p. 147; Jerome Blum, *The End of the Old Order in Rural Europe* (Princeton: Princeton University Press, 1978), p. 85.

30. Benecke, *Society and Politics*, pp. 80, 144.

31. Wunder, 'Peasant Organization', p. 53.

32. Carsten, *Origins*, pp. 151–6.

33. Ibid., pp. 163–4.

34. Brenner, 'Agrarian Roots', pp. 278–9.

35. Ibid., p. 278.

36. William Hagen, 'How Mighty the Junkers? Peasant Rents and Seigneurial Profits in Sixteenth Century Brandenburg', *Past and Present* no. 108 (August, 1985), p. 115.
A similar line of argument is pursued by the leading East German historian of east-Elbian agrarian relations. See Harmut Harnisch, 'Peasants and Markets: The Background to the Agrarian Reforms in Feudal Prussia East of the Elbe, 1760–1807', in Richard J. Evans and W. R. Lee, eds., *The German Peasantry* (New York: St Martin's Press, 1986), pp. 37–70.

37. Hagen, 'How Mighty the Junkers?', p. 94.

38. Ibid., pp. 104–5, 111.

39. Brenner, 'Agrarian Roots', p. 283.

40. Hagen, 'How Mighty the Junkers?', p. 113.

41. Ibid., p. 113; Carsten, *Origins*, p. 162.

42. Hagen, 'How Mighty the Junkers?', p. 114.

43. Over the longer term this was to have a significant impact on the transformation of agrarian relations on the *Junker* estates in the nineteenth century. However, it may be premature to see either markets or the end of serfdom as enough to precipitate the transition to agrarian capitalism. See Harnisch, 'Peasants and Markets'; William Hagen, 'The Junkers' Faithless Servants: Peasant Insubordination and the Breakdown of Serfdom in Brandenburg-Prussia, 1763–1811', *The German Peasantry* (New York: St Martins Press, 1986).

44. The most influential works in English which have insisted on the importance of *Junker* powers in the long-term development of Prussian absolutism are, Carsten, *Origins*, pp. 165–78; Hans Rosenberg, 'The Rise of the Junkers in Brandenburg-Prussia, 1410–1618', *American Historical Review* no. 49 (1943), pp. 1–22, 228–42. For a more extensive list of both German and English sources, see Hagen, 'How Mighty the Junkers?', n. 1, pp. 80–81.

45. Anderson, *Lineages*, p. 212.

46. Rosenberg, *Bureaucracy, Aristocracy, Autocracy*, p. 43.

47. Sagara, *Social History*, p. 5.

48. Benecke, *Society and Politics*, pp. 9, 34–5, 373–9.

49. Anderson, *Lineages*, p. 238; Sagara, *Social History*, p. 49.

50. Rosenberg, *Bureaucracy, Aristocracy, Autocracy*, pp. 35–7.

51. Carsten, *Origins*, p. 49.

52. Anderson, *Lineages*, p. 243; Carsten, *Origins*, pp. 186–7.

53. H. W. Koch, *A History of Prussia* (London: Longman, 1978), p. 57; Anderson, *Lineages*, p. 243; Carsten, *Origins*, p. 197.

54. Carsten, *Origins*, p. 187.

55. Anderson, *Lineages*, p. 240.

56. Rudolph Braun, 'Taxation, Socio-Political Structure, and State-Building: Great Britain and Brandenburg-Prussia', in Charles Tilly, ed., *The Formation Of National States in Western Europe* (Princeton: Princeton University Press, 1975), p. 312.

57. Anderson, *Lineages*, p. 218.

58. Ibid., pp. 217–18.

59. Carsten, *Origins*, p. 266; Rosenberg, *Bureaucracy, Aristocracy, Autocracy*, pp. 37–40.

60. On this point see Braun, 'Taxation, Socio-Political Structure and State-Building', pp. 312–13.

61. Carsten, *Origins*, p. 263.

62. Anderson, *Lineages*, p. 244.

63. Koch, *History of Prussia*, p. 66.

64. Rosenberg, *Bureaucracy, Aristocracy, Autocracy*, p. 59.

65. Koch, *History of Prussia*, p. 67.

66. Rosenberg, *Bureaucracy, Aristocracy, Autocracy*, p. 55.

67. Koch, *History of Prussia*, p. 72.

68. Rosenberg, *Bureaucracy, Aristocracy, Autocracy*, p. 47.

69. Ibid., p. 49.

70. Koch, *History of Prussia*, p. 81.

71. Rosenberg, *Bureaucracy, Aristocracy, Autocracy*, p. 77; Koch, *History of Prussia*, p. 90.

72. Rosenberg, *Bureaucracy, Aristocracy, Autocracy*, p. 74.

73. Ibid., p. 75.

74. Koch, *History of Prussia*, p. 82.

75. Ibid., p. 86.

76. Walther Hubatsch, *Frederick the Great: Absolutism and Administration* (London: Thames and Hudson, 1975), p. 173.

77. Koch, *History of Prussia*, p. 93.

78. Ibid., p. 94.

79. Anderson, *Lineages*, p. 246.

80. It seems to me that Perry Anderson overstates the degree of unanimity between the state and the nobility in the early eighteenth century when he writes that 'the Prussian landowning class was more stolidly at one with its State than any other in Europe. Bureaucratic unity and rural autonomy were uniquely reconciled in this cabbage paradise.' *Lineages*, p. 265. Hussain and Tribe, in a slightly different context, have described Anderson's view as 'Junker-centred' because it takes their 'economic and political position as the measure of all change'. Athar Hussain and Keith Tribe, *Marxism and The Agrarian Question* vol. 1 (London: Macmillan, 1981), p. 42. Although the authors are referring to the reform era of the early nineteenth century, their criticism can be applied to Anderson's general treatment of the relationship between the state and the nobility in·Prussia.

81. See Anderson, *Lineages*, p. 213, for Otto Hintze's judgement that the 'whole social system was placed in the service of militarism'; Rosenberg, *Bureaucracy, Aristocracy, Autocracy*, pp. 40–41, presents a more or less psychologistic explanation of Prussian militarism; Braun, 'Taxation, Socio-Political Structure and State-Building', p. 311, comments that 'war played a prime role in the development of taxation and public finance' in Prussia.

82. These institutional powers of the landlords, however, should not be exaggerated.

Frederick II, for example, only retained the office of *Landrat* because he thought it might be 'a useful counterweight to his own bureaucracy'. Hubatsch, *Frederick the Great*, p. 168.

83. Frederick II, quoted in C. B. H. Behrens, *Society, Government and the Enlightenment: The Experience of Eighteenth Century France and Prussia* (London: Thames and Hudson, 1985), p. 37.

84. Igomar Bog, 'Mercantilism in Germany', in D. C. Coleman, ed., *Revisions in Mercantilism* (London: Methuen, 1969), p. 175; Hubatsch, *Frederick the Great*, p. 72.

85. Frederick II, quoted in Hubatsch, *Frederick the Great*, p. 111.

86. Ibid., pp. 73, 97, 102–11.

87. Behrens, *Society and Enlightenment*, p. 60.

88. Hubatsch, *Frederick the Great*, p. 142; Behrens, *Society and Enlightenment*, p. 81.

89. Behrens, *Society and Enlightenment*, p. 33.

90. Sagara, *Social History*, p. 46.

91. Rosenberg, *Bureaucracy, Aristocracy, Autocracy*, p. 140.

92. Ibid., p. 147.

93. Hubert C. Johnson, *Frederick the Great and His Officials* (New Haven: Yale University Press, 1975), p. 256.

94. Behrens, *Society and Enlightenment*, p. 64.

95. Hubatsch, *Frederick the Great*, p. 161.

96. Ibid., p. 164.

97. Ibid., p. 212.

98. Rosenberg, *Bureaucracy, Aristocracy, Autocracy*, p.191.

99. Frederick II, quoted in Hubatsch, *Frederick the Great*, p. 166.

100. Ibid., p. 168.

101. Johnson, *Frederick and His Officials*, pp. 200–201.

102. Hubatsch, *Frederick the Great*, p. 143.

103. Ibid., p. 146.

104. Johnson, *Frederick and His Officials*, p. 204; Rosenberg, *Bureaucracy, Aristocracy, Autocracy*, pp. 172-4.

105. Blum, *End of the Old Order*, p. 373.

106. Hubatsch, *Frederick the Great*, p. 176.

107. Johnson, *Frederick and His Officials*, p. 208.

108. Frederick II, quoted in Koch, *History of Prussia*, p. 117.

109. Frederick II, quoted in Behrens, *Society, Government and Enlightenment*, p. 38.

110. Harnisch, 'Peasants and Markets', pp. 41–3.

111. Quoted in Blum, *End of the Old Order*, p. 361.

112. Harnisch, 'Peasants and Markets', p. 46.

113. Ibid., p. 53.

114. Marx, *Capital* vol. 1, p. 875.

115. Behrens, *Society, Government and Enlightenment*, p. 148.

116. Hagen, 'Faithless Servants', p. 93; Harnisch, 'Peasants and Markets', pp. 57–60.

117. John R. Gillis, 'Aristocracy and Bureaucracy in Nineteenth Century Prussia', *Past and Present* no. 41 (December, 1968), p. 111.

118. Sagara, *Social History*, p. 52.

119. Hussain and Tribe, *Agrarian Question*, p. 45.

120. Blum, *End of the Old Order*, p. 387.

121. Ibid., pp. 392–3.

122. Ibid., p. 394.

123. Hamerow, *Restoration, Revolution, Reaction*, p. 25.

124. Blum, *End of the Old Order*, p. 407.

125. Sagara, *Social History*, p. 153.

126. Hagen, 'Faithless Servants', p. 91.

127. Blum, *End of the Old Order*, p. 412.

128. Rosenberg, *Bureaucracy, Aristocracy, Autocracy*, chs 8 and 9.

129. Ibid., p. 200.

130. Ibid., p. 222.

131. Eckart Kehr, in Gordon A. Craig, ed., *Economic Interest, Militarism and Foreign Policy*, trans. Grete Heinz (Berkeley: University of California Press, 1977), p. 154.

132. Ibid., pp. 164–5.

133. Jane Caplan, '"The imaginary universality of particular interests": the "tradition" of the civil service in German history', *Social History* vol. 4, no. 2 (May, 1979), pp. 303-4.

134. Otto Hintze, quoted in Caplan, '"Imaginary universality"', p. 304.

135. Quoted in Draper, *Marx's Theory of Revolution* vol.1, pp. 488–9. Engels refers explicitly to 'the formation of a separate class of administrative government officers, in whose hands the chief power is concentrated, and which stands in opposition to all classes.' Quoted in Draper, p. 491. Draper adds to Engels's comment: 'This article illustrates the prevalent view of the absolutist bureaucracy as a class-like formation.... Clearly this state power involves so autonomous a social formation at its heart that the class label becomes a mere matter of terminology.' p. 491. He later concludes: 'Under the absolutist regime the state bureaucracy was seen as one of the estates of the realm. But it was also seen as a social class. This depends not on some superhistorical definition of class but on the concrete nature of the social system involved....' p. 507.

136. Alf Ludtke, 'The role of state violence in the period of transition to industrial capitalism: the example of Prussia from 1815 to 1848', *Social History* vol. 4, no. 2 (May, 1979), p. 185.

137. Ibid., pp. 186, 188. It was de Tocqueville who insisted that the French Revolution had disturbed little the social pattern of the *ancien régime*. Interestingly, he draws a comparison between the *Allgemeine Landrecht* and the Declaration of the Rights of Man. See Koch, p. 143.

138. Hamerow, *Restoration, Revolution, Reaction*, p. 188.

139. Ludtke, 'The Role of State Violence', p. 212.

140. Ibid., p. 202.

141. Braun, 'Taxation, Socio-Political Structure and State-Building', p. 316.

142. Ludtke, 'The Role of State Violence', pp. 210–11.

143. Frederick Engels, *Anti-Dühring* (Moscow: Progress Publishers, 1969), p. 126.

144. Blackbourn and Eley, *Peculiarities*, p. 190.

145. Hamerow, *Restoration, Revolution, Reaction*, p. 101; *The Social Foundations of German Unification 1858–1871* (Princeton: Princeton University Press, 1969), pp. 135–80.

146. James J. Sheehan, *German Liberalism in the Nineteenth Century* (Chicago: University of Chicago Press, 1978), p. 21.

147. Ibid., p. 24; See also Caplan, 'Imaginary universality', p. 312.

148. Eley, *Peculiarities*, p. 77.

149. Ibid., p. 75.

150. Ibid., p. 82.

151. Ibid., pp. 82–3.

152. Ibid., p. 83; See Gareth Stedman Jones, 'Society and politics at the beginning of the world economy', *Cambridge Journal of Economics* no. 1 (March, 1977), pp. 77–92.

Christopher Hill has adopted a similar view; 'A Bourgeois Revolution', in J G. A. Pocock, ed., *Three British Revolutions, 1641, 1688, 1796* (Princeton: Princeton University Press, 1980).

153. Eley, *Peculiarities*, p. 87.

154. Ibid., p. 88.

155. Ibid., p. 84.

156. Marx, quoted in Draper, *Marx's Theory of Revolution* vol. 2, p. 185.

157. Sheehan, *German Liberalism*, p. 43.

158. Ibid., p. 70.

159. J. A. S. Grenville, *Europe Reshaped 1848–1878* (London: Fontana Books, 1986), p. 135.

160. Ibid., p. 136.

161. Hamerow, *Restoration, Revolution, Reaction*, p. 188.

162. Grenville, *Europe Reshaped 1848–1878* (London: Fontana Books), p. 161; J. R. Gillis, *The Prussian Bureaucracy in Crisis, 1840–1866* (Stanford: Stanford University Press, 1971), p. 128.

163. Hamerow, *Restoration, Revolution, Reaction*, p. 191.

164. Grenville, *Europe Reshaped*, p. 162.

165. Gillis, *Prussian Bureaucracy*, pp. 150–51.

166. Kehr, *Economic Interest*, p. 156.

167. Gillis, *Prussian Bureaucracy*, p. 155.

168. Ibid., p. 155.

169. Eley, *Peculiarities*, p. 85.

170. Ibid., p. 85.

171. Frederick Engels, *The Role of Force in History* (New York: International Publishers, 1968), pp. 64–5.

172. Engels, quoted in Draper, *Marx's Theory of Revolution* vol. 1, p. 410.

173. Hans-Ulrich Wehler, *The German Empire 1871–1918*, trans. Kim Traynor (New Hampshire: Berg Publishers, 1985), pp. 57–9.

174. Ibid., p. 55. Engels used roughly similar terms. Bismarck sought 'to play the Bonaparte as against the bourgeois with the junkers behind him instead of peasants'. Quoted in Draper, *Marx's Theory of Revolution* vol. 1, p. 413.

175. Wehler, *German Empire*, p. 58.

176. Ibid., p. 64.

177. Blackbourn and Eley, *Peculiarities*, p. 132.

178. Ibid., p. 141. Perry Anderson takes a broadly similar position. Anderson argues that the German state was 'a capitalist apparatus, over-determined by its feudal ancestry, but fundamentally homologous with a social formation which by the early twentieth century was massively dominated by the capitalist mode of production.' *Lineages*, p. 278.

179. Eley, *Peculiarities*, p. 150.

180. Blackbourn, however, does note that the autonomy of the state also rested on certain independent criteria, though he does not specify whether these had anything to do with the absolutist origins of the state or not: 'The state retained a relative autonomy ... and was capable of acting against particular interests – including major capitalist interests – where that was judged appropriate.... The state had its own criteria of prestige, economic strength, and public order, which naturally changed in detail over time.' *Peculiarities*, p. 248.

181. There is a wealth of sources which detail developments in both agriculture and industry after 1850. Among the most valuable on industry see Hamerow, *The Social Foundations of German Unification* part 1; Helmut Bohme, *An Introduction to the Social and Economic History of Germany* trans. W. R. Lee (Oxford: Basil Blackwell, 1979); W. R. Lee, 'Tax Structure and Economic Growth in Germany 1750–1850', *Journal of European Economic History* vol. 4, no. 1 (Spring, 1975); W. O. Henderson, *The Rise of German Industrial Power 1834–1914* (London: Temple Smith, 1975); Martin Kitchen, *The Political Economy of Germany 1815–1914* (London: Croom Helm, 1978); R. H. Tilly, 'Capital Formation in Germany in the Nineteenth Century', in Peter Mathias and M. M. Postan, eds., *The Cambridge Economic History of Europe* vol. 7 (Cambridge: Cambridge University Press, 1978); Jurgen Kocha, 'Entrepreneurs and Managers in German Industrialization', *Cambridge Economic History* vol. 7; Karl Erich Born, 'Structural Changes in German Social and Economic Development at the End of the Nineteenth Century', in James J. Sheehan, ed., *Imperial Germany* (New York: New Viewpoints, 1976).

On changes in agriculture and the growth of agrarian capitalism, see J. A. Perkins, 'The Agricultural Revolution in Germany 1850–1914', *Journal of European Economic History* vol. 10 no. 1 (Spring, 1981); J. A. Perkins, 'Dualism in German Agrarian Historiography', *Comparative Studies in Society and History* vol. 28, no. 2 (April, 1986); R. A. Dickler, 'Organization and Change in Productivity in Eastern Prussia', in W. N. Parker and E. L. Jones, eds., *European Peasants and Their Markets* (Princeton: Princeton University Press, 1975); R. G. Moeller, 'Peasants and Tariffs in the Kaiserreich: How Backward were the Bauern?', *Agricultural History* 55 (1981); and various articles in Richard J. Evans and W. R. Lee, eds., *The German Peasantry: Conflict and Community in Rural Society from the Eighteenth Century to the Present* (London: Croom Helm, 1985).

182. See ch. 1, p. 33.

183. Evans, 'Myth of Germany's Missing Revolution', p. 79. Evans has in mind Engels's

treatment of Bismarck. For an example of Engels's almost panegyric assessment of Bismarck's historical foresight, see *Role of Force*, pp. 97–9.

Eley sometimes comes close to ascribing the same exaggerated foresight to Bismarck as well: 'Bismarck's radical solution to the German question, under circumstances of a constitutional confrontation with a resurgent German liberalism, is the classic instance of a successful revolution from above, substituting military unification and direct political negotiation with the opposition for the more confusing and volatile scenario of the English and French Revolutions.' *Peculiarities*, p. 85.

184. Alan Mitchell, 'Bonapartism as a Model for Bismarckian Politics', *Journal of Modern History* vol. 49, no. 2 (June, 1977), p. 198.

185. Sheehan, *German Liberalism*, p. 116.

186. Grenville, *Europe Reshaped*, p. 166.

187. Eley, *Peculiarities*, p. 145.

188. Grenville, *Europe Reshaped*, pp. 272–3.

189. Hussain and Tribe, *Marxism and the Agrarian Question*, p. 47. As Perkins points out, with the removal of 'the public functions of the *Junker* estate, ... the *Junkers* had come to form, in economic terms, an agrarian capitalist class, scarcely distinguishable – except perhaps relatively marginally in respect of the size of their holdings – from the large peasants occupying from 50 to 100 hectares of land.' 'Dualism in Agrarian Historiography', p. 306.

190. Hussain and Tribe, *Agrarian Question*, pp. 53–4.

191. The advent of agrarian capitalism among the *Junkers* in the 1870s meant that 'while the landed nobility continued to send their younger sons to the civil service, they were no longer the impoverished office-seekers so typical of the earlier years of the century.' Gillis, 'Aristocracy and Bureaucracy', p. 121.

192. Blackbourn, *Peculiarities*, p. 253.

193. Anderson, *Lineages*, p. 278. Eckart Kehr was largely responsible for popularizing the view that the German bureaucracy became 'refeudalized' in the 1880s under the direction of the Prussian minister of the interior, Robert von Puttkamer, a notorious conservative. See Kehr, 'The Social System of Reaction in Prussia under the Puttkamer Ministry', *Economic Interest*, pp. 109–31.

This view has recently been challenged by Margaret Anderson and Kenneth Barkin who have argued that no evidence exists for Kehr's claim that there was a 'refeudalization of the bourgeoisie' in the 1880s. See Margaret Lavinia Anderson and Kenneth Barkin, 'The Myth of the Puttkamer Purge and the Reality of the KulturKampf: Some Reflections on the Historiography of Imperial Germany', *Journal of Modern History* vol. 54, no. 4 (December, 1982), pp. 654–6. The details of Anderson and Barkin's argument are less important than the fact that the evidence they present helps to demonstrate how the social character of the state had changed, despite the continued prominence of '*Junker* interests' in the state bureaucracy in the 1880s, 1890s and beyond. It was not that the personnel of the bureaucracy had changed all that much, but that the role of the state itself had been transformed.

194. Anderson, *Lineages*, p. 278.

4

English State Formation and the Rise of Capitalism

Throughout the foregoing discussion of the evolution of politics and society in France and Germany, we have made periodic reference to the contrast between French and German developments and those which took place in England. Before we can draw any general conclusions about the relationship between state formation and the transition to capitalism on a Europe-wide scale, we should perhaps review some of the main aspects of English state formation.

I. The Agrarian Capitalist State

The protracted development of agrarian capitalism in England reviewed in chapter 1 also signalled the birth of a new form of state which was quite different from the absolutist states of the Continent. As Robert Brenner has written:

> The affirmation of absolute private property by the landlords over and against peasant possession went hand in hand ... with the gradual rise of a different sort of state, one which attained a monopoly of force over and against the privatized powers of feudal potentates. The state which emerged during the Tudor period was, however, no absolutism. Able to profit from rising land rents, through presiding over a newly emerging tripartite capitalist hierarchy of commercial landlord, capitalist tenant and hired wage labourers, the English landed classes had no need to recur to direct, extra-economic compulsion to extract a surplus. Nor did they require the state to serve them indirectly as an engine of surplus appropriation by political means (tax/office and war).[1]

One of the chief reasons for the Tudor monarchy's inability to construct

155

a viable absolutism lay in the fact that in attempting to offset the influence of the great territorial magnates, it strengthened the economic and social powers of the gentry – the very class which would be the driving force behind the ascendancy of Parliament and the eventual triumph of capitalism.[2] The Reformation had offered the Crown a rare opportunity to establish for itself an independent source of revenue through the exploitation of the vast tracts of church lands seized by the state. However, the war with France between 1543 and 1551 rapidly depleted this financial base as the Crown was forced to sell off most of its church properties, estimated to amount to a quarter of the country.[3] The chief beneficiary was the Tudor-created gentry who vastly expanded their own numbers and the size of their landed holdings. As Lawrence Stone observes:

> The central fact about English social history between 1540 and 1640, and in consequence of English political history, was the growth in numbers and wealth of the landed classes and the professions. The number of peers rose from 60 to 160; baronets and knights from 500 to 1,400; esquires from perhaps 800 to 3,000; and armigerous gentry from perhaps 5,000 to 15,000. The landed classes thus trebled in numbers at a time when the population scarcely doubled.[4]

Having sold off much of the church lands the Crown was also deprived of another major source of revenue, so lucrative for the French state during this period – the sale of offices. Although offices for purchase did exist, the right of English monarchs to create new offices above the meagre numbers which existed since the medieval period was strictly limited. Elizabeth's attempt to increase the numbers of offices for sale in 1587 was prohibited by the judges. Moreover, it was not the royal treasury which benefited from the sale of the few offices which did exist but the officials and courtiers of the court.[5]

Further attempts by James I to expand the sale of offices had some limited success, but the practice was continually attacked in Parliament. Sales of offices did, in fact, continue well after the Civil War. But it was no longer a practice which was designed to strengthen the powers of the Crown, but was rather under the control of the aristocracy and 'was primarily due to the habits of this class of the nation, and not to absolutism on the part of the king.'[6]

The persistence of such practices among the propertied classes has led some to assume that the aristocratic *ancien régime* had somehow survived the advance of capitalist relations on the land as well as the political and social upheavals of the seventeenth century. This is an important issue to which we shall return in greater detail below. For the present, it is sufficient to note that the very fact that it was the landed classes and not the Crown which controlled the sale of offices, patronage, and sinecures, tells us something of the social and political powers which the gentry had consolidated by the middle of the seventeenth century.

> By 1640, the gentry were neither faithful retainers of a local earl nor obedient servants of the political faction in control of power at Court. They were full citizens of the Commonwealth, independent men of substance. They were pouring into the universities and the Inns of Court, they were filling up the numbers on the bench of Justices, and they were crowding out the other social groups in the House of Commons. ... The rise of the gentry ... is politically the single most important social development of the age.[7]

That the gentry had greatly strengthened its social power against the Crown is clear. That they had also gained the upper hand against the peerage is less clear. Much debate has surrounded the question as to whether or not the peerage, which constituted the basis of the traditional aristocracy of the 'court', was a declining feudal aristocracy being outstripped by the rising capitalist gentry of the 'country' in the sixteenth and early seventeenth centuries. The growth of agrarian capitalism had not just altered social relations in the countryside, it was also beginning to shape the character of trade and commerce as well, from which much of the peerage drew their incomes. It has been estimated that two-thirds of the peerage, in the period 1560–1640, was engaged in colonial, trading or industrial enterprises.[8]

The important point is that the *entire* social structure was undergoing radical change which 'by the end of the seventeenth century ... had stamped upon the aristocracy of titled and armigerous landlords who formed the apex of the social and political hierarchy a new character that set them apart from their contemporaries in every other European monarchy.'[9] The peerage, like the gentry, were being transformed into a new type of ruling class:

> The class whose formation is the present focus of interest was being continuously recruited, and it naturally comprised diverse elements as to status, wealth and income. But despite these and other divergences, its members were species of the same genus. They constituted a single economic class, for what they had in common was the possession of capital for the end of profit and capital accumulation.[10]

But neither should the accumulating powers of the gentry be underestimated, for it was on the land that the real impetus for change was exerting itself. Through a combination of manoeuvres restricting the powers of the Crown by undercutting its independent sources of revenue, by strengthening its own powers at the national level in Parliament and at the local level through the justices of the peace (drawn from the ranks of the 'independent men of substance'), the gentry had built up a formidable set of political institutions in the years prior to the revolution which were able to withstand all attempts to establish royal absolutism. Both James I and Charles I ultimately failed to establish greater absolutist powers for the Crown. Charles I's attempts to undermine gentry power which included: his refusal to acknowledge Parliament's role in political decision making; the raising of taxes without consulting Parliament; his assault on the powers of the JPs; threats to gentry property rights inherent in the Crown's Irish policy as well as the perceived threat to Protestantism contained in Charles's pro-Catholic foreign policy, all helped to weld together a unified opposition against the Crown and royal absolutism by 1640.[11]

The crisis which finally precipitated the downfall of royal absolutism was sparked by Charles I's defeat in the war with Scotland. The king had succeeded in alienating both the large merchant oligarchies who refused to extend further funds to finance the war and the landed classes who suspected further assaults on their property rights. The financial crisis facing the Crown forced Charles to appeal to Parliament. But the elections to the Long Parliament in 1640 signalled a decisive defeat for the Crown. The threat of royal absolutism unified, to a remarkable degree, the men of property who dominated Parliament. It is testimony to the strength of this alternative political power that they achieved their main goals so swiftly:

> By the summer of 1641, the united opposition had achieved all its negative objectives. It had removed from the Crown the powers of taxation without consent; it had abolished the main organs of central government, the Councils of Wales and the North, the Courts of High Commission, Requests and Star Chamber; it had reversed the Laudian clerical and High Church policies and had stopped the persecution of dissenters; and it had punished the chief agents of royal policies.[12]

A victory of royal absolutism would have had a profound effect on the fortunes of the bourgeois opposition. It would have meant that those who owned property were not free to dispose of their wealth as they saw fit. The Crown had persistently attempted to intervene in relations between landowners and their tenants and to exert the prerogatives of the Crown over those of private property. As E.P. Thompson observed:

> What was at issue, from one aspect, was exactly a capitalist redefinition of 'the basic property statute,' from 'ancient right' to 'natural law' and purchase; of the mode and rationale of production from quasi-self-sufficiency to the marketing of commodities for profit; and of productive relations, from the organic compulsions of the manor and gild to the atomized compulsions of a free labour

market. .... And, from another aspect, the real movement was enormously complex and protracted, commencing ... with the great monastic wool farmers of Domesday, and passing through the enfeeblement of the barons in the wars, the growth of 'free labour,' the enclosure of the sheep-walks, the seizure and redistribution of Church lands, the pillaging of the New World, the drainage of the fens, and thence through revolution, to the eventual acceleration of enclosure and the reclamation of wastes.[13]

None of the gains of Parliament could have been won, however, without the intervention of the popular struggles which forced the men of property into sharper and sharper conflict with royal authority. In order to strengthen their hand against the king, parliamentary radicals appealed to the urban masses of London for support. The publication of the 'Grand Remonstrance' in 1641 represented a dramatic turn in the revolution. It brought onto the stage masses of ordinary citizens of London who participated in demonstrations, debates, and agitation. What became increasingly clear in the agitation around the Long Parliament was that there was a distinct set of demands emerging which went far beyond the narrow class interests of those who dominated Parliament. As Brian Manning points out, in London:

there was another agitation being conducted by religious radicals and separatists, amongst the apprentices and young men, the craftsmen and journeymen, and the lower classes generally. Its strength lay in the suburbs, where the industries were located and where the poorer people lived. It was designed not only to overcome the opposition of the Lords but also to pressure the Commons to go further than the limited demands for the removal of bishops and papists from Parliament, and to abolish episcopacy altogether and the prayer-book. It could not look to the power of wealth and influence to back its demands but only to the power of the numbers it could muster in the streets. ....[14]

Fear of this popular rebellion getting out of hand drove one section of Parliament into the royalist camp. Thus, Parliament was split into two parties, the party of order and a popular party. This division within the ruling class opened the door for Charles I's assault on Parliament and the beginning of the English Revolution. As Christopher Hill has written: 'In short, there was a quarrel between two groups of the ruling class; but looking on was the many-headed monster, which might yet be *tertius gaudens*. Once the unity of the parliamentary class was broken, social revolution would be possible.'[15]

Time after time during the years of the revolution, the intervention of the popular masses was decisive in defeating the forces of royal absolutism and for pushing the leaders of Parliament further along the path of full-scale revolution.

The civil war was transformed into a revolution by the pressure of the radical section of the 'middle sort of people', otherwise it would have been settled by some compromise between the gentry; they were that section of the bourgeoisie which represented the development of capitalism from amongst the petty producers; they led a revolutionary movement of some of the small peasants and artisans; but this movement became divided as the differences of interests were discerned between the upper layer of improving farmers and enterprising artisans who were becoming capitalists and the mass of small producers, peasants and artisans; and loss of popular support left the revolutionary bourgeoisie isolated as a counter-revolution developed in the 1650s and they were ground between the resurgence of the old ruling class and the resistance of the mass of the people.[16]

The years following the revolution up to the Restoration of 1660, and between 1660 and 1688, were ones of political instability as the landed classes attempted to defend their freedom to do as they pleased with their property against both the threat from below which had been unleashed in 1640 and renewed fears of absolutism:

The beneficiaries of the settlement were exactly those people who were represented in Parliament: that is, the men of substantial property, and especially landed property. Title to the enjoyment of their property was secured by the constitutional impedimenta with which the Crown was surrounded, and by the rule of a Law which was both dispassionate in its adjudication of substantial property-rights and passionately vengeful against those who transgressed them. . . .[17]

Even though 1660 represented the temporary triumph of a more pro-royalist section of the landed classes whose fear of popular dissent outweighed their fear of absolutism, legislation against non-Parliamentary taxation was confirmed. The Restoration also saw legislation passed against royal monopolies; abolition of the Court of Wards and feudal tenures 'turned lordship into absolute ownership.'[18] Further acts of 1661 and 1677 weakened the copyholds of small tenants, opening the way to rack-renting, evictions and enclosure.[19]

The Navigation Acts (1650–51; confirmed 1660, 1661) made possible the closed colonial system and provided for colonies to be subordinate to Parliament.[20] In sum, even the 'conservative' restoration greatly strengthened the forces of capitalism and the sovereignty of Parliament and further diminished any remaining hope of constructing an absolutist state on the pattern of France. The Settlement of 1688 saw a further retreat from the kind of 'popular' politics which had inspired the radicalism of the 1640s. But even though both the aristocracy and the Tories now feared popular insurrection more than they did the threat of absolutism, it was clear that neither section of the landed classes was prepared to let their trepidation of the former move them in the direction of strengthening the powers of the Crown in any meaningful way. Even though the Crown retained certain powers such as the right to appoint all state officials; to summon and dissolve Parliament; to make war and to veto Parliamentary legislation, these powers were strictly limited (the Crown veto was particularly ineffective since it was rarely enforced). What existed was a constitutional monarchy which was financially subordinate to Parliament. As Hill summarizes:

> What emerged was a state in which the administrative organs that most impeded capitalist development had been abolished: Star Chamber, High Commission, Court of Wards and feudal tenures; in which the executive was subordinated to the men of property, deprived of control over the judiciary, and yet strengthened in external relations by a powerful navy and the Navigation Act; in which local government was safely and cheaply in the hands of the national rulers, and discipline was imposed on the lower orders by a Church safely subordinated to Parliament.[21]

In sum, a new *type* of state, one which increasingly corresponded to the needs of a growing class of agrarian capitalists was coming into being in England by the end of the seventeenth century, which rested on fundamentally different social foundations than the tax/office state which existed in France during the same period. Unlike the absolutist states of the Continent, the English state no longer served as a vehicle for the aristocracy to extract economic surpluses from a subject peasantry through taxation and office-holding. As Brenner has emphasized,

> by the end of the seventeenth century the English evolution towards agrarian capitalism had brought about the end of the age-old 'fusion' of the 'economic' and the 'political', and the emergence of an institutional separation between 'state' and 'civil society'.[22]

II. Taxation and Office-holding in the English State

The English state was unique by European standards. And yet, as the eighteenth century wore on, its outward appearance seemed to belie certain similarities to the absolutist states of the Continent. But such superficial similarities could be deceiving. Taxation and office-holding in the English state now rested on a wholly different basis. The main form of taxation in England was the Land Tax, which was levied by the landed classes themselves through Parliament. Its collection was overseen by assessors and collectors drawn from the ranks of the lower gentry, tenant farmers and yeomanry.[23] Land Tax Commissioners, who oversaw assessment and collection in the counties, were drawn from the local gentry and the JPs. As Brooks notes:

> Appointment of Commissioners, and of their clerks, was a local matter, thrashed out between the county establishment and its MPs, and was based on 'one upmanship'.... Only rarely, in times of great political stress and party upheaval, was there any wholesale intervention from above. Lists of Commissioners went long unrevised. Parliament and the political nation was reluctant in the extreme to allow the Crown to name Commissioners.[24]

The jealousy with which the landed classes, both nationally and locally, guarded the administration of the Land Tax is an indication of the continuing hostility to the merest hint of Crown attempts to revive control over taxation. Indeed, the Land Tax was preferred over customs and excise precisely because of the latter's association with absolutism. Historically, the connection between the two had been very close. The proceeds of customs and excise had been applied to the army and the navy, long-standing symbols of Crown independence.[25] Once the threat of absolutism was effectively eliminated, hostility towards excise greatly diminished, as was the case by the beginning of the eighteenth century.[26]

The Land Tax, however, remained the centre-piece of the tax system because its operation was locally controlled and non-bureaucratically administered, even though it was supplemented with various indirect taxes and customs and excise duties. Between 1688 and 1714, over £46 million out of a total revenue of £122 million was raised from land and assessed taxes.[27] Assessments were remarkably low, amounting on average to four shillings in the pound. Under-assessment appears to have been habitual and widespread, though non-payment was less of a problem.[28] Overall, the tax was routinely paid with little complaint by the tenant, after which the amount was deducted from the rent paid to the landlord.[29] The Land Tax thus 'depended not upon force but upon consent. ...'[30] The reason for this was that the landed classes were levying these taxes upon *themselves* by annual votes in Parliament. Moreover, the Land Tax was a tax on *capitalist ground rents* paid to the owners of large estates by their *capitalist tenants* as a portion of the proceeds realized from the exploitation of rural wage-labour. In other words, it was a form of taxation which uniquely conformed to the tripartite structure of English agrarian capitalism which was emerging in the late seventeenth century. More than anything else, it was the compatibility between the Land Tax system, the political nation centred in a Parliament and dominated by the landed interest, and the emerging economic relations of agrarian capitalism, which underpinned the much-vaunted era of 'political stability' stretching between 1688 and 1714.[31]

The contrast with France during the reign of Louis XIV could not be greater. As Brooks observes:

> The localities were, after 1688, merging with the central government of the nation. How different the situation in France, where the role of the Intendant and his creatures on the one hand, and the extent of exemption and privilege on the other, divided and set apart the local community and the province from the central government. How different, too, the division between community and state created by the entering wedge of Interregnum finance and the men who administered it.[32]

Alienation from the state on the part of the French nobility was, of course, only one side of the story; this was merely an expression of the competition between state and nobility over peasant surpluses. At the same time, as we have seen, the nobility (as well as large sections of the bourgeoisie) was integrated into the structures of the state through office-holding and patronage; consequently, the divisions between the local community and the central government were greatly reduced.

But it is here, over the question of private office-holding, sinecures, and patronage, that the most apparent parallels between the English state and the tax/office states of the Continent might be thought to exist. However, in England, it was not the collection of taxes or the unwillingness of the landed classes to pay them which most often posed the greatest problem; it was the difficulty of getting the collected taxes and arrears from assessed taxes from the receivers and into the Treasury. Receivers often invested their balances and held back arrears for their personal profit. Thus receiverships became coveted sinecures which were coming to be seen as the private patrimonies of the powerful. After the Whig triumph, it became routine practice for receivers to hold back large balances, often investing them in ventures like the South Sea Company. By mid-century, it was rare for receivers to be dismissed for such practices; receiverships had become akin to 'private property'.

> By the middle of the century the whole attitude of public service had changed. ... A seat on the Taxes Board, in 1715 a most precarious asset, was regarded by Henry Keball as a freehold to be sold to the best bidder. Commissioners of Taxes, receiverships, surveyorships, became part of the patronage of the great, a fair reward for service by someone, commonly not the fortunate recipient. ... Some receivers were 'happy in the tranquillity of office' conducted by deputy; for others the place was less a public trust than an opportunity for private profit.[33]

Things were not much different with regard to customs and excise. Although tax-farming had been abandoned in customs in 1671, and excise in 1683, the growth of patronage and corruption within these departments grew apace after 1715. Edward Hughes argues, for example, that even though Walpole's excise scheme of 1732 which involved renewing the Salt Tax was designed as a substitute for reducing the Land Tax to one shilling, it was also motivated by a desire to preserve the positions of the salt commissioners. Moreover, patronage considerations became even more pronounced after Walpole's fall.[34] The persistence of such practices has led some to conclude that so far as office-holding and political patronage are concerned, the English state remained essentially an *ancien régime* type of state for the better part of the eighteenth century.

> The Revolution of 1688–89 had consolidated the position of that part of the nation which was primarily interested in the continuation of the sale of offices. Not before the power of the aristocracy was challenged by the middle classes and a more serious criticism of the *ancien régime* had developed, was a reform of the administrative abuses to take place.[35]

This view, however, seriously distorts the true nature of the relationship between office-holding and taxation in the English state. While it is true, for example, that indirect taxes grew at the beginning of the eighteenth century while direct taxation declined, an occurrence which seemed to parallel a similar explosion of indirect taxation in France during the same period, this should not be seen as proof that an *ancien régime* state was reconsolidating itself in the guise of 'Old Corruption'. It is true that there was considerable opposition to the growth of excise duties on basic items of consumption from among sections of the ruling class; but this was not out of an association of excise taxes with creeping absolutism. Rather, most of the opposition to taxes on necessities was based on the assumption that their introduction would raise *wages* and reduce *profits*. In other words, opposition to excise duties was motivated by a set of concerns which were distinctly *capitalist* in character. On the other hand, those who favoured a greater reliance on excise and indirect forms of taxation were motivated by a similar set of concerns. Walpole's argument for the Salt Tax was based on the assumption that *all men should pay* – the same rationale that underlay the Land Tax.[36] In short, excise taxes, like the Land Tax, were not feared by the bourgeoisie of the eighteenth century because it was they – and not an independent absolutist bureaucracy – who controlled and reaped the benefits of taxation.

III. 'Old Corruption': Parasitism and Capitalism

These considerations are critical to understanding the type of state form which dominated English society for much of the eighteenth century.

First of all, the state was not, in any sense, the instrument of the bourgeoisie as a whole; nor did it respond to the broader tasks of 'reproducing' the general conditions of capitalist production relations in any straightforward manner. It was, to use a common term, an *unrationalized* capitalist state which distinguished it from the 'rationalized' bureaucratic, but non-capitalist, states of the Continent. Nonetheless, this 'unrationalized' and immensely corrupt state was not a hindrance to the development of capitalism in the same way that the states of France and Germany certainly were.

> For much of the century, 'the State' was, not to put too fine a point on it, a racket, run by particular groups within the ruling class largely for their own benefit. But it is not enough to dismiss it with this observation, and see capitalist development as something that occurred entirely independently of this 'parasitism'. Old Corruption was conducive to capitalism, if in complex and contradictory ways.[37]

Understanding the precise character of the 'parasitism' which characterized the English state and its connection with capitalism is vital to understanding what marked it off from the fundamentally different 'parasitism' of office-holding, patronage and corruption which characterized the French state of the eighteenth century. According to E.P. Thompson, 'Old Corruption', as the eighteenth-century state was dubbed by its contemporaries, corresponded to a specific phase of capitalist development: 'This was a predatory phase of agrarian and commercial capitalism, and the State was itself among the prime objects of prey.'[38] That is to say, office-holding in the state, and the perquisites which came with it, was inseparably linked with the social relations which now dominated the economy. Landed property 'was both the jumping-off point for power and office, and the point to which power and office returned.'[39] A crucial link in this 'circuit' between landed property, money, politics, and office was the taxation system. Since the landed classes themselves consented to taxation and set the rate of the Land Tax in Parliament, they could look upon higher taxation with very little apprehension since their payments returned to them indirectly in the form of office or – where government loans were involved – in the form of interest.[40]

Unlike in France, where the price of absorption into the tax/office state by the aristocracy was a certain reduction in their independent class power, the English landed classes suffered no such limitation of their powers. Quite the contrary, for the English state was not in any sense a *competitor* of the landed classes as was indeed the case in France and

Germany; it was rather becoming the overseer of the capitalist transformation of 'civil society'. In this context Thompson considers that Old Corruption's

> greatest source of strength lay in precisely the weakness of the state itself: in the desuetude of its paternal, bureaucratic and protectionist powers; in the licence it afforded to agrarian mercantile and manufacturing capitalism to get on with their own self-reproduction; in the fertile soil which it afforded to laissez-faire.[41]

Although Thompson's use of the term 'weakness' to describe the English state may be problematic in this context, his argument is a useful one.[42] What was emerging at this time was a state uniquely suited to the needs of capitalism. Because economic self-reproduction was no longer tied up with the direct application of extra-economic coercive powers by the state, the parasitism of office-holding and patronage was subsidiary to the state's primary role of breaking down barriers to further capital accumulation. In stark contrast, office-holding under absolutism, where surplus extractive and political powers were combined, continued to represent an obstacle to capital accumulation; office-holding was not a by-product of economic processes which took place beyond the state, but rather a claim to a share of the surpluses extracted and redistributed directly by and through the state itself.

A characteristic of absolutism was the building-up of large standing armies under the direct control of the state, as both a means of territorial acquisition through warfare – which was an important form of feudal accumulation – and as an instrument of direct coercion for the extraction of peasant surpluses. In England, the fight against absolutism in the seventeenth century was tied up with restrictions on the size of the army by Parliament. This did not mean, however, that no armed force existed. On the contrary, the wars of the late seventeenth century and eighteenth century which established new territories and markets for England could not have been prosecuted without both a substantial army and navy. Between 1702 and 1714, 40 per cent of state expenditure went to the army, and 35 per cent to the navy.[43] The important point is that control of the army was securely in the hands of the landed interest in Parliament and not the Crown. Secondly, the maintenance of the army and navy were relatively slight since their cost was ultimately underwritten by the expanding wealth being generated through the expansion of capitalism. The fact that a doubling of tax revenues for war between 1688 and 1697, and by a further 75 per cent between 1702 and 1714, did not undermine the fiscal stability of the state is testimony to the critical role of this growing prosperity.[44]

At home, the role of the standing army had also been similarly transformed.

> England was of course never without a standing army in the eighteenth century.
> ... But for purposes of internal control this was often a small and emergency
> force. . . . The weakness of the state was expressed in an incapacity to use force
> swiftly, in an ideological tenderness towards the liberties of the subject, and
> in a sketchy bureaucracy so riddled with parasitism and clientage that it scarcely
> offered an independent presence.[45]

The English state was thus weak in the specific sense that, unlike the
absolutist state, its bureaucracy and coercive apparatus was not geared
to the needs of surplus-extraction for its own 'self-reproduction'. Rather,
it was geared to the needs of the class which controlled it but whose
surplus-extractive powers were now *independent* of the 'public power'
of the state. In securing the conditions for the 'self-reproduction' of the
capitalist class, the English state was not 'weak' but 'strong'.

> Indeed that State, weak as it was in its bureaucratic and rationalizing functions,
> was immensely strong and effective as an auxiliary instrument of production
> in its own right: in breaking open the paths for commercial imperialism, in
> imposing enclosure upon the countryside, and in facilitating the accumulation
> and movement of capital, both through its banking and funding functions and,
> more bluntly, through the parasitic extractions of its own officers. It is this
> specific combination of weakness and of strength which provides the 'general
> illumination' in which all colours of that century are plunged . . .[46]

It was this state – parasitic, corrupt, and riddled by patronage –
which oversaw the consolidation of agrarian capitalist social relations
in eighteenth-century England. 'In the eighteenth century,' Thompson
writes, 'agrarian capitalism came fully into its inheritance. . . .'[47] During
the period from 1690 to 1750, there was a significant shift of property
away from the lesser gentry and yeomanry into the hands of the largest
landowners as land values doubled.[48] Returns from enclosure – although
an expensive undertaking itself – were high enough to make it one of
the most profitable uses of capital.[49] Such considerations pushed landlords
in the direction of enclosure on a massive scale by the turn of the eighteenth
century. The year 1710 saw the first private enclosure act presented in
Parliament. Between 1720 and 1750, 100 acts were passed and a further
139 acts in the following decade. Between 1760 and 1779, 900 acts were
passed. Enclosure reached its peak between 1793 and 1815, when 2,000
acts were approved in Parliament.[50] Before 1760, 400,000 acres of open
field had been enclosed; between 1761 and 1844, approximately 4 million
acres were enclosed and a further 2 million acres were added to this

with the passage of the General Enclosure Act of 1845. After 1700, almost half the arable land of England was subject to enclosure or nearly six million acres. During the same period it is estimated that between 40,000 and 50,000 small farms disappeared through engrossing.[51]

The expropriations, which were a natural part of enclosure, created a huge mass of rural proletarians who provided the labour force for the large capitalist farms which now dominated the English countryside. By 1750, between 40 and 50 per cent of English families worked for wages.[52] By the end of the century, approximately one million people were working as wage-labourers on the land.[53] These changes in rural social relations in turn prompted the growth of rural industries and the home market. Such industries, which began often on a modest scale, employed small artisans who produced cloth, hosiery or metal products. In addition, landowners began to exploit the mineral wealth, such as coal, which lay beneath their holdings. As Hobsbawm writes:

Most of the new technical inventions and productive establishments could be started economically on a small scale, and expanded piece-meal by successive addition. That is to say, they required little initial investment, and their expansion could be financed out of accumulated profits. Industrial development was within the capacities of a multiplicity of small entrepreneurs and skilled traditional artisans. No twentieth-century country setting about industrialization has, or can have, anything like these advantages.[54]

What was unique about the growth of domestic industry was not its size but the fact that it was symbiotically connected to the growth of capitalist relations on the land. The expansion of wage-labour also meant an expansion of the money economy and a growing demand for the necessities of life on the part of those who no longer spent the bulk of their time producing for their own consumption. On the other hand, the needs of capital were also changing. Even if increases in productivity were still chiefly gained through lengthening the working day, some measure of technological innovation was essential since individual capitalists were increasingly enmeshed in a web of *competitive* market relations which compelled them to innovate lest they lose their position in the marketplace. The 'secret' of the home market was that it emerged hand in hand with agrarian capitalism; its importance lay in the fact that it 'provided the broad foundations for a *generalized* industrial economy. ... The domestic market may not have provided the spark, but it provided fuel and sufficient draught to keep it burning.'[55]

These momentous changes in both the physical and social geography of England were facilitated by a host of well-documented changes in the English legal system. There was a growth in statute law which came to replace customary rights. Statute law was particularly important with regard to enclosure. As Porter observes: 'the complex bundle of users' rights (usufruct) tended to be simplified into absolute property right, to the benefit of the landowner. Customary tenures were also assailed.'[56] There was a concomitant growth in the number of capital offences written into the criminal code dealing with crimes against property whose implementation was overseen by JPs drawn from the ranks of local men of property.[57] Perhaps the clearest expression of how the law was being made to conform to the requirements of capitalist property relations was contained in the famous Waltham Black Act of 1724 which created, at a single stroke, fifty new capital offences governing poaching and game laws. The act itself had a wider significance though; it also expressed the special role of the 'rule of law' in mediating the separation of 'economics' and 'politics' which characterized the new social relations.

> The Act registered the long decline in the effectiveness of old methods of class control and discipline and their replacement by one standard recourse of authority: the example of terror. In place of the whipping-post and the stocks, manorial and corporate controls and the physical harrying of vagabonds, economists advocated the discipline of low wages and starvation, and lawyers the sanction of death. Both indicated an increasing impersonality in the mediation of class relations, and a change, not so much in the 'facts' of crime as in the *category* – 'crime' – itself, as it was defined by the propertied. What was now to be punished was not an offence between men ... but an offence against property. ... As, in the eighteenth century, labour became more and more free, so labour's product came to be seen as something totally distinct, the property of landowner or employer, and to be defended by the threat of the gallows.[58]

Thompson and others have emphasized the powerful ideological role played by the law in securing ruling-class hegemony in England during this period. Because direct coercion for purposes of exploitation was no longer a 'face to face' affair but was rather mediated through the 'faceless' and 'impersonal' forces of the market, it was much easier for the law to appear impartial and unbiased by class interest. The gentry, of course, continued to play a central part in the dispensation of justice; but they were able to do so from behind a cloak of seeming goodwill and 'patrician benevolence'.[59] The 'rule of law' was coming to play a dual role: on the one hand, it was an instrument of naked class interest designed to secure the capitalist's absolute claim to property; on the other hand, it was a subtle and powerful means of *masking* the true nature of class exploitation, in a way which would have been impossible under pre-capitalist conditions. As Douglas Hay observes:

A ruling class organizes its power in the state. The sanction of the state is force, but force that is legitimized, however imperfectly, and therefore the state deals alşo in ideologies. Loyalties do not grow simply in complex societies: they are twisted, invoked and often consciously created. Eighteenth-century England was not a free market of patronage relations. It was a society with a bloody penal code, an astute ruling class who manipulated it to their advantage, and a people schooled in the lessons of Justice, Terror and Mercy. The benevolence of rich men to poor, and all the ramifications of patronage, were upheld by the sanction of the gallows and the rhetoric of the death sentence.[60]

In an important sense, it was the historical novelty of the English state which allowed it both to directly intervene in the transformation of economic and legal relations on behalf of capital, and at the same time, to maintain the façade of a seeming impartiality and neutrality. However, the 'night watchman' state which arose on the foundations of agrarian capitalism was, by European standards, relatively modest in size. The tradition of decentralized government meant that the size of the administration remained small. At the beginning of the nineteenth century, the English state had only 16,000 civilian employees, the bulk of which were employed in the collection of customs and excise. Ministry staffs were small; the Treasury, the Home Office, the Foreign Office, the Colonial Office all had staffs of 25 or less. Approximately half of the total of 1,500 central government employees were employed by War, Ordinance and Navy.[61]

The small size of the bureaucracy, however, was more than outweighed by its achievements. Foreign policy became the engine which drove forward the expanding boundaries of British capitalism in the eighteenth century. Unlike her continental rivals, Britain:

was prepared to subordinate *all* foreign policy to economic ends. Her war aims were commercial and (what amounted to much the same thing) naval ... unlike all its other rivals, British policy in the eighteenth century was one of systematic aggressiveness – most obviously against the chief rival, France. Of the five great wars of the period, Britain was clearly on the defensive in only one. The result of this century of intermittent warfare was the greatest triumph ever achieved by any state: the virtual monopoly among European powers of overseas colonies, and the virtual monopoly of world-wide naval power. Moreover, war itself – by crippling Britain's major competitors in Europe – tended to boost exports; peace, if anything, tended to slow them up.[62]

Britain's singular success in the prosecution of war was unique among European powers. If Britain's rulers feared a standing army because of its associations with absolutism, it did not fear a standing navy. As Michael Mann observes: 'Armies can be used for internal repression, navies cannot. Thus the English Parliament never feared the professional

navy the way it feared standing armies.'[63] More importantly, war finance
was a relatively routine affair since the English ruling class itself controlled
the levying of taxes. In the absolutist states, on the other hand, taxation
was levied on the peasantry without their consent which made the raising
of funds for war an uncertain and potentially explosive undertaking.[64]
British state finances were dominated by war finance. And yet, not once
in the entire century did the state face bankruptcy as a result of war.
From 1700 to 1820, a period which saw six major wars, state expenditure
on war never outstripped its ability to pay. The biggest increase in total
expenditure over peacetime conditions never exceeded 50 per cent and
was considerably lower than the 200 per cent to 1,000 per cent increases
which characterized English war finance in previous centuries. The
systematic way in which debt-repayment overtook military expenditure
in the final years of warfare in every conflict in which Britain was involved
in the eighteenth century, is truly remarkable.[65] Only a society which
was just as systematically generating new sources of wealth could possibly
achieve such a pattern. If the English state had become a 'permanent
war state' in the eighteenth century, as Mann contends,[66] it was because
it was sustained and underwritten by the exceptional vitality of capitalism.

In all of its major aspects – Parliament and the civil service, taxation,
property and criminal law, foreign policy and war – the British state
in the eighteenth century was uniquely suited to the requirements of
capitalism. The corruption of the state during much of the century did
not prove a major hindrance. The fact that the state could withstand
such massive corruption and still serve the needs of capital so effectively
is testimony to this. As Perry Anderson has recently commented:

> no major structural change was needed in the state for the purposes of mill-
> owners or manufacturers. The basic design transmitted by laissez-faire landlords
> proved eminently adaptable and suitable to the needs of the first Industrial
> Revolution. The tensions between aristocratic and bourgeois politics within
> the post-reform framework did not coincide with any conflict over the role
> of the state in the common capitalist economy.[67]

IV. The Anderson–Nairn Thesis

Given this last judgement it is surprising – in Anderson's case especially
– that so much emphasis by Marxist writers has been placed on the supposed *backwardness* of the English state and English capitalism. The
original exposition of this view took place in a series of articles which
sought to provide a comprehensive historical explanation for the looming
social and political crisis of British capitalism in the 1960s.[68] At the centre
of this analysis was the notion that English evolution was marked by

a 'mediated' and less 'pure' variety of capitalist development than elsewhere. Tracing the causes of this to the English Revolution, Anderson
argued that the main protagonists in the revolution were two different
sections of the land-owning class; the ideological expression of the struggle
was religious and not political; and, the main social forces which
triumphed were not urban but rural.[69]

> The distinctive facets of English class structure, as it has evolved over three
> centuries, can thus be summed up as follows. After a bitter cathartic revolution,
> which transformed the structure but not the superstructures of English society,
> a landed aristocracy underpinned by a powerful affinal group, became the first
> dominant class in Britain. This dynamic agrarian capitalism expelled the English
> peasantry from history. Its success was economically the 'floor' and sociologi-
> cally the 'ceiling' of the rise of the industrial bourgeoisie. Undisturbed by a
> feudal state, terrified of the French Revolution and its own proletariat, mes-
> merized by the prestige and authority of the landed class, the bourgeoisie won
> two modest victories (in 1832 and 1846, the Great Reform Act and the repeal
> of the Corn Laws), lost its nerve and ended by losing its identity. The late
> Victorian era and the high noon of imperialism welded aristocracy and bour-
> geoisie together in a simple social bloc. The working class fought passionately
> and unaided against the advent of industrial capitalism; its extreme exhaustion
> after successive defeats was the measure of its efforts. Henceforward it evolved,
> separate but subordinate, within the apparently unshakeable structure of British
> capitalism, unable, despite its great numerical superiority, to transform the
> fundamental nature of British society.[70]

The explicit theme running through the whole of Anderson's account,
then, is that of bourgeois failure. While it is impossible to take up all
of the issues raised by such an analysis, it is worthwhile examining its
implications for the role and nature of the state, since it is supposedly
the unreformed 'superstructures' of British society which explain its relative backwardness vis-à-vis other capitalist states.[71]

As Edward Thompson noted in his initial reply to Anderson and Nairn,
there is 'throughout their analysis an undisclosed model of Other
Countries, whose typological symmetry offers a reproach to British exceptionalism. . . . The Anderson–Nairn model clearly approximates most closely to the French experience, or to a particular interpretation of that
experience. . . .'[72] In Nairn's work we find constant comparisons between
the supposedly 'incomplete' and partial character of the English Revolution and the 'truly modern doctrine of the abstract or "impersonal" state'[73]
which emerged out of the French Revolution. The latter is judged to
be the only genuinely complete bourgeois revolution:

> The most common pattern in the formation of modern states was that the
> middle classes, whether in a social revolution or in a nationalist movement,

turned for help to the people in their effort to throw off the burden of 'traditional society' (absolutism, feudalism, or the imported oppression of colonial regimes). During the 'classic period' the French Revolution had given the sharpest and most influential definition to this conflict. However, developmental priority was to impose and retain quite a different pattern in England. The Civil War of the 1640s was the English conflict that most nearly corresponded to the later model (the 'first bourgeois revolution'). Yet, while ending absolutism and opening the way to capitalism, it had given in many respects the weakest and least influential definition to the general movement which followed in Europe. In spite of its importance, its *political* imprint on subsequent developments was almost nil.[74]

There are, as our earlier analysis has shown, strong reasons for rejecting *both* the proposition that the English state was in some abstract sense 'pre-modern' or backward *and* the view that the 'classic period' of the French Revolution can be elevated to the status of an 'ideal type'. As is typical of such generalizations, Nairn leaves out crucial differences between the English and French Revolutions. When the balance-sheet of the French Revolution is tallied, what is striking are the paradoxes it contains. The *politically* advanced character of the revolution, and to a certain extent, those which succeeded it, were to a large extent an expression of what was yet to be achieved, in capitalist terms, by the bourgeoisie. The revolution was vital to the advance of capitalism. But, in the immediate post-revolutionary era, capitalism advanced haltingly as a result of the revolutionary settlement with the peasantry.

The English Revolution occurred *after* a considerable period of capitalist development. The bourgeoisie had already forged a largely independent economic identity from the monarchy as well as an array of semi-independent political institutions. In France only the beginnings of such a process could be glimpsed. In England, as well, the popular revolution, although crucial to the victory of the bourgeoisie over the Crown, was more decisively defeated than in France. The degree to which ruling classes were able to subordinate popular mobilizations to the aims of the bourgeois leadership, determined to a large extent the relative freedom which the bourgeoisie would enjoy in the pursuit of its interests in the post-revolutionary era. In England, this meant the relatively untrammelled consolidation of capitalism. In France, it meant a period of slow and tortuous advance.

Nairn also exaggerates the modern and impersonal character of the continental states. Marx railed against the pre-modern aspects of the French state for good reason; the parasitism of the French state with a bureaucracy of 670,000 in the 1840s, made the parasitism of Old Corruption look like small potatoes.

It is vital to insist upon these differences since a number of other writers have sought to extend the Anderson–Nairn thesis to cover all of the European states up to 1914. Arno Mayer, for example, has written that

> neither England nor France had become industrial-capitalist and bourgeois civil and political societies by 1914. . . . All alike were *ancien régimes* grounded in the continued predominance of landed elites, agriculture or both.[75]

Anderson himself has recently endorsed a similar view, apparently departing from his earlier position. Of European development up to the First World War, Anderson writes:

> Agriculture remained the largest employer of labour in every country save Britain. Land typically generated the larger part of the revenue of the propertied classes. Industry generally remained small in scale, its principal trades traditional consumer goods – textiles, food or furniture. Modern capital-goods sectors nowhere dominated equity, output or employment in manufacturing. It was on these at best semi-industrialized foundations that the superstructures of aristocratic or notable politics retained their extensive material pedestal.[76]

In contrast with his earlier view, which stressed the relative backwardness of England compared with the ostensibly more progressive bourgeois states of the Continent, Anderson now proclaims that 'agrarian paramountcy' was characteristic of *every* European state down to the First World War.[77] As a generalization, however, this statement tells us very little and may actually obscure the essential *differences* between English and continental development, for we still need to know to what extent these agrarian interests were penetrated by capitalism. Anderson's latest work emphasizes much more than his previous writings the capitalist character of English agriculture and its decisive importance in shaping the English state in the eighteenth and nineteenth centuries.[78] Many of the conclusions he draws now seem to accord with those of his harshest critics, like Thompson and others.

Only now, Anderson locates the sources of English backwardness precisely where others have located its earliest capitalist success: in the early growth and consolidation of agrarian capitalism. As in his earlier analysis, Anderson traces this to the 'incomplete' character of the English revolution which he now, somewhat paradoxically, links with the early defeat of absolutism in England. Rather than seeing the latter as a sign of the strength of capitalism, it is presented as one of the central reasons for the supposed aristocratic backwardness of the Victorian state and beyond:

> The peculiar profile of the English state owed its origins to the interdiction of royal Absolutism in the seventeenth century. The creation of an extensive corps of office-holders heavily, but not exclusively, recruited from the nobility, laid the foundations for the subsequent emergence of a permanent professional

bureaucracy in the continental monarchies. The victory of decentralized gentry rule, through a landowner Parliament and unpaid justices of the peace blocked this path towards a modern state in England. ... Thus neither major army nor bureaucracy was bequeathed by the pre-history of agrarian power in nineteenth century Britain. Nor, on the other hand, did the industrial upheaval that now occurred substantially alter the traditional parameters of the state.[79]

The continental countries, having laid the foundations of the modern state by building up huge central bureaucracies and standing armies during the absolutist era, experienced successive waves of revolution in the nineteenth century, after the initial conquering of power by the bourgeoisie. 'Britain alone,' according to Anderson 'had now never experienced a modern "second revolution", abruptly or radically remoulding the state inherited from the first.'[80] The English Revolution and the subsequent development of the English state we are told, 'slowly modified the structures of traditional power and privilege, without ever radically redrawing them at a stroke.'[81] On the Continent just the opposite occurred:

The experience of every other capitalist state was very different. ... The French Revolution was followed by the Parisian risings of 1830 and 1848, putting an end to the Restoration and the July Monarchy, and by the military defeat and popular insurrection of 1870–71 which ushered in the Third Republic. ... The Bismarckian Monarchy disintegrated in the November Revolution. ... The general significance of these 'revolutions after the revolution' was everywhere the same. They were essentially phases in the modernization of the state, which thereby permitted the reinvigoration of the economy. The most conservative or regressive social elements of the ruling order ... French legitimists, Japanese landlords, Prussian *Junkers*, Italian latifundists – were eliminated amidst a drastic recomposition of the dominant bloc.[82]

In sum then, Anderson's original thesis which contrasted English backwardness with continental 'modernity' has changed very little. Having assimilated aristocratic hegemony in England to a general pattern of aristocratic dominance throughout Europe which prevailed down to the First World War, we are now informed that more or less complete 'bourgeois revolutions' did indeed occur on the Continent but not in England. Even though 'notable politics' survived just as long in countries like France and Germany, it was incapable of holding back the modernization of the state since its influence was undercut by a series of bourgeois revolutionary ruptures in the fabric of civil society. What we are left with in the end is an only slightly modified version of the model of 'other countries' which informed Anderson's earlier analysis, coupled with an account of English 'exceptionalism'. Britain's failure to carry through its 'second revolution' shielded it from the 'gale of creative destruction' that had pushed the continental states along the path towards modern capitalist development.

V. Britain versus the Continent

What is interesting in all of this is that Anderson's most recent account falters and retreats in the face of precisely those historical factors which are most relevant to understanding the contrasting paths of development followed by Britain and the states of continental Europe.

We have argued that bourgeois revolutions should not be judged on the basis of the social forces which made them, or their degree of consciousness, but rather by their consequences. Bourgeois revolutions are political transformations of the state which facilitate the accumulation of capital and the domination of the capitalist class. As a generalization, this definition is sufficiently broad to capture the similarities between the three cases we have examined. But there are obvious differences as well. What form each revolution took had mainly to do with the phase of development of the world economy and how far the internal development of class relations prepared the way for the ascendancy of capitalism.

Thus, if it is at all useful to construct typologies of bourgeois revolutions, it is arguably only England that stands as the 'classic' example in both its form and outcome. England is the 'purest' example of what Marx described as the 'really revolutionizing path' to capitalism. The early development of capitalism out of the ranks of the small producers prepared the ground for the revolutionary coalition which overthrew the Stuart monarchy in 1640. Without the intervention of the 'middle sort of people', comprised of sections of the petty bourgeois urban masses and the yeomanry, the more conservative gentry and big landlords would undoubtedly have sought some compromise with the old order. These were the forces of petty capitalism which ultimately fell victim to their own success. Cromwell turned on the Leveller movement and crushed it decisively. Political defeat paved the way for economic defeat as big landlords began to consolidate large capitalist farms. In terms of its outcome, therefore, the English Revolution was a decisive event in the creation of a political framework, a new type of state, which allowed the more or less unfettered development of capitalism in the eighteenth and nineteenth centuries.

One could well ask, therefore, why Anderson seems to believe that Britain required a second revolution in the first place. As David Nicholls points out:

> Anderson seems to have forgotten here the quintessential point about the English aristocracy. . . . namely, its remarkable wealth, enterprise and longevity

as a *capitalist* class. It is precisely this fact which makes a second revolution unnecessary.[83]

England's lack of a second revolution, should not be seen as a source of its backwardness, but rather as an indication of the advanced character of its capitalist development when set against that of the continental countries. The separation of the state and civil society which was the hallmark of British capitalism from the seventeenth century onwards produced a dual effect: on the one hand, the consolidation of the market as the mechanism through which labour was bought and sold had the effect of masking the true nature of the relations of exploitation between labour and capital. On the other hand, it had the effect of obscuring the class character of the state as well. As Johnson observes, 'it is a feature of the British route that the bourgeois thrust in the domains of production and material life has been masked at the levels of ideology and the state, especially perhaps, at the level of political society and party.'[84]

This does not mean, however, that class struggle was any less a feature of British society than elsewhere. It simply means that the struggle between appropriators and producers over the distribution of economic surplus does not appear as a political struggle, but as one over the conditions of production. Since the state is no longer directly involved in the extraction of surplus, the process of exploitation between capital and wage-labour is concentrated in the 'private sphere' and only indirectly linked to that of the 'public sphere' of the state. Class struggle under capitalism, unlike under pre-capitalist conditions where 'politics' is directly implicated in the exploitation of labour, only becomes *political* when it moves beyond the confines of the individual unit of production to confront the apparently 'autonomous' and 'neutral' forces of the capitalist state. Thus, on the one hand, while capitalism lays the foundations for a higher level of class identity and consciousness by concentrating masses of workers in large units of production, it also more perfectly 'hides' its political and coercive aspects than is possible in pre-capitalist societies and, therefore, acts as a partial break on the development of class-consciousness within the working class.[85] Therefore, while it may be true that the British working class became relatively quiescent after the mid nineteenth century when compared with its counterparts on the Continent, this can be seen as an expression of the more highly advanced character of British capitalism and not the result of an underdeveloped 'socialist' culture amongst British workers.[86]

At best these observations are only partial indicators of some of the material factors which underlay the reformist practices which overtook the British labour movement after 1850. But it is interesting to note that it was at roughly the same point that the state succeeded in removing, in John Saville's words, the last 'obstacles of any significance to the pursuit of profit by the owners of capital'.[87] In addition to this, the ruling class seems to have adopted a less coercive approach to managing the working class. After the defeat of Chartism, employers attempted to replace repression with cooptation, by enticing sections of the working class into an acceptance of Parliamentarism under the guidance of bourgeois parties. Although this strategy had a limited degree of success, it did foreshadow two important developments: the emerging appeal of working-class reformism and the conscious recognition, by sections of the ruling class at least, that the institutional framework for the encouragement of reformism was the price to be paid for social peace.[88]

Attempts to install working-class reformism in the political sphere were in part a response to larger-scale shifts in the balance of forces between capital and labour at the point of production. The development of a highly-skilled industrial working class meant that the potential for the disruption of production in areas such as coal, textiles, and iron and steel was considerable. Employers often had no choice but to accommodate to some extent working-class demands in order to secure cooperation.[89] The net effect of this situation had far-reaching implications:

> The institutionalization of such accommodationist relationships did not of itself prevent British capital from embracing mass production techniques or introducing payment-by-results systems in industry in response to the competitive pressures from the international economy from the 1870s onwards. What it did mean, however, was that any concerted and sustained move in this direction by industrial capital would necessitate a general 'employers' offensive' directed against the most powerful industrial labour movement in Europe and aimed at a radical redrawing of the existing pattern of industrial politics in Britain. This in turn would have required dramatic changes both to the legal framework and the strategical framework of bourgeois politics. Taken together, these could have posed a devastating threat to the carefully constructed edifice of management and negotiation that lay at the core of capital and wage-labour in Britain.[90]

The point that needs emphasizing here is that just as British capitalism was the most advanced in Europe so also was the working class to which it had given birth. The potential power of workers at the point of production set definite limits to the burdens which capital could impose on British workers. It was within the boundaries of these 'structural limits' that capital was forced to operate.[91] Anderson seeks the reasons for British decline in the defects of the ruling class without seriously considering that the relationship between the classes – the dynamics of class struggle – may be the real key.[92]

If England was a 'classic' bourgeois revolution, France represents some-

thing of an intermediate case. Like England, the coalition of small producers and the bourgeoisie was a critical factor in the overthrow of the
ancien régime. But in the case of France, both the petty producers and
the bourgeoisie were much less developed in capitalist terms. However,
the political character of the revolution was, in one sense, more advanced.
The mobilization of the urban and rural masses was certainly more intense
and lasting than in the English Revolution. In part, this was due to the
fact that the old ruling class was more firmly entrenched than in England.
This was complicated by the fact that large sections of the bourgeoisie
were similarly, if to a lesser extent, entrenched in the structures of the
absolutist state. This, of course, had much to do with the form which
the revolution took in its early phases; 'politics' was at a premium because
growing numbers of the bourgeoisie were threatened with exclusion from
political office.

The 'political precocity' of the revolution also anticipated a pattern
which would become much more common in the nineteenth century. As
backward societies sought to close the gap between themselves and more
advanced capitalist countries, the state became the natural ideological
focus for those who aspired to make good their competitive disadvantage
in a comparatively short space of time. 'Rather than rationalizing an
accumulation of existing change, revolutionary programmes become an
attempt to anticipate the desirable future.'[93] But the advanced character
of the revolution also had the paradoxical effect of limiting the expansion
of capitalism in the post-revolutionary period. The bourgeoisie, having
relied on the peasantry and the urban masses to defeat the old ruling
class, was now forced to make major concessions, especially to the
peasantry.

The revolutionary land settlement and the continued reliance of the
state bureaucracy on revenues drawn from landed property meant that
early nineteenth-century capitalism in France was forced along a different
path from that which had been followed by England. The relatively developed character of the merchant capitalist sector, combined with the
growing compulsions of international competition, meant that French
capital was forced to pursue alternative strategies of accumulation which
often combined older forms of artisanal production with newer forms
of productive organization and technique. In its initial phases at least,
French capitalism conformed most closely to what Marxists have come
to refer to as 'Way II', wherein 'the merchant establishes direct sway
over production.'

However, the slow and contradictory development of French capitalism
in the first half of the nineteenth century meant that it still had not
caught up with British capitalism by mid-century. Moreover, the parasitic character of the state still represented a considerable drag on the

expansion of the economy. The revolutionary upheavals of 1830 and 1848 had, in Marx's words, only 'perfected this machine instead of smashing it.' Ironically, it was the Bonapartist state which brought to full fruition the achievements of the French Revolution. It completed 'from above' what the first revolution had begun 'from below'.

Germany, on the other hand, represents a classic example of bourgeois revolution from above. No coalition of petty producers and bourgeois forces combined to overthrow the old aristocratic order in Germany. The effects of 'combined and uneven development' had created a considerable degree of social differentiation between the industrial bourgeoisie and petty producers. Consequently, bourgeois fear of revolution from below often outstripped the desire to engage in revolutionary adventures against absolutism. The failed bourgeois revolution of 1848, as Marx recognized, sowed the seeds of Bismarck's revolution from above.

But there was also another side to the story. Fear of revolution from below only exacerbated the inherent conservatism of leading sections of German liberalism. Many of the leading spokesmen for liberalism in 1848 came from the ranks of the state bureaucracy. Consequently, they displayed a strong ambivalence towards capitalism. In as much as their immediate material interests were tied to the absolutist state, it is understandable that their commitment to a system which was eroding the social foundations of absolutism was, at best, lukewarm. Even so, from the time of Frederick the Great's agrarian reforms, each attempt to renovate absolutism had only further undermined the social structures on which it rested. That was the dilemma faced by Frederick II's advisers when they reported on social conditions which had spawned Britain's agricultural revolution in the eighteenth century.

The contradictory dialectic between the conscious aims of reformers and the actual outcome of their actions can only ultimately be understood in the context of the structural changes which had taken place in the international economy with the triumph of capitalism. By the late eighteenth century, national histories, walled off from the effects of the world economy, were a thing of the past. By the second half of the nineteenth century, Germany was under immense pressure from the bourgeois states which surrounded it. The great achievement of the Bismarck era was that the revolutionary transformation of the German state from above took place at a time when Germany could take the fullest advantage of the expansion of the world economy.

It may be an irony of history that Bismarck's greatest accomplishment was an unintended consequence of the last and perhaps most spectacular attempt to reinvigorate the faltering structure of Prussian absolutism. But the fact that it was unintentional in no way diminishes its revolutionary character from the standpoint of what it meant for the future of capitalism in Germany. 'Bourgeois revolutions', Callinicos argues, 'occur at the intersection between objective historical processes and conscious human agency.'[94] It is a characteristic feature of bourgeois revolutions from above that the gap between the intentions of those who carry through the revolution and its objective consequences tends to be greater than in bourgeois revolutions which involved the active intervention of the bourgeoisie. This should not be surprising, given that revolutions from above have tended to occur in countries (Germany, Meiji Japan) which are relatively economically backward. Consequently, the social forces that prosecute revolutions from above are very often the same social forces that, for generations, resisted the penetration of capitalism.

Seen in this light, the 'revolutions after the revolution' referred to by Anderson are not so neatly linear as his account suggests. In France, the revolutions of 1830 and 1848, were only partially successful in removing the obstacles standing in the way of capitalism. Their 'advanced' political character was more an expression of what remained to be achieved than what they had actually accomplished. Paradoxically, it was when the parasitism of the French state was at its zenith, during the Second Empire, that the most dramatic advances of capitalism occurred. In Germany, as we have seen, the transformation of the state under Bismarck was conditioned by objective circumstances, largely outside the control of the actors involved. Revolution from above was a response to Germany's comparatively late transition to capitalism. Thus, the 'revolutions after the revolution' in both France and Germany serve as a poor yardstick for measuring the supposedly incomplete 'modern "second revolution" of England'.[95]

In conclusion, something should be said about the long-term consequences of the divergent paths of development followed by England and the continental states from the seventeenth century onwards. Both the French and German states played a central role in the development of capitalist infrastructures in the form of rail and communications networks and both states actively encouraged the concentration and cartellization of capital in the last decades of the nineteenth century through tariff and banking policies. The English state, by contrast, played only a minor role in these areas; only in the 1930s did the English state begin to encourage the monopolization of British industry – and then, only half-heartedly.[96] Although the reasons for the declining power of British capitalism in the late nineteenth century are complex, involving, among other factors, shifts in the balance of power between labour and capital, declining foreign investment and obsolete technologies, it seems undeniable that one of the main impediments to the 'rationalization' of British capital was the character of the laissez faire state itself. The British state was accustomed to facilitating the growth of capital through legislation at home and plunder abroad; it was not accustomed to, nor did it have the bureaucratic resources to undertake, intervention in the affairs of capital in order to carry through a large-scale restructuring of the economy. This impediment only became more acute once the rival capitalist powers of the Continent began seriously to challenge British hegemony over the world economy.

By the turn of the twentieth century, the historical roles played by the dominant states of Europe had been reversed. The English state, like much of English capitalism, had begun to suffer from 'the disadvantages of priority'.[97] In the cases of France and Germany, what had formerly been a hindrance to capitalism – their bloated bureaucratic and military state structures – now became superior instruments deployed in the service of capital. For the twentieth century, the full implications of that historic role reversal have indeed been immense.

Notes

1. Brenner, 'The Agrarian Roots of European Capitalism', in T. H. Aston and C. H. E. Philpin, eds., *The Brenner Debate* (Cambridge: Cambridge University Press, 1987), p. 298.

2. Lawrence Stone, *The Causes of the English Revolution* (New York: Harper & Row, 1972), p. 63.

3. Ibid., p. 61; Christopher Hill, *Reformation to Industrial Revolution* (Harmondsworth: Penguin Books, 1969), p. 31.

4. Stone, *Causes*, p. 72.

5. K. W. Smart, *Sale of Offices in the Seventeenth Century* (Utrecht: HES Publishers, 1980), pp. 49–50; Stone, *Causes*, p. 61.

6. Smart, *Sale of Offices*, p. 54.

7. Stone, *Causes*, p. 75.

8. Pauline Gregg, *Black Death to Industrial Revolution* (Harrap, 1976). Quoted in Colin Barker, 'Notes on Pre-Industrial England', Manchester Polytechnic, 1983. (Mimeographed)

9. Perez Zagorin, 'The Social Interpretation of the English Revolution', in Lawrence Stone, ed., *Social Change and Revolution in England, 1540–1640* (London: Longman, 1965), p. 50.

10. Ibid., p. 51.

11. Stone, *Causes*, pp. 118–35.

12. Ibid., p. 137.

13. E. P. Thompson, 'Peculiarities of the English', *Socialist Register* (1965), p. 316.

14. Brian Manning, *The English People and the English Revolution* (Harmondsworth: Penguin Books, 1978), pp. 80–1.

15. Christopher Hill, *The Century of Revolution 1603–1714* (London: Sphere Books, 1973), p. 89.

16. Brian Manning, 'Class and Revolution in Seventeenth Century England', *International Socialism* no. 2:38 (Spring, 1988), p. 50.

17. E. P. Thompson, 'Peculiarities of the English', p. 317.

18. Christopher Hill, 'A Bourgeois Revolution', in J. G. A. Pocock, ed., *Three British Revolutions, 1641, 1688, 1796* (Princeton: Princeton University Press, 1980), p. 116.

19. Ibid., p. 116; Philip Corrigan and Derek Sayer, *The Great Arch* (Oxford: Basil Blackwell, 1985), p. 82.

20. Hill, *Reformation to Industrial Revolution*, pp. 158–61; Corrigan and Sayer, *Great Arch*, p. 83.

21. Hill, 'A Bourgeois Revolution', p. 134.

22. Brenner, 'Agrarian Roots of European Capitalism', p. 299.

23. Colin Brooks, 'Public Finance and Political Stability: The Administration of the Land Tax, 1688–1720', *The Historical Journal* vol. 17, no. 2 (1974), pp. 288–9; William Reginald Ward, *The English Land Tax in the Eighteenth Century* (Oxford: Oxford University Press, 1953), p. 4.

24. Brooks, 'Public Finance', p. 293.

25. Edward Hughes, *Studies in Administration and Finance 1528–1825* (Manchester: Manchester University Press, 1934), p. 122.

26. William Kennedy, *English Taxation 1640–1799* (London: G. Bell and Sons, 1913), p. 72.

27. Brooks, 'Public Finance', p. 283.

28. Ibid., p. 282.

29. Ward, *English Land Tax*, p. 7.

30. Brooks, 'Public Finance', p. 284.

31. The best introduction to the political conflicts of this period and their subsequent decline is J. H. Plumb, *The Growth of Political Stability* (London: Macmillan, 1967). The link between the Land Tax and 'political stability' forms the main theme of Brooks's analysis of public finance, though he does not explicitly connect this with the development of capitalism on the land.

32. Brooks, 'Public Finance', p. 300.

33. Ward, *English Land Tax*, p. 176.

34. Hughes, *Studies*, pp. 294–312.

35. Smart, *Sales of Offices*, p. 61; A similar view can be found in P. G. M. Dickson and J. Sparling, 'War Finance, 1689–1714', in J. S. Bromley, ed., *The New Cambridge Modern History* (Cambridge: Cambridge University Press, 1975). They argue that war taxation gave rise to a general pattern of state finance such that 'its consequences were European and not merely of English extent, leading, at the expense of the smaller gentry and peasantry, to consolidation of the great landowners, financiers and merchants, and the state bureaucracies which everywhere in Europe after 1715 were extending their scope and power.'

36. See Kennedy, *English Taxation*, pp. 99–101.

37. Corrigan and Sayer, *Great Arch*, p. 89.

38. E.P. Thompson, 'Eighteenth Century English Society: Class Struggle Without Class?', *Social History* vol. 3, no. 2 (May, 1978), p. 139.

39. Thompson, 'Eighteenth Century English Society', p. 139.

40. Roy Porter, *English Society in the Eighteenth Century* (London: Pelican Books, 1982), p. 132.

41. Thompson, 'Eighteenth Century English Society', p. 141.

42. See Corrigan and Sayer, *Great Arch*, p. 91.

43. Dickson and Sparling, 'War Finance', p. 285.

44. Ibid., p. 286.

45. E. P. Thompson, 'Patrician Society, Plebeian Culture', *Journal of Social History* (Summer, 1974), p. 402.

46. Thompson, 'Eighteenth Century English Society', p. 162.

47. Thompson, 'Peculiarities of the English', p. 317.

48. See H. J. Habakkuk, 'English Landownership, 1680–1740', *Economic History Review* vol. 9 (1940); Porter, *English Society*, pp. 70–1.

49. J. D. Chambers and G. E. Mingay, *The Agricultural Revolution 1750–1850* (London: Batsford, 1966), p. 84.

50. William Lazonick, 'Karl Marx and Enclosures in England', *The Review of Radical Political Economics* vol. 6, no. 2 (Summer, 1974), pp. 26–7.

51. Corrigan and Sayer, *Great Arch*, p. 87.

52. Porter, *English Society*, p. 100.

53. John Saville, 'Primitive Accumulation and Early Industrialization in Britain', in Ralph Miliband and John Saville, eds., *The Socialist Register* (1969).

54. Eric Hobsbawm, *Industry and Empire* (Harmondsworth: Penguin Books, 1983), p. 39.

55. Ibid., pp. 47–8.

56. Porter, *English Society*, p. 150.

57. On this point, see the important essay by Douglas Hay, 'Property, Authority and Criminal Law', in D. Hay et al, *Albion's Fatal Tree: Crime and Society in Eighteenth Century England* (New York: Pantheon Books, 1975).

58. E. P. Thompson, *Whigs and Hunters* (Harmondsworth: Penguin Books, 1977), pp. 206–7.

59. Corrigan and Sayer, *Great Arch*, p. 100; Thompson, 'Patrician Society', pp. 388–90.

60. Hay, 'Property', pp. 62–3.

61. Perry Anderson, 'Figures of Descent', *New Left Review* 161 (January–February, 1987), p. 36.

62. Hobsbawm, *Industry and Empire*, pp. 49–50.

63. Michael Mann, *States, Wars and Capitalism* (Oxford: Basil Blackwell, 1988), pp. 116–17.

64. Ibid., pp. 117–18.

65. Ibid., p. 108. Mann provides a graph, charting war and debt expenditures for the British state in the eighteenth century, on p. 106.

66. Ibid., p. 108.

67. Anderson, 'Figures', p. 36.

68. The original articles published in *New Left Review* were: Tom Nairn, 'The British Political Elite', and Perry Anderson, 'Origins of the Present Crisis', in *NLR* 23 (January–February 1964); Tom Nairn, 'The English Working Class', *NLR* 24, (March–April 1964); Tom Nairn, 'The Anatomy of the Labour Party', *NLR* 27–8 (September–October and November–December, 1964). The main response to the position developed in these articles was contained in Thompson, 'Peculiarities', republished in *The Poverty of Theory* (New York: Monthly Review Press, 1978). Further articles included Perry Anderson, 'Socialism and Pseudo-Empiricism', *NLR* 35 (January–February 1966) and 'Components of the National Culture', *NLR* 50 (July–August 1968); Tom Nairn, 'The British Meridian', *NLR* 60 (March–April 1970) and 'The Twilight of the British State', *NLR* 101 (February–April, 1976). The latter is also contained in Tom Nairn, *The Break-Up of Britain* (London: Verso, 1977).

69. Anderson, 'Origins', p. 28.

70. Ibid., pp. 38–9.

71. There are two general summaries of the original Anderson–Nairn–Thompson debate which are exceptionally useful in illuminating some of the broader issues at stake. See Keith Neld, 'A Symptomatic Dispute? Notes on the Relation between Marxian Theory and Historical Practice in Britain', *Social Research* vol. 47, no. 3 (Fall, 1980) and Richard Johnson, 'Barrington Moore, Perry Anderson and English Social Development', in Stuart Hall, ed., *Culture, Media, Language* (London: Hutchinson, 1984).

72. Thompson, 'Peculiarities', p. 312.

73. Nairn, *Breakup of Britain*, p. 17.

74. Ibid., p. 30.

75. Arno Mayer, *The Persistence of the Old Regime* (New York: Pantheon Books, 1981), p. 11. Still others have attempted to broaden the scope of the original thesis put forward by Anderson and Nairn specifically with regard to Britain. Two notable works are: Colin Leys, *Politics in Britain* (London: Heinemann, 1983). Leys's debt to Anderson and Nairn is explicit: 'Anderson and Nairn grasped and articulated the existence of a crisis in a way that has hardly been surpassed almost two decades later', p. 13; Martin J. Weiner, *English Culture and The Decline of the Industrial Spirit 1850–1980* (Cambridge: Cambridge University Press, 1981). This work, like Mayer's, places much emphasis on the influence of elite culture on economic and political development.

76. Anderson, 'Figures', p. 27.

77. Ibid., p. 26.

78. Ibid., pp. 28–36.

79. Ibid., p. 37.

80. Ibid., p. 47.

81. Ibid., p. 48.

82. Ibid., p. 48.

83. David Nicholls, 'A Subordinate Bourgeoisie? The Question of Hegemony in Modern British Capitalist Society', in Colin Barker and David Nicholls, eds., *The Development of British Capitalist Society: a Marxist Debate* (Manchester: Northern Marxist Historians Group, 1988), p. 49.

84. Johnson, 'English Social Development', p. 62.

85. See Ellen Wood, 'The Separation of the Economic and Political in Capitalism', *New Left Review* 127 (May–June, 1981), pp. 92–3.

86. See Anderson, 'Figures', pp. 48–51.

87. John Saville, 'Some Notes on Perry Anderson's "Figures of Descent" ', *Development of British Capitalist Society*, p. 36.

88. Robert Looker, 'Shifting trajectories: Perry Anderson's Changing Account of the Pattern of English Historical Development', *Development of British Capitalist Society*, pp. 18–19.

89. Ibid., p. 20.

90. Ibid., p. 20.

91. Ibid., p. 21.

92. David Coates, 'In Pursuit of the Anderson Thesis', *Development of British Capitalist Society*, p. 75.

93. David Blackbourn and Geoff Eley, *The Peculiarities of German History* (New York: Oxford University Press, 1984), p. 86.

94. Alex Callinicos, 'Bourgeois Revolutions and Historical Materialism', *International Socialism*, no. 43 (June, 1989), p. 126.

95. Ibid., p. 47.

96. See Eric Hobsbawm, *Industry and Empire*, pp. 225–48. Similar points are made by Anderson, 'Figures', on pp. 37–8, 42–3.

97. Alex Callinicos, 'Exception or Symptom? The British Crisis and the World System', *New Left Review* 169 (May–June, 1988), p. 103.

Bibliography

This bibliography is divided into four sections: the first section deals with sources on general theory and history; the second with France; the third with sources on Germany; and the last with sources on England.

General Theory and History

Abrams, Philip. *Historical Sociology.* London: Open Books, 1982.
Anderson, Perry. *Lineages of the Absolutist State.* London: Verso, 1979.
—— *Passages From Antiquity to Feudalism.* London: Verso, 1978.
—— *Arguments Within English Marxism.* London: Verso, 1980.
Andrews, Bruce. 'The Political Economy of World Capitalism:Theory and Practice', *International Organization* vol. 36, no. 1, 1982. pp. 135–51.
Balibar, Étienne. 'The Basic Concepts of Historical Materialism', in *Reading Capital* translated by Ben Brewster. London: Verso, 1979.
Banaji, Jairus. 'Modes of Production in a Materialist Conception of History', *Capital and Class* 3, 1977. pp. 1–42.
—— 'Gunder Frank in Retreat?' *Journal of Peasant Studies* vol. 7, no. 4, 1980. pp. 514–18.
—— 'The Peasantry in the Feudal Mode of Production: Towards an Economic Model', *Journal of Peasant Studies* vol.3, 3, 1976. pp. 299–521.
Barker, Colin. 'A Note on the Theory of Capitalist States', *Capital and Class* 1978.
Blackburn, Robin. *The Overthrow of Colonial Slavery.* London: Verso, 1988.
Blum, Jerome. *The End of the Old Order in Rural Europe.* Princeton: Princeton University Press, 1978.
Bois, Guy. 'Against Neo-Malthusian Orthodoxy.' In T. H. Ashton and C. H.

E. Philpin, eds., *The Brenner Debate*, Cambridge: Cambridge University Press, 1987.

Braudel, Fernand. *The Wheels of Commerce: Civilization and Capitalism, 15th to the 18th Century.* New York: Harper and Row, 1982.

—— *Afterthoughts On Capitalism and Material Life.* New York: Harper and Row, 1977.

Brenner, Robert. 'Agrarian Class Structure and Economic Development in Pre-Industrial Europe.' T. H. Ashton and C. H. E. Philpin, eds., *The Brenner Debate.* Cambridge: Cambridge University Press, 1987. pp. 10–63.

—— 'The Origins of Capitalist Development: A Critique of Neo-Smithian Marxism.' *New Left Review*, 104, 1977. pp. 25–92.

—— 'The Agrarian Roots of European Capitalism.' *The Brenner Debate.* pp. 213–325.

—— 'Dobb on the Transition from Feudalism to Capitalism.' *Cambridge Journal of Economics* 2, 1978. pp. 121–40.

—— 'The Social Basis of Economic Development.' In John Roemer, ed., *Analytic Marxism.* Cambridge: Cambridge University Press, 1986.

Burke, Peter., ed., *Economy and Society in Early Modern Europe.* London: Routledge & Kegan Paul, 1972.

Callinicos, Alex. *Is There A Future For Marxism?* London: Macmillan Press, 1982.

Chase-Dunn, Christopher. 'Interstate System and Capitalist World-Economy: One Logic or Two.' *International Studies Quarterly* vol. 25 no. 1, 1981.

Clarke, Simon. 'Althusserian Marxism.' In *One-DimensionalMarxism: Althusser and the Politics of Culture.* London: Allison and Busby, 1980. pp. 7–102.

—— 'Socialist Humanism and the Critique of Economism.' *History Workshop Journal*, 8, 1979. pp. 137–56.

Cohen, G. A. *Karl Marx's Theory of History: A Defence.* Oxford: Clarendon Press, 1978.

Colletti, Lucio. 'Bernstein and the Marxism of the Second International.' In *From Rousseau to Lenin: Studies in Ideology and Society.* trans. John Merrington and Judith White. New York: Monthly Review Press, 1972.

Clay, G. A. *Economic Expansion and Social Change 1500–1700.* Cambridge: Cambridge University Press, 1984.

Croot, Patricia and Parker, David. 'Agrarian Class Structure and Economic Development.' *Past and Present*, 78, 1978. pp. 37–46.

Dobb, Maurice. *Studies in the Development of Capitalism.* New York: International Publishers, 1963.

—— 'A Reply.' In *The Transition From Feudalism to Capitalism*, ed. Rodney Hilton. London: Verso, 1978. pp. 57–67.

Draper, Hal. *Karl Marx's Theory of Revolution: State and Bureaucracy* vol. 1. New York: Monthly Review Press, 1977.

—— *Karl Marx's Theory of Revolution: The Politics of Social Classes* vol. 2. New York: Monthly Review Press, 1978.

Droz, Jacques. *Europe Between Revolutions 1815–1848.* London: Fontana Press, 1985.

Dyson, Kenneth. *The State Tradition in Western Europe.* Oxford: Martin Robertson, 1980.

Engels, Frederick. *The Role of Force in History.* New York: International Publishers, 1968.

—— *Anti-Dühring.* Moscow: Progress Publishers, 1954.

—— *The Origins of the Family, Private Property and the State.* Moscow: Progress Publishers, 1977.

Fulbrook, Mary and Skocpol, Theda. 'Destined Pathways: The Historical Sociology of Perry Anderson.' In *Vision and Method in Historical Sociology,* ed. Theda Skocpol. New York: Cambridge University Press, 1984.

George, C. H. 'The Origins of Capitalism: A Marxist Epitome and A Critique of Immanuel Wallerstein's Modern World System.' *Marxist Perspectives* 3, 1980. pp. 71–100.

Grenville, J. A. S. *Europe Reshaped 1848–1878.* London: Fontana Books, 1976.

Gunder Frank, André. *Capitalism and Underdevelopment in Latin America.* New York: Monthly Review Press, 1969.

—— *World Accumulation 1492–1789.* New York: Monthly Review Press, 1978.

Gourevitch, Peter. 'The International System and Regime Formation.' *Comparative Politics* vol. 10, 1978. pp. 419–38.

Hegel, G.W.F. *The Philosophy of Right,* ed. T. M. Knox. Oxford: Oxford University Press, 1952.

Hechter, Michael. 'Lineages of the Capitalist State.' *American Journal of Sociology* vol. 82, no. 5, pp. 1057–85.

Hilton, Rodney, ed. *The Transition From Feudalism to Capitalism.* London: Verso, 1978.

Hilton, Rodney. *Bond Men Made Free: Medieval Peasant Movements and the English Rising of 1381.* London: Methuen, 1973.

—— *The English Peasantry in the Later Middle Ages.* Oxford: Oxford University Press, 1975.

—— 'A Crisis of Feudalism.' *Past and Present* 78, 1980.

—— 'Feudalism in Europe: Problems for Historical Materialists.' *New Left Review,* 147, 1984.

Hill, Christopher. *Reformation to Industrial Revolution.* Harmondsworth: Penguin Books, 1969.

—— *The Century of Revolution 1603–1714.* London: Sphere Books, 1973.

Hobsbawm, Eric. 'The Crisis of the Seventeenth Century.' In *Crisis in Europe 1560–1660.* ed. Trevor Aston. London: Routledge & Kegan Paul, 1965.

—— *The Age of Revolution.* London: Abacus, 1977.

—— *The Age of Capital.* London: Abacus, 1977.

—— *Industry and Empire.* Harmondsworth: Penguin Books, 1983.

Holton, Robert J. 'Marxist Theories of Social Change and the Transition From Feudalism to Capitalism.' *Theory and Society* vol. 10, 1981. pp. 854–62.

Hindess, Barry and Hirst, Paul. *Pre-Capitalist Modes of Production.* London: Routledge & Kegan Paul, 1975.

Hussain, Athar and Tribe, Keith. *Marxism and the Agrarian Question.* 2 vols. London: Macmillan, 1981.

Hussain, Athar *et al. Marx's Capital and Capitalism Today.* London: Routledge & Kegan Paul, 1977.

Jessop, Bob. *The Capitalist State.* Oxford: Martin Robertson, 1982.

Jones, Gareth Stedman. 'Society and Politics at the Beginning of the World Economy.' *Cambridge Journal of Economics* 1, 1977. pp. 77–92.

Kiernan, Victor. *State and Society in Europe 1550–1650.* New York: St. Martin's Press, 1980.

Kindelberger, Charles. *A Financial History of Western Europe.* London: George Allen and Unwin, 1984.

Kula, Witold. *An Economic Theory of the Feudal System.* London: Verso, 1976.

Laclau, Ernesto. *Politics and Ideology in Marxist Theory.* London: Verso, 1979.

Landes, David. *The Unbound Prometheus: Technological Change and Industrial Development in Western Europe from 1760 to the Present.* Cambridge: Cambridge University Press, 1969.

Lenin, V. I. *The Development of Capitalism in Russia.* Moscow: Progress Publishers, 1977.

Lis, C. and Soly, H. *Poverty and Capitalism in Pre-Industrial Europe.* New Jersey: Humanities Press, 1979.

Mair, Charles. *Recasting Bourgeois Europe.* Princeton: Princeton University Press, 1975.

Marx, Karl. *Capital* 3 vols. Moscow: Vintage Books 1977.

—— *Theories of Surplus-Value.* Moscow: Progress Publishers, 1977.

—— *The German Ideology.* New York: International Publishers, 1974.

—— *The Grundrisse.* Harmondsworth: Penguin Books, 1973.

—— 'Russia's Pattern of Development.' In *Marx and Engels: Basic Writings on Politics and Philosophy*, ed. Lewis S. Feuer. New York: Doubleday, 1959. pp. 438–40.

—— 'A Contribution to the Critique of Political Economy.' In *Marx and Engels: Basic Writings on Politics and Philosophy*, ed. Lewis S. Feuer. New York: Doubleday, 1959. pp. 42–7.

—— *The Poverty of Philosophy.* Moscow: Progress Publishers, 1975.

—— 'The Eighteenth Brumaire of Louis Bonaparte.' In *Surveys From Exile*, ed. David Fernbach. Harmondsworth: Penguin Books, 1977. pp. 143–225.

—— 'The Class Struggles in France 1848 to 1850.' In *Surveys From Exile*, ed. David Fernbach. Harmondsworth: Penguin Books, 1977. pp. 35–142.

Mathias, Peter and Postan, M.M., eds. *The Cambridge Economic History of Europe: The Industrial Economies* vol. VII. Cambridge: Cambridge University Press, 1977.

Mayer, Arno. *The Persistence of the Old Regime.* New York: Pantheon Books, 1981.

McNally, David. *Political Economy and the Rise of Capitalism: A Reinterpretation.* Berkeley: University of California Press, 1988.

Merrington, John. 'Town and Country in the Transition to Capitalism.' In *The Transition From Feudalism to Capitalism*, ed. Rodney Hilton. London: Verso, 1978. pp. 170–95.

Moore, Barrington. *The Social Origins of Dictatorship and Democracy.* Boston: Beacon Press, 1966.

Nell, E. J. *Growth, Profits and Property.* Cambridge: Cambridge University Press, 1980.

Polanyi, Karl. *The Great Transformation.* Boston: Beacon Press, 1957.

Pirenne, Henri. *Medieval Cities.* New York: Doubleday Anchor Books, 1956.

—— *Economic and Social History of Medieval Europe.* London: Routledge & Kegan Paul, 1978.

Postan, Michael. *The Medieval Economy and Society.* London: Penguin Books, 1975.

Poulantzas, Nicos. *Political Power and Social Classes.* London: Verso, 1978.

Rosdolsky, Roman. *The Making of Marx's Capital.* London: Pluto Press, 1977.

Rudé, George. *Revolutionary Europe 1783–1815.* New York: Meridian Books, 1964.

—— *Ideology and Popular Protest.* New York: Pantheon Books, 1980.

Sayer, Derek. *Marx's Method: Ideology, Science and Critique in 'Capital'.* Brighton: Harvester Press, 1983.

Supple, Barry. 'The State and the Industrial Revolution 1700–1914.' In *The Fontana Economic History of Europe.* ed. Carlo M. Cipolla. London: Fontana, 1973. pp. 301–57.

Skocpol, Theda. *States and Social Revolutions.* Cambridge: Cambridge University Press, 1979.

—— 'Wallerstein's World Capitalist System: A Theoretical and Historical Critique.' *American Journal of Sociology* vol. 82, 5, 1977. pp. 1075–90.

—— and Trimberger, Kay. 'Revolutions and the World-Historical Development of Capitalism.' *Berkeley Journal of Sociology* 22, 1977–8. pp. 101–13.

—— 'A Critical Review of Barrington Moore's Social Origins of Dictatorship and Democracy.' *Politics and Society* vol. 4, 1, 1973. pp. 1–34.

Sweezy, Paul. 'A Critique.' In *The Transition From Feudalism to Capitalism,* ed. Rodney Hilton. London: Verso, 1978. pp. 33–56.

Takahashi, Kahachiro. 'A Contribution to the Discussion.' In *The Transition From Feudalism to Capitalism.* London: Verso, 1978.

Taylor, John G. *From Modernization to Modes of Production.* London: Macmillan, 1979.

Tilly, Charles., ed. *The Formation of National States in Western Europe.* Princeton: Princeton University Press, 1975.

Therborn, Goran. *What Does The Ruling Class Do When It Rules?* London: Verso, 1978.

Tribe, Keith. *Geneologies of Capitalism.* Atlantic Highlands, New Jersey: Humanities Press, 1981.

Williams, E. N. *The Ancien Régime In Europe.* Harmondsworth: Penguin Books, 1972.

Wallerstein, Immanuel. *The Modern World System: Capitalist Agriculture and the Origins of the European World Economy in the Sixteenth Century* vol. 1. New York: Academic Press, 1974.

—— *The Modern World System.* vol. 2. New York: Academic Press, 1976.

—— 'The Rise and Future Demise of the Capitalist World System: Concepts for Comparative Analysis.' *Comparative Studies in Society and History* 4, 1974. pp. 387–415.

—— *Historical Capitalism*. London: Verso, 1983.

Watts, Sheldon. *A Social History of Western Europe 1450–1720*. London: Hutchinson, 1984.

Weber, Max. *Economy and Society*, ed. G. Roth and C. Wittich. New York: Bedminster Books, 1968.

Wood, Ellen Meiksens. 'The Separation of the Economic and the Political in Capitalism.' *New Left Review* 127, 1981. pp. 66–95.

France

Aminzade, Ronald. 'Reinterpreting Capitalist Industrialization: A Study of Nineteenth Century France.' *Social History*. vol. 9, 3, 1984. pp. 329–50.

Behrens, C.B.A. *The Ancien Régime*. London: Harcourt and Brace, 1967.

Bergeron, Louis. *France Under Napoleon*. trans. R.R. Palmer. Princeton: Princeton University Press, 1981.

Bloch, Marc. *French Rural History*, trans. Janet Sondheimer. London: Routledge & Kegan Paul, 1966.

Bois, Guy. *Crise du Feodalisme*. Paris: Presses de la Fondation Nationale Des Sciences Politiques, 1976.

Bois, Paul. *Paysans de l'Ouest*. Paris: Mouton, 1960.

Bosher, John. *French Finances 1770–1795: From Business to Bureaucracy*. Cambridge: Cambridge University Press, 1970.

Bury, J. P. T. *Napoleon III and the Second Empire*. New York: Harper and Row, 1964.

Callinicos, Alex. 'Bourgeois Revolutions and Historical Materialism.' *International Socialism*. no. 43, 1989, p. 143.

Carlisle, Robert B. 'Saint-Simonian Radicalism: A Definition and a Direction.' *French Historical Studies*. vol. 5, no. 4, 1968. pp. 430–45.

Church, Clive. *Revolution and Red Tape: The French Ministerial Bureaucracy 1770–1850*. Oxford: Oxford University Press, 1981.

—— *Europe in 1830: Revolution and Political Change*. London: George Allen and Unwin, 1983.

—— 'The Social Basis of the French Central Bureaucracy Under the Directory 1795–1799.' *Past and Present* 36, 1967. pp. 59–72.

—— 'In Search of the Directory.' In *French Government and Society 1500–1850*, ed. J. F. Bosher. London: Athlone Press, 1973.

Clapham, J. H. *Economic Development in France and Germany*. Cambridge: Cambridge University Press, 1963.

Clout, Hugh D. *The Land of France 1815–1914*. London: George Allen and Unwin, 1983.

Cobban, Alfred. *A History of Modern France 1789–1871*. Harmondsworth: Penguin Books, 1965.

—— *The Social Interpretation of the French Revolution.* Cambridge: Cambridge University Press, 1968.

Comninel, George C. *Rethinking the French Revolution: Marxism and the Revisionist Challenge.* London: Verso, 1987.

De Tocqueville, Alexis. *The Old Regime and the French Revolution*, trans. Stuart Gilbert. New York: Anchor Books, 1955.

Doyle, William. 'Was There An Aristocratic Reaction in Pre-Revolutionary France?' In *French Society and the Revolution*, ed. Douglas Johnson. Cambridge: Cambridge University Press, 1976.

—— *Origins of the French Revolution.* New York: Oxford University Press, 1980.

Dupeux, Georges. *French Society 1789–1970*, trans. Peter Wait. London: Methuen, 1976.

Ellis, Geoffrey. 'The "Marxist Interpretation" of the French Revolution.' *English Historical Review*, vol.9, 367, 1978. pp. 353–76.

Farmer, Paul. 'The Second Empire in France.' *The New Cambridge Modern History Vol. 10.* ed. J. P. T. Bury. Cambridge: Cambridge University Press, 1960.

Fisher, H. A. L. *Bonapartism.* Oxford: Oxford University Press, 1961.

Forster, Robert. *The Nobility of Toulouse.* Baltimore: Johns Hopkins Press, 1960.

—— 'Survival of the Nobility During the French Revolution.' In *French Society and the Revolution.* ed. Douglas Johnson. Cambridge: Cambridge University Press, 1976. pp. 130–52.

—— and Ranum, Orest. *Rural Society in France.* Baltimore: Johns Hopkins Press, 1977.

Fox-Genovese, Elizabeth and Genovese, Eugene. *The Fruits of Merchant Capital.* New York: Monthly Review Press, 1983.

Furet, François. *Interpreting the French Revolution.* Cambridge: Cambridge University Press, 1979.

Goubert, Pierre. *The Ancien Régime.* trans. Steve Cox. London: Weidenfeld and Nicolson, 1973.

—— *Louis XIV and Twenty Million Frenchmen.* trans. Ann Carter. New York: Vintage Books, 1970.

—— 'The French Peasantry in the Seventeenth Century: A Regional Example.' In Isser Woloch, ed. *The Peasantry in the Old Regime.* New York: Robert Krieger Publishing, 1977.

Hampson, *A Social History of the French Revolution.* Toronto: University of Toronto Press, 1963.

Hobsbawm, Eric. 'The Making of a "Bourgeois Revolution"'. *Social Research* vol. 56, no. 1, 1989.

Hunt, David. 'Peasant Politics in the French Revolution.' *Social History.* vol. 9, 3, 1984. pp. 277–99.

Johnson, Christopher. 'The Revolution of 1830 in French Economic History.' In *1830 In France.* ed. John M. Merriman. New York: New Viewpoints, 1975.

Jones, P.M. *The Peasantry in the French Revolution.* Cambridge: Cambridge University Press, 1988.

Kemp, Tom. *Economic Forces in French History.* London: Dobson Books, 1971.

Lefebvre, Georges. *The French Revolution: From its Origins to 1793*. 2 vols., trans. Elizabeth Moss Evanson. New York: Columbia University Press, 1962.

—— *The Coming of the French Revolution*. trans. R. R. Palmer. Princeton: Princeton University Press, 1967.

Le Goff, T. J. A. *Vannes and Its Region: A Study of Town and Country in Eighteenth Century France*. Oxford: Oxford University Press, 1981.

Le Roy Ladurie, Emmanuel. *The Peasants of Languedoc*, trans. John Day. Urbana: University of Illinois Press, 1974.

Lublinskaya, A. D. *French Absolutism: The Crucial Phase 1620–1629*. Cambridge: Cambridge University Press, 1967.

Lucas, Colin. 'Nobles, Bourgeois and the Origins of the French Revolution.' *Past and Present* 60, 1973.

McGarr, Paul *et al. Marxism and the Great French Revolution*. Special Issue, *International Socialism* 43, June 1989.

Magraw, Roger. *France 1815–1914: The Bourgeois Century*. Oxford: Fontana, 1983.

Mandrou, Robert. 'Porchnev, Mousnier and the Significance of Popular Uprisings.' In *The Peasantry In the Old Regime*, trans. Linda Kimmel and Isser Woloch. New York: Robert Krieger Publishing, 1977.

Mousnier, Roland. 'The Financial *Officers* During the Fronde.' In *France in Crisis 1620–1675*. ed. P. J. Coveney. London: Macmillan, 1977. pp.136–68.

—— 'Conjuncture and Circumstance in Popular Uprisings.' In *The Peasantry In the Old Regime*, trans. and ed. Linda Kimmel and Isser Woloch. New York: Robert Krieger Publishing, 1977.

Napoleon III, *Napoleonic Ideas*, ed. Brison D. Gooch. New York: Harper Torchbooks, 1967.

Palmade, Guy. *French Capitalism in the Nineteenth Century*. Newton Abbot: David and Charles, 1972.

Parker, David. *The Making of French Absolutism*. London: Edward Arnold, 1983.

—— 'The Social Foundation of French Absolutism.' *Past and Present* 53, 1971. pp. 67–89.

Pinkney, David. *The French Revolution of 1830*. Princeton: Princeton University Press, 1972.

—— 'The Myth of the Revolution of 1830.' In *A Fetschrift for Frederick B. Artz*. Durham, N.C.: Duke University Press, 1964.

Porchnev, Boris. 'The Bourgeoisie and Feudal-Absolutism in Seventeenth Century France.' In *France in Crisis 1620–1675*, trans. and ed. P. J. Coveney. London: Macmillan, 1977. pp. 103–35.

—— 'Popular Uprisings in France Before the Fronde.' In *France In Crisis 1620–1675*, trans. and ed. P. J. Coveney. London: Macmillan, 1977. pp.78–102.

Price, Roger. *The Economic Modernization of France 1730–1880*. London: Croom Helm, 1975.

Ratcliffe, Barrie M. 'Napoleon III and the Anglo-French Commercial Treaty of 1860: A Reconsideration.' *The Journal of European Economic History*, vol. 2, 3, 1973. pp. 582–613.

Salmon, J. H. M. *Society in Crisis: France in the Sixteenth Century.* London: Methuen, 1975.
—— 'Venality of Office and Popular Sedition in Seventeenth Century France.' *Past and Present* 37, 1967. pp. 21–43.
Sewell, William. *Work and Revolution in France 1789–1848.* Cambridge: Cambridge University Press, 1980.
Skocpol, Theda. 'Reconsidering the French Revolution in World-Historical Perspective.' *Social Research* vol. 56, 1, 1989.
Soboul, Albert. *The French Revolution 1787–1799*, trans. Alan Forrest and Colin Jones. New York: Vintage Books,1974.
—— 'Du feodalisme au capitalisme: la Revolution française et la problematique des vois de passage,' *La Pensee* 196, 1977.
—— *The Sans-Culottes*, trans. Remy Inglis Hall. Princeton: Princeton University Press, 1980.
Sutherland, D. M. G. *France 1789–1815: Revolution and Counter-revolution.* London: Fontana, 1985.
—— *The Chouans: The Social Origins of Popular Counter-Revolution in Upper Brittany.* Oxford: Oxford University Press, 1982.
Taylor, George V. 'Types of Capitalism in Eighteenth Century France.' *English Historical Review*, vol. 79, July 1964. pp. 479 97.
—— 'The Paris Bourse on the Eve of the Revolution.' *American Historical Review*, vol. 67, no. 3, 1962. pp. 951–77.
—— 'Non-Capitalist Wealth and the Origins of the French Revolution.' *American Historical Review*, vol. 72, no. 2, 1967. pp. 469–96.
Vovelle, Michel. *The Fall of the French Monarchy 1787–1792.* Cambridge: Cambridge University Press, 1987.
Wallerstein, Immanuel. 'The French Revolution as a World-Historical Event.' *Social Research*, vol. 56, no. 1, 1989.
Weber, Eugen. *Peasants into Frenchmen: The Modernization of Rural France, 1870–1914.* Stanford: Stanford University Press, 1976.

Germany

Anderson, Margaret and Barkin, Kenneth. 'The Myth of the Puttkamer Purge and the Reality of Kulturkampf: Some Reflections on the Historiography of Imperial Germany.' *Journal of Modern History*, vol. 54, no. 4, 1982. pp. 617–85.
Benecke, G. *Society and Politics in Germany 1500–1750.* Toronto: University of Toronto Press, 1974.
Behrens, C. B. H. *Society, Government and Enlightenment: The Experience of Eighteenth Century France and Prussia.* London: Thames and Hudson, 1985.
Blackbourn, David and Eley, Geoff. *The Peculiarities of German History.* Oxford: Oxford University Press, 1984.
Blackbourn, David. 'The *Mittelstand* in German Society and Politics, 1871–1914.' *Social History* 4, 1977. pp. 409–33.
Blickle, Peter. 'Peasant Revolts in the German Empire in the Late Middle Ages.' *Social History*, vol.4, no. 1, 1979. pp. 223–39.

Bog, Igomar. 'Mercantilism in Germany.' In *Revisions in Mercantilism*, ed. D. C. Coleman. London: Methuen, 1969.

Bohme, Helmut. *An Introduction to the Social and Economic History of Germany*, trans. W. R. Lee. Oxford: Basil Blackwell, 1979.

Born, Karl Erich. 'Structural Changes in German Social and Economic Development at the End of the Nineteenth Century.' In *Imperial Germany*, ed. James J. Sheehan. New York: New Viewpoints, 1976.

Braun, Rudolph. 'Taxation, Socio-Political Structure and State-Building: Great Britain and Brandenburg-Prussia.' In *The Formation of National States in Western Europe*, ed. Charles Tilley. Princeton: Princeton University Press, 1975.

Caplan, Jane. ' "The Imaginary Universality of Particular Interests": the "Tradition" of the Civil Service in German History.' *Social History*, vol. 4, no. 2, 1979. pp. 299–317.

Carsten, F. L. *The Origins of Prussia*. Oxford: Oxford University Press, 1954.

Catt, Cathleen. 'Farmers and Factory Workers: Rural Society In Germany, The Example of Maudach.' In *The German Peasantry*, ed. Richard Evans. New York: St Martin's Press, 1986.

Dahrendorf, Ralf. *Society and Democracy in Germany*. New York: Anchor, 1969.

Dickler, R. A. 'Organization and Change in Productivity in Eastern Prussia.' In *European Peasants and Their Markets*, ed. W. N. Parker and E. L. Jones. Princeton: Princeton University Press, 1975.

Dorn, W. L. 'The Prussian Bureaucracy in the Eighteenth Century.' *Political Science Quarterly*, 46, 1931; 47, 1932.

Eley, Geoff. 'Memories of Under-Development: Social History in Germany.' *Social History*, October 1977. pp. 785–91.

—— 'Capitalism and the Wilhelmine State: Industrial Growth and Political Backwardness in Recent German Historiography, 1890–1918.' *The Historical Journal*, vol. 21, no. 3, 1978. pp. 737–50.

Evans, Richard, ed. *Society and Politics in Wilhelmine Germany*. London: Croom Helm, 1978.

Evans, Richard. 'The Myth of Germany's Missing Revolution.' *New Left Review*, 149, 1985. pp. 67–95.

Farr, Ian. ' "Tradition" and the Peasantry: On the Modern Historiography of Rural Germany.' In *The German Peasantry*, ed. Richard Evans. New York: St Martin's Press, 1986.

Fletcher, Roger. 'Recent Developments in West German Historiography: The Bielefeld School and its Critics.' *German Studies Review*, vol. 7, no. 3, 1984. pp. 451–80.

Gerschenkron, Alexander. *Bread and Democracy in Germany*. New York: Howard Fertig, 1966.

Gillis John R. *The Prussian Bureaucracy in Crisis 1840–1866*. Stanford: Stanford University Press, 1971.

—— 'Aristocracy and Bureaucracy in Nineteenth Century Prussia.' *Past and Present* 41, 1968. pp. 105–29.

Hagen, William. 'How Mighty the *Junkers*? Peasant Rents and Seigneurial Profits in Sixteenth Century Brandenburg.' *Past and Present* 108, 1985. pp. 80–116.

——— 'The *Junkers* Faithless Servants: Peasant Insubordination and the Breakdown of Serfdom in Brandenburg-Prussia, 1763–1811.' In *The German Peasantry*, ed. Richard Evans and W. R. Lee. New York: St Martin's Press, 1986.

Hamerow, Theodore. *Restoration, Revolution and Reaction: Economics and Politics in Germany 1815–71*. Princeton: Princeton University Press, 1958.

——— *The Social Foundations of German Unification: Ideas and Institutions 1858–1851*. Princeton: Princeton University Press, 1969.

Harnisch, Harmut. 'Peasants and Markets: The Background to the Agrarian Reforms in Feudal Prussia East of the Elbe, 1760–1807.' In *The German Peasantry*, ed. Richard Evans and W. R. Lee. New York: St Martin's Press, 1986.

Henderson, W. O. *The Rise of German Industrial Power 1834–1914*. London: Temple Smith, 1975.

——— *The Zollverein*. Cambridge: Cambridge University Press, 1939.

——— *Studies in the Economic Policy of Frederick the Great*. London: Frank Cass, 1963.

Hintze, Otto. 'Military Organization and the Organization of the State.' In *The Historical Essays of Otto Hintze*, ed. Felix Gilbert. New York: Oxford University Press, 1975.

Holborn, H. *A History of Modern Germany*. 2 vols. London: Eyre and Spottiswoode, 1966.

Hubatsch, Walther. *Frederick the Great: Absolutism and Administration*. London: Thames and Hudson, 1975.

Johnson, Hubert. *Frederick the Great and His Officials*. New Haven: Yale University Press, 1975.

Kehr, Eckart. *Economic Interest, Militarism, and Foreign Policy: Essays on German History*. Berkeley: University of California Press, 1977.

Kitchen, Martin. *The Political Economy of Germany 1815–1914*. London: Croom Helm, 1978.

Koch, H. W. *A History of Prussia*. London: Longman, 1978.

Kocha, Jurgen. 'Entrepreneurs and Managers in German Industrialization.' In *The Cambridge Economic History of Europe*, vol. 7, ed. Peter Mathias and M. M. Postan. Cambridge: Cambridge University Press, 1978. pp. 492–555.

——— 'Capitalism and Bureaucracy in German Industrialization Before 1914.' *Economic History Review*, vol. 34, no. 3, 1981. pp. 453–68.

Lee, W. R. 'Tax Structure and Economic Growth in Germany 1750–1850.' *Journal of European Economic History*, vol. 4, no. 1, 1975. pp. 153–78.

Ludtke, Alf. 'The Role of State Violence in the Period of Transition to Industrial Capitalism: The Example of Prussia from 1815 to 1848.' *Social History*, vol. 4, no. 2, 1979. pp. 175–221.

Mitchell, Allan. 'Bonapartism as a Model for Bismarckian Politics.' *Journal of Modern History*, vol. 49, no. 2, 1977. pp. 181–99.

Moeller, Robert G. 'The Kaiserreich Recast?: Continuity and Change in Modern German Historiography.' *Journal of Social History*, Summer, 1984. pp. 655–83.

—— 'Peasants and Tariffs in the Kaiserreich: How Backward Were the Bauern?' *Agricultural History* 55, 1981.

Perkins, J. A. 'The Agricultural Revolution in Germany 1850–1914.' *Journal of European Economic History*, vol. 10, no. 1, 1981. pp. 71–118.

—— 'Dualism in German Agrarian Historiography.' *Comparative Studies in Society and History* vol. 28, no. 2, 1986. pp. 287–306.

Retallack, James. 'Social History with a Vengeance? Some Reactions to H.-U. Wehler's "Das Deutsche Kaiserreich".' *German Studies Review* vol. 7, no. 3, 1984. pp. 423–450.

Rosenberg, Hans. *Bureaucracy, Aristocracy and Autocracy: The Prussian Experience 1660–1815*. Boston: Beacon Press, 1966.

—— 'Political and Social Consequences of the Great Depression of 1873–1896 in Central Europe.' *The Economic History Review*, vol. 13, nos. 1–2, 1943. pp. 58–73.

—— 'The Rise of the *Junkers* in Brandenburg-Prussia, 1410–1618.' *American Historical Review* 49, 1943. pp. 1–22, 228–42.

Sagara, Eda. *A Social History of Germany*. London: Methuen, 1977.

Sheehan, James J. *German Liberalism in the Nineteenth Century*. Chicago: University of Chicago Press, 1978.

Tilley, R. H. 'Capital Formation in Germany in the Nineteenth Century.' In *The Cambridge Economic History of Europe*, vol. 7, ed. Peter Mathias and M.M. Postan. Cambridge: Cambridge University Press, 1978. pp. 382–429.

Veblen, T. *Imperial Germany and the Industrial Revolution*. London: Macmillan, 1939.

Wehler, Hans-Ulrich. *The German Empire 1871–1918*, trans. Kim Traynor. New Hampshire: Berg Publishers, 1985.

Wunder, Heide. 'Peasant Organization and Class Conflict in East and West Germany.' *Past and Present* 78, 1978. pp. 47–55.

England

Anderson, Perry. 'Origins of the Present Crisis.' *New Left Review* 23, 1964. pp. 26–52.

—— 'Socialism and Pseudo-Empiricism.' *New Left Review* 35, 1966. pp. 2–42.

—— 'Components of the National Culture.' *New Left Review*, 50, 1968.

—— 'Figures of Descent.' *New Left Review*, 161, 1987. pp. 20–76.

Ashton, T. S. *An Economic History of England: The 18th Century*. New York: Barnes and Noble, 1954.

Barker, Colin and Nicholls, David *et al. The Development of British Capitalist Society: A Marxist Debate*. Northern Marxist Historians Group. Manchester, 1988.

Bindhoff, S. T. *Tudor England*. Harmondsworth: Penguin Books, 1950.

Brooks, Colin. 'Public Finance and Political Stability: The Administration of the Land Tax, 1688–1720.' *The Historical Journal* vol. 17, no. 2, 1974. pp. 281–300.

Callinicos, Alex. 'Exception or Symptom? The British Crisis and the World System.' *New Left Review* 169, May–June, 1988.

Campbell, Mildred. *The English Yeoman*. London: Merlin Press, 1942.

Chambers, J. D. and Mingay, G. E. *The Agricultural Revolution 1750–1850*. London: Batsford, 1966.

Corrigan, Philip and Sayer, Derek. *The Great Arch: English State Formation as Cultural Revolution*. Oxford: Basil Blackwell, 1985.

Day, Christopher. 'A Redistribution of Incomes in Fifteenth Century England.' In *Peasants, Knights and Heretics*. ed. Rodney Hilton. Cambridge: Cambridge University Press, 1976. pp. 192–215.

Dickson, P. G. M. and Sparling, J. 'War Finance, 1689–1714.' In *The New Cambridge Modern History*. ed. J. S. Bromley. Cambridge: Cambridge University Press, 1975. pp. 284–315.

Elton, G. R. *England Under the Tudors*. 2nd. edn. London: Methuen, 1974.

Habakkuk, H. J. 'English Landownership, 1680–1740.' *Economic History Review*, vol. 9, 1940. pp. 2–17.

Hay, Douglas. 'Property, Authority and Criminal Law.' In *Albions Fatal Tree: Crime and Society in Eighteenth Century England*, ed. D. Hay *et al*. New York: Pantheon Books, 1975.

Higgins, J. P. P. and Pollard, Sydney. *Aspects of Capital Investment in Great Britain 1750–1850*. London: Methuen, 1971.

Hilton, Rodney. *The Decline of Feudalism in Medieval England*. London: Macmillan, 1969.

—— *The Economic Development of Some Leicestershire Estates in the Fourteenth and Fifteenth Centuries*. Oxford: Oxford University Press, 1947.

Hill, Christopher. *Intellectual Origins of the English Revolution*. London: Granada, 1972.

Hobsbawm, Eric, and Rudé, George. *Captain Swing: A Social History of the Great English Agricultural Rising of 1830*. New York: W. W. Norton, 1975.

Hughes, Edward. *Studies in Administration and Finance 1528–1825*. Manchester: Manchester University Press, 1934.

John, A. H. 'Aspects of English Economic Growth in the First Half of the Eighteenth Century.' *Economica*, 28, 1961. pp. 176–90.

Johnson, Richard. 'Barrington Moore, Perry Anderson and English Social Development.' In *Culture, Media and Language*, ed. Stuart Hall. London: Hutchinson, 1984. pp. 48–70.

Jones, A. H., ed. *Agriculture and Economic Growth in England 1650–1815*. London: Methuen, 1967.

—— 'Agriculture and the Origins of Industry.' *Past and Present* 40, 1968. pp. 58–71.

Kennedy, William. *English Taxation 1640–1799*. London: G. Bell and Sons, 1913.

Kerridge, Eric. 'The Movement of Rent, 1540–1640.' *Economic History Review*, 2nd Series, 6, 1953. pp. 16–34.

Lazonick, William. 'Karl Marx and Enclosures in England.' *The Review of Radical Political Economics* vol. 6, no. 2, 1974. pp. 1–58.

Leys, Colin. *Politics in Britain*. London: Heinemann, 1983.

—— 'The Formation of British Capital.' *New Left Review* 160, 1986. pp. 114–20.

Mann, Michael. *States, Wars and Capitalism.* Oxford: Basil Blackwell, 1988.

Manning, Brian. *The English People and the English Revolution.* Harmondsworth: Penguin Books, 1978.

—— 'Class and Revolution in Seventeenth Century England.' *International Socialism* 38, 1988.

Mingay, Gordon. *English Landed Society in the Eighteenth Century.* London: Routledge & Kegan Paul, 1963.

—— 'The Size of Farms in the Eighteenth Century.' *Economic History Review*, 2nd Series, 14, 1961–2. pp. 469–88.

Nairn, Tom. 'The British Political Elite.' *New Left Review* 23, 1964. pp. 19–25.

—— 'The English Working Class.' *New Left Review* 24, 1964.

—— 'The Anatomy of the Labour Party.' *New Left Review*, 27–8. 1964. pp. 38–65.

——— 'The British Meridian.' *New Left Review* 60, 1970.

—— 'The Twilight of the British State.' In *The Break-Up of Britain.* London: Verso, 1977. pp. 11–91.

Neld, Keith. 'A Symptomatic Dispute? Notes on the Relation Between Marxian Theory and Historical Practice in Britain.' *Social Research*, vol. 47, no. 3, 1980. pp. 479–506.

Porter, Roy. *English Society in the Eighteenth Century.* Harmondsworth: Pelican, 1982.

Plumb, J. H. *The Growth of Political Stability.* London: Macmillan, 1967.

Rogers, Nicholas. 'Money, Land and Lineage: the Big Bourgeoisie of Hanoverian London.' *Social History* vol. 4, no. 3, 1979. pp. 437–54.

Saville, John. 'Primitive Accumulation and Early Industrialization in Britain.' In *The Socialist Register*, ed. Ralph Miliband and John Saville. 1969. pp. 247–71.

Smart, K. W. *Sale of Offices in the Seventeenth Century.* Utrecht: HES Publishers, 1980.

Speck, W. A. *Stability and Strife: England 1714–1760.* London: Edward Arnold, 1977.

—— 'Conflict in Society.' In *Britain after the Glorious Revolution*, ed. Geoffrey Holmes. London: Macmillan, 1969. pp. 135–54.

Stone, Lawrence. *The Causes of the English Revolution.* New York: Harper and Row, 1972.

—— *The Crisis of the Aristocracy 1558–1641.* Abridged edn. Oxford: Oxford University Press, 1967.

Tawney, R. H. *The Agrarian Problem in the Sixteenth Century.* New York: Harper and Row, 1967.

Thirsk, Joan. *Economic Policy and Projects.* Oxford: Oxford University Press, 1978.

Thompson, E. P. *Whigs and Hunters.* London: Penguin Books, 1977.

—— 'Eighteenth Century English Society: Class Struggle without Class?' *Social History* vol. 3, no. 2, 1978. pp. 133–65.

—— 'Patrician Society, Plebian Culture.' *Journal of Social History*, Summer 1974. pp. 382–405.

—— 'The Peculiarities of the English.' *Socialist Register*, 1965. pp. 311–62.

Ward, William Reginald. *The English Land Tax in the Eighteenth Century.* Oxford: Oxford University Press, 1953.

Weiner, Martin. *English Culture and the Decline of the Industrial Spirit 1850–1980.* Cambridge: Cambridge University Press, 1981.

Willman, Robert. 'The Origins of "Whig" and "Tory" in English Political Language.' *The Historical Journal* vol. 17, no. 2, 1974. pp. 247–64.

Zagorin, Perez. 'The Social Interpretation of the English Revolution in England.' In *Social Change and Revolution in England 1540–1640*, ed. Lawrence Stone. London: Longman, 1965.

Index

Printed in the United States
by Baker & Taylor Publisher Services